DOODLEBUGS *and* ROCKETS

The Battle of the Flying Bombs

This is the story of the flying bomb (doodlebug and rocket) attacks on Great Britain as it has never been told before. A wealth of photographs, maps and diagrams alongside stories of tragedy, endurance and courage help to recreate the atmosphere of life as it was in those remarkable days between June, 1944 and March, 1945. The work of the Royal Observer Corps, Civil Defence, the fire, police and ambulance services, the men on the anti-aircraft guns, the ATS, the boys and girls of Balloon Command and the "women in green" (WVS) is told in detail. So, also, is the role of the RAF who played their part by photographing and bombing the launching sites and then meeting and repulsing the foe in this new Battle of London.

by Bob Ogley

Froglets Publications

Froglets Publications

Brasted Chart, Westerham,
Kent, TN16 1LY

Tel: 0959 562972
Fax: 0959 565365

© Bob Ogley 1992

ISBN 1 872337 22 8 (Casebound)
ISBN 1 872337 21 X (Paperback)

Front Cover shows a Tempest V, piloted by
Squadron Leader Roland Beamont chasing
a V1 flying bomb above the Kentish
countryside in the summer of 1944 painted
by Geoffrey Nutkins, Shoreham Air
Historical Museum, High Street, Shoreham
by courtesy of Group Captain Hugh Tudor

Back Cover: The Battle of London painted
by Frank Salisbury.
by courtesy of Mr Julian Sandys

This book was originated by Froglets Publications Ltd and printed and bound by Staples of Rochester Ltd. Environmentally friendly paper 40% straw without chlorine. A catalogue record for this book is available from the British Library.

Jacket design by Alison Stammers
First published: September 1992

Acknowledgements and Credits

THE flying bomb was a unique, brilliantly conceived, indiscriminate and short-lived weapon that was launched by the Germans in a last-ditch orgy of terror, designed to turn the tide of war. The main thrust of the V1 campaign began on June 12, 1944 and lasted only ten weeks. It was followed by the V2, the rocket projectile that brought a new dimension to air warfare, and cast a shadow that still hangs over the world today. By March, 1945 when the last missile appeared out of the stratosphere and crashed onto the town of Orpington, the war had virtually been won by the Allies and history was being made in almost every corner of the globe.

The flying bomb campaign, then overshadowed by events and of no real military significance, was largely ignored by historians until the writer, Norman Longmate, with an enormous wealth of official material which had been denied to earlier historians because of the "thirty year rule", published his books *The Doodlebugs* and *Hitler's Rockets* — two full investigations into the concept, development and subsequent effects of the flying bomb menace.

Mr Longmate discovered that the V1 and V2, short-lived as they were, made an extraordinary and lasting impact on all who lived in Southern England in 1944 and 1945. I have had the same reaction. Appealing in the local press for reminiscences and photographs, I was overwhelmed by the response. Hundreds of letters, scores and scores of telephone calls and many stirring stories from those I casually met in the street. Thousands of people remember the Doodlebugs and Rockets. It's not surprising -- everyone living in southern and eastern England at the time was on the receiving end.

This book is not intended to be a military history or a full account of the great intelligence hunt but an attempt to recreate the atmosphere of life as it was at the time using photographs and maps from newspapers, museums, libraries and private sources -- many of which have never been published before. Interwoven with these is a brief history and some of the more fascinating anecdotes and letters. The picture is completed by contemporary documents and statistics and colour photographs of some of those who "played a leading part".

I am grateful for the professional help I received from local newspapers, particularly the *Kent Messenger* whose photographic archives have been preserved with great care. I have used more than 30 pictures taken in Kent in 1944 or 1945, the locations of which could not be named in the newspaper at the time because of the censorship policy which then applied. This book could not have been written without the co-operation of those who printed my appeal for reminiscences and those who responded.

In May 1945, Winston Churchill said: "The lights went out and the bombs came down. But every man, woman and child in the country had no thought of quitting the struggle." I hope that all those who experienced the flying bombs, those who missed them by virtue of being elsewhere and the young people who have inherited an enormous interest in the war years will find something in these pages to remind them that we didn't quit, despite the late arrival on the scene of Hitler's miracle weapons.

Photographs in this book are the copyright of the following: Kent Messenger Newspapers: pages 28, 29, 43, 46, 47, 54, 60, 62, 69, 70, 80, 81, 98, 99, 101,105, 109,111, 113, 114,116, 118, 121, 122, 124, 126, 127,128,132-133, 145, 152, 153,155, 160, 162, 183,182top, 191,192. Imperial War Museum 4, 7, 11, 12, 14, 17, 22, 25, 36, 37, 40, 41, 42, 44, 49, 53, 56, 57, 72, 73, 76, 77,82, 84, 85, 88R, 94, 106, 107R, 115,119, 120, 123,129, 140, 151, 156, 161, 163, 176, 177, 180, 186, 187, 188, 189. Deutsches Museum, München 6, 8, 9, 10, 18, 27, 139, 203. Towner Art Gallery, Eastbourne 38, 117; Topham Picture Agency 35, 39, 58, 79, 158, 159, 165, 171, 185. Railway Museum 31. R.V. Jones 20. RAF Biggin Hill 45L. Bromley Library 63, 71, 172. Croydon Library (Croydon Advertiser) 65, 67, 68, 100. Beckett Newspapers, Hastings 74. East Grinstead History Museum 86. London Fire Brigade 91, 142. Newham Library 90. Syndication International 96. Kentish Mercury (Lewisham Local Studies) 103. The Ted Carter Collection (Waltham Abbey Historical Society) 146, 178. Bexley Local History Studies 147, Southend Library 154. Fern Flynn 97, 102, 125, 195, 198, 199, 202, 207. Other photographs come from private, individual sources. Artwork by Alison Stammers.

A special thank you to Jill Goldsworthy who helped with the research and the typesetting and was greatly involved with the production at all stages.

THE CONTENTS

Various maps, charts, diagrams and statistics which may be helpful in following the story of the flying bomb campaign are contained on the following pages:

The V1 was a pilotless mid-wing monoplane, 25 ft 4 in long, constructed of plywood and sheet steel. Its wing span was 17 ft 6 in and it was propelled by a pulse-jet engine. The direction of the bomb was governed automatically by a gyroscopic unit that gave signals to the air-operated rudder and elevator which stabilised it. Directional information was obtained from a pre-set compass. An air-log measured the pre-set distance after which the elevators were depressed and the robot dived to the ground. The nose was armed with 850 kg of high explosive, bolted to the forward end of the fuel tank.

INTRODUCTION

V for Vengeance

ON June 6, l944, only a few hours after the D Day landings, the German High Command gave orders for an immediate assault on Britain. Six days later the first of the new Vengeance Weapons made its appearance. This was the V1 or *Vergeltungswaffe 1*, better known to Londoners and those in south-east England as the flying bomb or "doodlebug".

The V1 was launched on a country still showing terrible scars from the 1940-41 blitz. It was a novel but deadly weapon, a pilotless mid-wing monoplane armed with an explosive nose and propelled by a pulse-jet engine. Coming directly after D Day, when everyone in England thought the war was almost won, it had a devastating effect on morale. During the summer of 1944 several thousand missiles landed in southern England killing almost 5,500 civilians and inflicting enormous damage to property in London and the Home Counties.

Day after day, night after night, the ungainly monsters, would speed across the skies, sometimes just above rooftop height. Resembling a wooden cross in the sky and spitting red flames from its tail, the missile made a noise like a badly-tuned motorbike engine that became louder and louder as it approached. To the people below it was a once-heard-never-forgotten sound as it clattered along on its deadly mission towards the capital. When the engine cut out the missile would fall silently to earth followed, several seconds later, by an ear-shattering explosion.

The loss of life in London, was considerable. 121 died in the middle of a morning service in the Guards Chapel, 48 died when a bomb fell in The Aldwych and 74 were killed when the US Army billets in Sloane Court, Chelsea received a direct hit. It was the London Civil Defence Region which bore the brunt of the assault. The 2,419 V1's which dropped in the London boroughs killed 5,126 people. Outside London, 2,789 flying bombs caused another 350 deaths. In terms of casualties the "doodlebugs" were worse than the Blitz.

In the face of this German offensive the defences in England were strengthened immediately. Anti-aircraft guns and barrage balloons were massed on the approaches to London and fighter aircraft patrolled an outer defensive screen. Between them they destroyed

Between June 13, 1944 and March 29, 1945 a total of 9,251 V1 flying bombs were plotted. Of these 2,419 reached London. The total number destroyed was 4,261 — 1,971 by anti-aircraft, 1,979 by the Royal Air Force, 278 by balloons and 33 by the Royal Navy

many V1's, gradually gained the upper hand and the threat diminished.

But Hitler had another, more deadly, revenge weapon. This was the long-range rocket, known as the V2, which flew at around 3,600 miles an hour and arrived without warning via the stratosphere. It was 46 feet long with four stabilising fins, a cylindrical body and a warhead of one ton. The V2 took just five minutes from launch to impact and travelled too high and too fast to be tracked down. There was no time to give an anti-aircraft warning. It was a weapon with which Hitler could have won the war.

From September 1944 to March 1945, 1,115 V2 rockets were fired at Britain killing 2,612 people in London and 212 civilians elsewhere. London received 517 rockets and 537 fell outside the capital, the remainder in the sea. Many more rockets were destined to land on British soil but the Allied armies gained the initiative, the launching sites and rocket pads were overrun and, late in March 1945, the ordeal came to an end.

With the V1 and V2 Hitler brought the war to Britain as the Luftwaffe had done in 1940 and German Minister of Propaganda, Dr Josef Goebbels boasted of the great destruction of London. But Londoners and others throughout the south-east faced the onslaught with courage and with a defiance that was, by 1944, their hallmark.

Those who lived through the summer and autumn of 1944 and the winters of 1944 and '45 will never forget the Vengeance Weapons. Many loved ones lie in communal graves, beneath headstones on which are inscribed the words 'By enemy action', and others still bear the scars of injury. Thousands of families, who lost precious possessions when their homes were destroyed, can look back with a slender slice of comfort — the battle of the flying bomb was a victory for the Allies. Victory at a price.

CHAPTER 1: SECRET WEAPONS

"There are serious indications that Germany has been developing bacterial warfare, gases, flame weapons, glider bombs and pilotless aircraft, and long range guns, and it is recommended that necessary precautions be taken".

Dr R.V. Jones, November, 1939

As a scientific adviser to the Air Ministry, Dr R.V. Jones was the man responsible for the early investigations into the feasibility of "secret weapons" in Germany. In November, 1939 he completed a report for the Secret Intelligence Services with this sombre warning. He was right. The Germans had been designing novel weapons including a long range guided missile which had been on the drawing board since 1930. Photograph shows one of the earliest research rockets, the Winkler HWZ. Test firing took place in 1931 on the small island of Greifswalder Oie in the Baltic Sea.

A national joke

Sleeping beauty

Rocket age arrives

Operation Cherrystone

The "Wunderwaffe"

Mid-summer photocalls

Raid on Peenemunde

The "ski sites"

No-ball assault

Sinister activities

A national joke

IT was Adolf Hitler in one of his hysterical broadcasts who first mentioned the existence in Germany of a secret weapon. The war was little more than two weeks old when the Führer spoke in the city of Danzig on Tuesday September 19, 1939. He reflected: "The moment might very quickly come for us to use a weapon with which we ourselves could not be attacked".

In Britain, Hitler's "secret weapon" made headlines everywhere and the Secret Intelligence Services (SIS) with headquarters in Broadway, London were instructed to find out more. After painstaking investigations through SIS files, Dr R.V. Jones, a scientific adviser to the Air Ministry, came up with these conclusions: "There are a number of weapons to which general references occur, and of which some must be considered seriously. They include — bacterial warfare, new gases, flame weapons, gliding bombs, aerial torpedoes and pilotless aircraft, long range guns and rockets, new torpedoes, mines and submarines, death rays, engine-stopping rays and magnetic guns."

As the weeks passed by there was no sign of the "secret weapon" and it became a national joke, dismissed by newspapers as German bluff, possibly by the Propaganda Minister, Dr Joseph Goebbels.

It was no bluff at all. For many years, German scientists had been designing two novel weapons. One was a pilotless jet-propelled aircraft; the other was a long-range guided missile — a sophisticated and brilliant conception that had been on the drawing boards since 1930 and was known as the *Aggregat 1* or *A1*.

Director of the rocket programme was Walter Dornberger, an artillery officer in the German Army, the Wehrmacht, which, by the Treaty of Versailles, had been limited to just 10,000 men. Dornberger's assistant from 1932 was Werner von Braun, a young scientist with a passion for rocketry and space exploration. The two men worked at the Army Weapons Department at Kummersdorf, just south of Berlin.

By 1932 the *A1* was designed and built but plagued by considerable teething troubles which Dornberger sought to solve while von Braun, with an independent team, developed another rocket, the liquid-filled *A2*, stabilised by gyro-mechanism and capable of reaching an altitude of 7,000 feet.

In 1933 Adolf Hitler gained control of the German Government and became the Führer of the Third Reich. Although he was not greatly enthusiastic about the rocket programme — he considered it to be little more than an elaborate toy — he was nonetheless

Dr Josef Goebbels, with a Nazi party armband and Adolf Hitler on the Führer's 55th birthday, April 20, 1944

anxious that it should be developed in the strictest secrecy. As von Braun began work on an even larger and heavier missile, the *A3*, it became clear that Kummersdorf was too large, too heavily populated with too many prying eyes for the testing of such a weapon. Another site would have to be found.

In 1935, von Braun, now 27 years old, visited the island of Usedom on the Baltic sea where his father used to shoot ducks. He considered it the perfect place for guided missile tests. Walter Dornberger agreed and recommended that the northern peninsular of the island be purchased immediately.

Within 12 months the new rocket base was taking shape close to a small fishing village called Peenemunde.

Sleeping beauty

PEENEMUNDE is a name synonymous with the German rocket industry. It presents an image of liquid-fuelled long-range missiles on vertical ramps, each carrying a warhead of high explosive. It conjures up visions of brilliant scientists and engineers with the skills to develop, perfect and build a secret weapon capable of winning the war.

Before 1937, few people had heard of this small German fishing village where the River Peene flows into the Baltic Sea. Some visitors knew it as a beautiful and healthy area of northern Germany; a nature reserve set on a small peninsula, surrounded by dense forest and inhabited only by birds and deer.

Peenemunde really was the ideal site for the rocket men. Here, among the thickly growing trees 110 miles north of Berlin, over an uninterrupted 300-mile stretch of German-controlled sea, the new weapon could be designed and tested in complete secrecy. By the end of 1937 Peenemunde's place in the history of rocket research was assured.

The cost of building the military experimental centre with its laboratories, workshops, office blocks and living quarters was shared between the German Army and the Air Force, the *Luftwaffe*. Few trees were cut down so much of the work was concealed at ground level. The area which housed the Experimental Works was known as Peenemunde East.

Further to the north, close to the forest and the sea, a number of launching stands were constructed. To the west, and of vital importance to the *Luftwaffe*, was an airfield. Peenemunde West became the centre for the test-flying of new aircraft and pilotless flying bombs.

In the centre of the peninsula, south of the airfield, the forest was cleared and homes built for all who worked at Peenemunde. There was a school, a community centre, a sports field and shops. In the south-west corner a coal-fired steam turbine power house was constructed to be joined later by a factory producing liquid oxygen, the rocket fuel. Each area was linked by a new road and rail system and all around were pine forests, sand dunes and the sea.

As the years passed by the new Peenemunde grew. The housing estate expanded and great halls were built for assembling the rockets. The skilled and unskilled German workers were joined by hundreds of foreigners, Russians, Ukrainians and Poles — slave labourers conscripted to the military units. By 1943 there were

A4 rockets being prepared for launch. on the foreshore at Peenemunde

between 17,000 and 20,000 people working at Peenemunde. A security cordon which surrounded the whole area was manned by SS Guards. There were two checkpoints and a drawbridge over the River Peene.

Security was tight, so tight in fact, that few of this vast army of people knew what was being made at Peenemunde.

The rocket age arrives

DORNBERGER, von Braun and their team of rocket scientists learned a lot from the testing of their first three experimental, but temperamental, missiles and were excited about the capabilities of the fourth. The *A4* was on the drawing board at the outbreak of war but the German advance into France and the Low Countries early in 1940 was so successful that Hitler and his officers were convinced they would quickly overrun England. They were sure the *A4* would never have to be fired in anger.

Ironically, by winning the Battle of Britain, it was the Royal Air Force who put the project back in business. TheWehrmacht gave the *A4* top priority and by March, 1942 test firing began in earnest. The first blew up on its stand, the second crashed into the Baltic Sea and the third exploded after launching.

On October 3, 1942 Dornberger and von Braun tested their fourth *A4*. This time the black and white painted missile lifted off powerfully and increased in speed as it rose into the sky with flames and smoke billowing from the stern. The scientists watched anxiously as it continued its ascent and disappeared from sight high over the Baltic. As it splashed down on target the two scientists shook hands. The rocket age had truly arrived.

More successful tests followed and the Peenemunde leaders were quickly rewarded for their pioneering work.

Dornberger was promoted to Colonel, von Braun was awarded the War Service Silver Cross, lst Class with Swords. At a dinner to celebrate the first successful launch, theWehrmacht sent them a congratulatory telegram. Now all they had to do was convince Adolf Hitler that the *A4* could reach England.

The opportunity came on July 7, 1943; a meeting with Hitler in his "wolf's lair" in East Prussia. Dornberger and von Braun took along scale models of the *A4* and launchers, maps, drawings and a colour film of the October launch. Hitler and his High Command listened as von Braun added the commentary to the film and watched with growing interest as the great *A4* rocket took off and burst through the clouds, travelling faster than sound.

The film was designed to capture the Führer's enthusiasm and it had just that effect. He shook hands, gave his approval to the whole concept, apologised for not recognising its potential, demanded that the scientists should build a rocket carrying ten tons of explosives, ordered concrete launching bunkers to be built at once and insisted on mass production of the *A4*.

At the dinner to celebrate the first successful launch, Dornberger (left) and von Braun read the telegram from the Wehrmacht.

Although the rocket men favoured mobile launchers and lighter warheads they had achieved another great breakthrough. Hitler, now beside himself with excitement, was giving top priority to the missile programme.

It was agents of the Polish Underground Intelligence Service who gave the first information about rocket research being carried out on the Baltic coast. Their informant was a drunken German soldier, stationed at a rocket training centre, who boasted that the Third Reich was in possession of powerful "Air Torpedoes" which would enable the Führer to conquer the world. About the same time the Poles learned that the Nazis had built a secret base at Peenemunde and on March 28, 1943 the first coded radio message about experiments with "V" weapons reached London.

The A4 rocket is towed into position and erected by a Meiller trailer next to the inspection platform. Many of the early launch attempts failed but a thorough investigation of these failures led to constant improvements in performance, and on October 3, 1942 the breakthrough success was attained.

IMPULSE DUCT ENGINE

GRILL INCORPORATING SHUTTERS
& PETROL INJECTION JETS

FUEL TANK,
(CAPACITY 180 GALLS, PETROL)

WIREBOUND SPHERICAL
COMPRESSED AIR BOTTLES

PNEUMATIC SERVO
MECHANISM OPERATING
RUDDER & ELEVATORS

LIFTING LUG

FUEL ... ER CAP

AUTOMATIC PILOT:
3 AIRDRIVEN GYROS:
HEIGHT & RANGE SETTING CONTROLS

WARHEAD: APPROX. 1000 Kg.

PRESSED STEEL WING RIBS

SHEET STEEL WING COVERING

LAUNCHING RAIL

LIGHT ALLOY NOSE FAIRING
PROBABLY CONTAINING COMPASS

STEEL TUBULAR MAIN SPAR
PASSING THROUGH FUEL TANK

Operation Cherrystone

AS the German Army continued to test-fire and perfect the *A4* rocket, the Luftwaffe were by no means idle in the business of weapon development. Forced on the defensive by the Battle of Britain and then by the opening salvoes in the offensives against their cities, they were keen to retaliate and any restraints on using indiscriminate weapons against civilians were rapidly disappearing.

The opportunity came in March, 1942 when the Argus Motorenwerke Company asked the Air Ministry in Berlin if it were still interested in pilotless aircraft — a project that had been on the drawing boards just before the outbreak of war. The idea appealed to Field Marshal Erhard Milch, deputy to Reichsmarshal Hermann Goering, Commander-in-Chief of the Luftwaffe. On May 28, 1942, Milch met Robert Lusser, an aircraft designer and outlined his plan for an Argus-tube-propelled pilotless missile.

Lusser's designs met Milch's needs to perfection. It would make no demand on the aluminium industry, being made of thin steel plate, it would burn low-grade petrol instead of scarce and costly high-octane aviation spirit and the labour would be extremely small, only 550 man hours per robot — excluding the explosive and auto-pilot.

The idea of a flying bomb became a firm project on June 9, 1942. Fieseler Flugzeugbau, makers of the 196 or Storch, a small high-wing monoplane powered by an Argus engine, received specifications of the new aircraft which, they were told, should be able to carry a warhead of around 200 lbs and was to be driven by a pulse-jet engine. The project was code-named *"Kirschkern,"* or *"Cherrystone"*.

On July 19, 1942 representatives of Argus and Fieseler met Milch in Berlin where the decision was made to go straight into production as soon as the development work was completed. The designation, Fieseler Fi 103 was adopted and the date given was the end of 1943.

The "Wunderwaffe"

ON Christmas Eve, 1942 the first launching of a V1 powered missile took place at Peenemunde followed, early in 1943, by a series of tests. The results were disappointing and frequent crashes occurred due to errors in the design. It was discovered that the missile went out of control when subjected to a cross wind — a malady corrected after one of the most courageous acts in the history of aviation.

Test Pilot, Flugkapitan Hanna Reitsch volunteered to fly in an observation capsule built into the robot so that she could determine, by means of a periscope, what was causing the missile to be thrown out of control. Hanna lay on the floor of the fuselage and operated makeshift controls with her hands. After several days of this perilous work she discovered the fault and the design was changed. By May, 1943 sustained flights were achieved and the project pronouced as "very hopeful".

Operation *Gomorrah*, the devastating series of raids on Hamburg, began on July 24, 1943 and, at a meeting with his advisers the following day, Hitler screamed for retaliation. "The only thing that will have any effect is a systematic attack on their villages and towns. You can only smash terror with counter terror." By then 68 Fi 103's had been test-launched and 28 had been entirely successful. One had flown 152 miles and another had reached 375 mph.

Following Hitler's demands, positive steps were taken to use the flying bomb as a revenge weapon. The Flak Regiment was established and given responsibility for the actual launchings in France. It comprised 48 platoons in 13 batteries, involving a total of 4,000 men. In charge of the unit was Colonel Max Wachtel.

In France, preparations were under way for the erection of concrete bunkers and ramps for the discharge of large numbers of flying bombs to south-east England. Christmas, 1943 was the date nominated for the first assault.

Josef Goebbels was taking an intense interest in the progress of what he called the "*Wunderwaffe*" or "miracle weapon". During a speech at the Sports Palace in Berlin, he said: "All German people have only one idea. To retaliate in an equal fashion....The British nation has no reason for triumph. It will have to foot the bill, which its leaders have incurred here; only blood can pay for their guilt in bloodshed."

Field-Marshal Erhard Milch, Inspector-General of the Luftwaffe and deputy to Reichmarshal Hermann Goering, its Commander-in-Chief. Milch and Robert Lusser, an aircraft designer, were the first men to produce plans for an Argus-tube-propelled pilotless aircraft.

Mid-summer photocalls

There have recently been indications that the Germans may be developing some form of long-range projectors, capable of firing on this country from the French coast. There is unfortunately little concrete evidence on the subject except that the projector may be similiar in form to a section of railway track. It is obviously of great importance to obtain the earliest possible warning of the existence of any such device, and we should therefore be grateful if you would keep a close watch for any suspicious erections of rails or scaffolding and consult M.I.10, through us, on any doubtful cases.

War Office memo to Major Norman Falcon, Central Photographic Interpretation Unit, Medmenham: February 13, 1943

HOW long would it be before Allied Intelligence realised exactly what was happening at Peenemunde ? The answer was six years. From 1937 when the Army Weapons Department established the new base on the Baltic peninsula to the last month of 1942, Peenemunde buzzed with activity and not one agent involved in the intelligence hunt knew of the enormous threat that it posed.

Information contained in an anonymous packet and delivered to the British Naval Attaché in Oslo in November 1939 actually gave details of large long-range rockets being tested at Peenemunde but the "Oslo Report" as it became known was considered to have been planted by the Germans, inciting the British to waste intelligence resources. It was not followed up and Peenemunde was not heard of again for three years.

From December 1942 various reports from underground units in occupied Europe and intelligence agents in Germany mentioned secret weapons and a site at Peenemunde. In the spring of 1943 the London Bureau of the Polish General Staff received the message about "mysterious happenings" at Usedom Island in the Baltic. Finally, there was the now-famous conversation in a room wired for sound between two German prisoners-of-war who expressed surprise that the rocket attack on London had not yet commenced.

To Dr Jones this was the turning point in his investigations into the possibility of a German rocket site. The Generals were being held as prisoners of war at Latimer Park in Buckinghamshire. Their cell was bugged with microphones and on Saturday March 27, 1943 they mentioned the "rocket business" and "things that go 15 km into the stratosphere". Dr Jones was convinced that the rocket site existed at Peenemunde. He needed photographic evidence.

On April 20, 1943, some weeks after the German Generals' gaffe, Winston Churchill accepted a recommendation from the Chiefs of Staff and appointed Duncan Sandys MP — his son-in-law — to investigate the possibility of long-range rocket development. Sandys, then 35, had been Commander of Britain's first experimental anti-aircraft rocket unit but he was injured in a motor accident and invalided out of the army. Sandys had returned to the House of Commons and become the Minister responsible for weapon research and development. He began the investigation of a possible rocket base at Peenemunde, but real evidence was difficult to find.

Eventually it was RAF photo-reconnaissance pilots, flying Mosquitoes, who gave Duncan Sandys a clear picture of what was happening at Peenemunde. On June 12, Flight Lt R.A.Lenton took pictures of a rocket lying horizontally on a trailer and on June 23, Flight Sergeant Peek came back with superbly clear photographs which so delighted André Kenny and his colleagues at the photographic interpretation unit at Medmenham that they rushed the news to the Prime Minister. They had been assigned to search for signs of experimental work at Peenemunde; Peek's photographs showed rockets lying on road vehicles. Above the rockets towered a structure resembling a massive observation tower and the steep encircling slope of elliptical earthworks. Beyond were the woods, and seawards, at the end of an approach road, there was the fan-shaped stretch of foreshore.

On subsequent sorties, photographs showed more rockets and several unusual looking aircraft, possibly jet-propelled. This was the Messerschmitt liquid-filled fighter, the Me 163, identified by Constance Babington Smith, being test-flown at Peenemunde. At that time nothing was known of the existence of a flying bomb at Peenemunde.

In all six Mosquito pilots of 540 Squadron A Flight, based at Leuchars on the east coast of Scotland, were involved in the mid-summer photocalls over Peenemunde. Tragically, all the pilots were to die within the next six months.

On June 27, Mr Sandys completed his investigation and reported to the War Cabinet. He said that the development of jet-propelled aircraft was probably proceeding side by side with the work on rockets. He advised that the sites be destroyed in a bombing raid as soon as possible. It took a month of lengthy debates and sometimes bitter argument before the War Cabinet agreed.

"Peenemunde must be obliterated."

High above the clouds, this Mosquito of 540 Squadron, based at Leuchars on the east coast of Scotland, was on its way to photograph Peenemunde. Reconnaissance pictures became a vital part of RAF operational work in the bid to solve the mystery of the "secret weapons". Hour after hour, day after day, airmen of the service reconnaissance units flew their Mosquitoes over the North Sea and then on to Peenemunde.

ON April 20, 1943 Mr Duncan Sandys was officially appointed by the Prime Minister to head the *Bodyline* Committee (later to become *Crossbow*) and review the evidence for German long-range rocket development. His appointment met with a hostile reaction from Lord Cherwell (formerly Professor Lindemann), the Prime Minister's Scientific Advisor, who wanted Dr Jones, as a scientist, to direct the inquiry. Cherwell considered that such devices could not be fired over long ranges with any degree of accuracy and dismissed the rocket notion as "fantastic" and "unreal." He persued a trenchant campaign for Mr Sandys removal as Britain's supremo in the hunt for rocket clues.

Mr Sandys and his military advisor, Colonel Kenneth Post, stuck to their task, initiating numerous photographic missions over Peenemunde and France, working closely with the interpreters at Medmenham, and making inspection tours of Normandy.

In November 1943, Mr Sandys' responsibilities were transferred to the Deputy Chief of Air Staff and a Joint Intelligence Sub-Committee was instructed to initiate counter measures against pilotless aircraft, which by now had been indentified. With his retirement from the scene, the rocket inquiry, for which there was still much scepticism at high level, lost its momentum.

A few days after the V1 offensive began, on June 19, 1944, Duncan Sandys returned to the fray to chair the *Crossbow* Committee, with even wider powers to co-ordinate British counter measures.

Peenemunde — the photograph taken in June, 1943 on which A4 rockets were first recognised. General Dornberger later confirmed this 'test stand' as the one from which the first successful launching of the A4 took place.

The raid on Peenemunde

BOMBER Command received orders to attack three separate areas of Peenemunde in what was to be the only operation of the war in which the entire force was employed at night. The Air Ministry made it clear to Sir Arthur Harris, Commander-in-Chief of Bomber Command, that the idea of the raid was to destroy the workshops and laboratories where the missile was designed and assembled, and kill or incapacitate as many scientists or technicians as possible, by bombing their sleeping quarters. There were no instructions to attack the airfield at Peenemunde West, or the large camp for foreign workers.

The rocket site was 500 miles from Britain — a difficult, almost impossible target for the Army or Navy — but well within range for the squadrons of Bomber Command, whose men had never heard of Peenemunde and had no idea of its great threat to the civilian population and the Allies' prospects of invading Europe.

The operation had to wait several weeks for suitable weather conditions — a full, or nearly full moon with no cloud over Peenemunde, was essential. The forecasters recommended Tuesday August 17, 1943 and on the afternoon of that historic day final orders were issued to the Main Force of Bomber Command. Of the 58 squadrons, 54 were to go into action that night in an operation code-named *Hydra*. A diversionary attack on Berlin by a few Mosquito Pathfinders to decoy the Luftwaffe night fighters was code-named *Whitebait*.

The route chosen for the bombers was over the North Sea, Denmark and the Baltic Sea. It was to be a high-explosive raid using a Master Bomber who would remain in the target area throughout the raid to radio advice to his Pathfinders and then to the Main Force. The tactics also included a "timed run" on a fixed bearing from a known position.

The Master Bomber technique had been pioneered by Guy Gibson VC on a raid of the Ruhr Dams. The dangerous but highly responsible task on this occasion was to go to Group Captain John Searby commanding 83 Squadron. Two deputy master bombers were selected in case Searby was shot down. The briefing took place with neither the briefers nor aircrew knowing what there was at Peenemunde but they were told that the work on the base was so important that the raid would have to be repeated night after night until the site was razed to the ground.

Some hours later, 596 bombers carrying 1,650 tons of high explosive and 274 tons of incendiaries set off across the North Sea on what was to be the only precision raid undertaken by the RAF at night during the whole of the second world war. It was to be a night of action and drama with many lives lost.

The first bomber to take off was a Stirling of 90 Squadron based at West Wickham, Cambridgeshire, piloted by Flight Lieutenant George Crew. Behind him were 324 Lancasters, 218 Halifax's and 53 Stirlings, each squadron taking a different path across the North Sea to the point marked on the navigators' map as Position A.

A few hours later Peenemunde was burning. The raid was considered by the RAF to be a huge success. At least 25 buildings which formed the Experimental Works — the scientific heart of Peenemunde — were destroyed, including the headquarters office block and the design office. There were direct hits on the assembly buildings where the V2 rocket was about to be mass produced. Valuable documents were destroyed and Dr Walter Thiel, engineer responsible for the rocket propulsion department, was killed.

Tragically many bombs fell in the area which contained the camp for foreign workers; very few were allowed to take shelter and the death toll was appalling — more than 600 Polish labourers or Russian prisoners of war. In another area a large dormitory building, occupied by young women, was destroyed by blast and there was great loss of life. Some of the girls, forced out of the building by fire or terror, were killed while running to the beach.

Apart from Herr Thiel most of the leading German scientists survived including Walter Dornberger and Werner von Braun, who courageously rescued many of his documents from the flames. According to the Germans few items of scientific importance were lost. However, one objective of the raid was to delay the production of the V2 rocket and this was achieved.

It was decided not to rebuild Peenemunde immediately and the base was left with a deliberately damaged appearance. The test-firing of rockets was moved to Poland and mass production to underground caves.

So ended the raid on Peenemunde -- a mission that had nothing to do with the Vl for the British did not know of the link between the Flying Bomb and Peenemunde until after the operation. Many stray bombs fell well beyond the area selected for attack but, ironically, the airfield at Peenemunde West where the Flying Bomb tests were carried out did not receive a single hit.

Dr Jones was not consulted about the aiming points in the raid but, in retrospect, he wished he had been. Bomber Command had originally intended to make its main attack on the development works and installation at Peenemunde but Duncan Sandys convinced the Command that it was even more important to attack the housing estate where the scientists lived.

"I would probably not have agreed", said Dr Jones, "because the main emphasis should have been to smash up the research and manufacturing facilities. But with the emphasis on the housing estate, a substantial portion of our bombs fell to the south of the establishment itself, and particularly on the camp which housed the foreign labourers, including those who had risked so much to get information through to us. We never had another report from them and some 600 of them were killed compared with 130 or so German scientists, engineers and other staff. On the debit side there was the fact that we lost 41 aircraft out of 596."

How much vital production time did the Germans lose by the British raid on their military experimental site at Peenemunde ? Six months, or more, said General Eisenhower. At least two months, said Dr Jones. Six to eight weeks, said Dr Joseph Goebbels. Two months, say the official British history books.

Master bomber, Group Captain John Searby of 83 Squadron who remained in the target area throughout the raid on Peenemunde

A view of the Karlshagen community after the raid on Peenemunde. Most of these houses were occupied by scientists or engineers.

The "ski site" at Bois Carré, near Yvrench — the first V1 launching site in France to be analysed on photographs This one was taken on November 9, 1943 and shows the long. low building of heavy concrete which was used for the storage of flying bomb components. Within a few weeks, similar constructions were identified on photographs between Dieppe and Calais.

Launch pads and "ski sites"

JUST before the raid on Peenemunde a new suspicious construction site was discovered on reconnaissance photographs taken in the Pas de Calais area, near St Omer.

The site was hidden in Foret d'Eperlecques at Watten and, although no-one at the time knew what its purpose would be, instructions were given to the US Eighth Air Force to bomb it.

It was later discovered that the Germans were building a bomb-proof concrete launch pad for the V2 rocket and the Americans' daylight attack on August 27, 1943 so thoroughly smashed it up that the project had to be abandoned. In its place the Germans built a massive bomb-proof concrete factory for the manufacture of the liquid oxygen needed to fuel the rockets.

A few weeks later, in November, another "suspicious erection" was discovered on a new set of photographs. These showed a long, low building with a curved end and was christened "ski site" by photographic interpreters. Again, no-one knew for what purpose it would be used but orders were issued to destroy it.

Crossbow and the No-Ball assault

One of the many problems facing British Intelligence was to discover a coherent theme running through the information coming in from France, Poland and elsewhere, for many agents were confusing the rocket with the pilotless aircraft. On September 3, 1943 one agent, known simply as "Amniarix", managed to send through a remarkably detailed account of the "stratospheric bomb tests" which contained information also of Colonel Wachtel's regiments and the "catapult sites". Dr Jones tried to find the source of this valuable new information but was only told it came from a young girl. After the war the secret was unveiled. Jeanne Rousseau, aged 23, was "Agent Amniarix". She spoke five languages and worked as an interpreter. In 1976, Yorkshire Television traced her and arranged for Dr Jones to meet her for the first time (see picture). Jeanne was now Vicomtesse de Clarens.

THE massive jigsaw, presented piece by piece to military intelligence from agents on the ground was still not fully taking shape, but early in November, 1943 came a new twist in the chain of events. A contact working at a building site in the Abbeville district of France, noticed "a different type of construction". Camera-equipped Mosquitoes confirmed it was something a little under 300 feet in length and from the air looked "like a ski site".

More photographic sorties were made; in fact the whole area of north-west France within 150 miles of London was subject to the most careful scrutiny and thousands of pictures were taken. By November 22, 95 ski sites had been positively identified but no-one could be certain for what sinister purpose they would be used. It was now obvious that these sites, more than 250 feet long and 10 feet wide, were connected with Hitler's most-vaunted secret weapons, but were they launching sites for glider bombs, pilotless aircraft or long-range rockets ?

On November 28, 1943 a new set of photographs of Peenemunde was taken by Squadron Leader Merifield. They appeared to show little that was new but Flight Officer Constance Babington Smith, a young WAAF officer who specialised in enemy aircraft recognition, compared the new set of prints with previous photographs of the same area. She noticed a sort of ramp banked up with earth, supporting rails that inclined towards the water's edge. She reported her find to Wing Commander Douglas Kendall, the interpreter in charge of the investigation.

"Don't you think it might be a catapult for pilotless aircraft?" Kendall replied: "Babs, I know it is". On another photograph her trained eye fastened onto a tiny cruciform shape, set exactly on the lower end of the inclined rails — a midget aircraft actually in place for launching. It was an observation that was to earn her a place in history. Flight Officer Babington Smith had made the first British sighting of a flying bomb.

Before daylight the next morning Wing Commander Kendall's report report was on its way to London with the news that the most imminent cross-Channel threat was established beyond doubt. It was going to be a flying bomb. At this point it seemed that the attacks, when they came, would be of an appalling magnitude. The ski-buildings provided storage space for 20 flying bombs, and as there were nearly 100 sites, it seemed likely that something like 2,000 bombs would be launched each day.

Britain's secret weapon inquiry, codenamed *Bodyline*, was replaced

Wing Commander Leonard Cheshire, commanding 617 (Dambusters) Squadron led the first serious attack on the No-Ball sites on the night of December 16, 1943. The target was near Abbeville and was marked by Mosquitos of the Pathfinder Force. Cheshire, leading the main force of nine Lancasters, delivered the bombs within 150 feet of the markers. Two were actually within 90 feet, but it was still not close enough to destroy the site. In later sorties Cheshire's low-level marking technique, flying Mosquitos and Mustangs, made pin-point attacks possible. For his outstanding and extensive period of operational low-level flying in the most dangerous circumstances, Leonard Cheshire was later to be awarded the Victoria Cross.

by *Crossbow*; the ski sites, now a target for Fighter Command, were called *No-Ball* sites and orders were issued to eliminate them forthwith. Fighters alone, however, could not destroy the massive concrete buildings, now spreading rapidly across northern France, so reinforcements were introduced. Heavy bombers of the recently-established Allied Expeditionary Air Force, supported by bombers of the US Air Force, joined the *No-Ball* counter attack. The Americans were ordered "to get the job done in days, not weeks". It was not that easy. The novelist, H.E.Bates, then working in the Public Relations Department of the Air Ministry wrote:

"Such small targets demanded a far greater degree of accuracy than was needed to knock out a factory. The Germans' favourite site was a small wood of five to ten acres close to a hard road, where trees in both summer and winter gave them perfect cover. In such woodland sites the Germans built hundreds of sites and supply depots. But they also chose more domestic sites. Orchards of apples and pears were favourite places. Nor had they any compunction whatsoever about putting them in the back gardens of French peasants in remote villages. And on at least one occasion they built an entire launching site in a village street."

Bombing was dangerous and wildly inaccurate. On Christmas Eve, a year after the first successful flying bomb test, 672 American Fortresses attacked 24 separate sites. Other attacks that day brought the number involved to 1,300 — the largest single operation ever undertaken by the US Eighth Air Force. The results were disappointing. By the end of December only seven sites had been destroyed and the Germans were still completing new sites faster than the Allies could destroy them.

The New Year proved more successful but defences were strong and losses heavy. In one attack alone, near Cherbourg, 160 out of 217 Marauders were damaged by flak. By the end of May, 1944, 82 *No-Ball* sites were believed to have been neutralised but the Allies had lost 154 aircraft and 771 aircrew were dead or missing. This included 48 heavy bombers and 462 men of the US Eighth Air Force. There were other victims of the *Crossbow* campaign. Some sites had attracted as many as 4,000 bombs and the countryside around them was bleak with tragedy.

H.E.Bates, who visited the Pas de Calais, wrote: "Its villages have crumbled into heaps of stone and plaster; its fields are like miniature alpine ranges....village streets are chains of ponds after heavy rain, gardens and orchards have been obliterated. For the night and day bombing which caused all this, the French had a single and terribly expressive word — 'Effrayant!' Yet again and again the observer talking to them in the days immediately after their liberation heard them say: 'We did not mind....however often you came and however much you bombed us. We knew it had to be done and that it had to be done to us'. "

An air reconnaissance photograph of part of the experimental station at Peenemunde taken on November 28, 1943 by Squadron Leader John Merifield (inset). It shows a launching ramp on which, less than three weeks later, the trained eye of Constance Babington Smith who worked at the Photographic Interpretation Unit at Danesfield Medmenham, detected a miniature aeroplane at the end of the ramp, in position for launching. Hitler's secret was out.

Sinister activities

FLIGHT Officer Constance Babington Smith, the young WAAF who first identified the photograph of a "midget aircraft" sitting on its launching ramp at Peenemunde, was a girl who came from a background of firm dedication to her country. She was the daughter of Sir Henry Babington Smith, former private secretary to the Viceroy of India, and fiercely proud of the part being played by photographic intelligence in analysing and assessing the threat of V-weapons.

It was in May 1942 that Constance, as a photographic interpreter, flipped through a stack of pictures taken by Flight Lieutenant D.W. Steventon. Something unusual caught her eye — a collection of circular embankments at a place called Peenemunde. No-one knew what they could possibly be so the photographs were placed in the print library at Medmenham for possible future reference.

A year later with the "secret weapon" threat out in the open, Constance remembered the mysterious rings. More photographs were taken of Peenemunde and, on the evidence these provided, Operation Bodyline was established.

The Interpretation Unit at Medmenham buzzed with activity. Mr Sandys had ordered that the whole area of north-west France within 150 miles of London should be photographed — and there were hundreds of separate sorties, yielding thousands of pictures. Box files stacked up in mountains, the interpretation team worked long hours and almost every day there were sinister new activities to be examined.

It was later in 1943, months after the raid on Peenemunde, that Miss Babington Smith made her two greatest discoveries. One was a midget aircraft, smaller than a fighter, sitting in a small enclosure. The other was a sort of ramp, banked up with earth, supporting rails that inclined upwards.

With the agents who risked their lives in Germany and the occupied countries, the interrogators who questioned the prisoners of war, the men and women who combed through trade magazines and monitored German broadcasts, the technical wizards, the airmen of photographic reconnaissance and the intelligence experts, the interpreters were only part of the huge team involved in this great, often frustrating, hunt.

The vigilance of Constance Babington Smith and her colleagues contributed to the ultimate success of the Allied cause.

The photograph of the flying bomb on the launching ramp (left), interpreted by Constance Babington Smith, provided the link between Peenemunde and the launching sites in France and finally proved that the "ski sites" were for launching flying bombs.

Wing Commander Douglas Kendall, expert photographic interpreter. From 1943 onwards he co-ordinated the work on the V weapons at RAF Medmenham

CHAPTER 2:   THE DOODLEBUGS

"After months of waiting the time has come for us to open fire. Today your wait and your work will have their reward. The order to open fire has been issued. Now that our enemy is trying to secure at all costs his foothold on the Continent, we approach our task supremely confident in our weapons; as we launch them today, and in the future let us always bear in mind the destruction and the suffering wrought by the enemy's terror bombing."

Col Max Wachtel to his Flak Regiment 155 (W) on June 12, 1944

Colonel Max Wachtel, Commanding Officer of Flak Regiment 155 (W). In the 1914-18 war, Wachtel had been an artillery officer. He rejoined the army in 1936 and eventually became commander of technical development projects and later the Anti-Aircraft Artillery School.

V1 launching site

Order to attack

Allied Landings

Diver, Diver, Diver !

Battle of London

Falling like flies

Flaming tails

Modified sites

THE Nazis were now confident that flying bombs would provide them with a chance to snatch victory out of the jaws of defeat, and thousands of construction workers, who had been engaged on the erection of defences against the anticipated invasion of the Continent by the Allies, were transferred to the building of launching areas for the new weapons.

In the meantime attacks on the *No-Ball* sites, in the first few months of 1944, continued with some success and a further reconnaissance over Picardy, Normandy and Artois indicated that work on the majority had been abandoned. Those that did show signs of activity received more visits from the RAF but the War Office believed that a much simplified system of launching the pilotless aircraft was under construction.

This was the case. Flakregiment 155(W), now almost mobile, was building "modified sites" of minimal construction with a ramp, concrete roads and a few essential buildings. Each site took about six days to erect and could be abandoned when discovered by the Allied bombers.

The Germans were certainly not cricket enthusiasts but many of the officers in High Command knew of a word straight from cricket anthology, No-Ball. By January, 1944, the codename for the Allied bombing of the flying bomb sites was hardly a secret but to confuse the enemy two new words were introduced — Diver for flying bombs and Big Ben for rockets.

At the end of April, 1944, the interpreters at Medmenham spotted a totally new development — a long concrete platform with a pair of studs embedded between it. This was a much simpler launching arrangement, labelled by Wing Commander Kendall as a "modified site". As photographic reconnaissance work continued, Kendall put more interpreters on duty. Picture shows a Mosquito pilot returning with yet another set of photographs for the Crossbow jigsaw.

Any time now

UNTIL April, 1944 no detailed official information of the likely attack by flying bombs or rockets had been received in England by anyone, other than Civil Defence Controllers and Chief Constables. Now the picture was to change. The rank and file were told of "the possibility of an attempt at a preliminary use of the new weapon, at any time now".

On April 26, police, wardens and members of the Royal Observer Corps were given appropriate instructions and a notice was issued to "prevent publication of any report which would indicate to the enemy where his missiles may fall". The notice was for distribution to all police stations and wardens' posts in an area covering the whole of Southern England.

INSTRUCTIONS

The pilotless aircraft is believed to resemble a small monoplane having a wing span of about 20 feet and an overall length of about 18 feet. No pilot's cockpit will be visible. The aircraft will be jet-propelled and consequently no propeller will be fitted....The pilotless aircraft will probably cause a shallow crater.

Maximum speed: Is likely to exceed 400 m.p.h.

Average speed: Speed increases with range from launching point. Probable speeds are:
At 10 miles from launching point.....230 m.p.h.
at 30 miles from launching point.....330 m.p.h.

Operational height: Between 500 and 10,000 feet. 6,000 feet with a cruising speed of 330 m.p.h. is considered probable.

Flight path: Steady climb to about 6,000 feet for 25 miles and then level flight in both vertical and horizontal plane.

Hitler's order to attack

From the Chief of The High Command of the Armed Forces:

The Führer has ordered

1: The long range bombardment of England will begin in the middle of June. The exact date will be set by Commander-in-Chief West who will also control the bombardment with the help of LXV Army Corps and 3rd Air Fleet.

2: The following weapons will be employed.
(a) FZG 76
(b) FZG 76 launched from He 111
(c) Long-range artillery
(d) Bomber forces of 3rd Air Fleet

3: Method
(a) against the main target, London
The bombardment will open like a thunderclap by night with FZG 76 combined with bombs (mostly incendiary) from the bomber forces, and a sudden long-range artillery attack against towns within range. It will continue with persistent harassing fire by night on London. When weather conditions make enemy air activity impossible, firing can also take place by day. This harassing fire, mingled with bombardments of varying length and intensity, will be calculated so that the supply of ammunition is always related to our capacities for production and transport. In addition, six hundred FZG 76 will be regarded as a reserve of the High Command of the Armed Forces, to be fired only with the approval of the High Command of the Armed Forces.
(b) Orders will be given in due course for switching fire to other courses.

4: Bomber planes of the Air Force will co-operate to the exclusion of other tasks, at least at the beginning of the bombardment. Fighter and anti-aircraft defence of firing-points and dumps will be completed and organised at the beginning of the bombardment. All preparations will be made on the assumption that communications with the firing points will come under heavy enemy attack and may be destroyed.

5: The orders laid down for secrecy in Paragraph 7 of the order of 25 December, 1943 No. 663082/43 for Senior Commanders will apply.

16th May, 1944   *KEITEL*

Allied Landings and Nazi shells

"THE bombardment will open like a thunderclap at night", says part of the directive (on the left) issued by Field Marshal Keitel, Chief of the German High Command. The date for the start of the "thunderclap" was to be April 20, The Führer's birthday, but not enough bombs were ready so a new date in mid-June was fixed.

The people of Folkestone, like other front-line towns, had forgotten about Hitler's "secret weapons" and were more concerned with the good news from Normandy, where the Allies had landed on the beaches and were driving the Germans from the Cherbourg Peninsula. There was now every sign that the war might soon cease; certainly the shelling, which Folkestone had endured for so long, had ended. Or had it?

Soon after midnight on Tuesday June 13, the Nazis' cross-Channel batteries started up again and within the first hour eight shells had fallen into the sea. German radar, used for target precision, corrected the elevation and the shells began to fall in the borough of Folkestone. One hit the George Spurgeon School in Sidney Street, another exploded on the Warren Road level crossing and a number reached Cheriton and Morehall. A hardware store in George Street and the old Grammar School at Grace Hill received direct hits and the bowling club pavilion collapsed from the blast.

More shells struck built-up areas. By this time the townsfolk were in their shelters listening to the shells crashing down, while outside there was complete chaos. On this night, Folkestone's heaviest-ever shell bombardment, many shops were demolished and more than 1,000 homes damaged by blast. Six men and four women were injured.

To prove that the shells had a far longer range, and to direct attention away from the imminent arrival of the robot weapons that were being prepared by Flakregiment 155(W) in Pas de Calais, another Kentish town was bombarded — Maidstone. Eight landed in the borough, causing astonishment and considerable damage. One fell in the village of Otham.

Field Marshal Keitel, chief of the German High Command (in the foreground) inspecting Peenemunde in the Spring of 1944. The missile centre had been rebuilt and rocket trials recommenced. From left: General Warlimont, OKW, Field Marshal Keitel, General Fromm, Commander Ersatzheer and Major Dornberger.

Diver, Diver, Diver !

LOCAL farmer Edwin Woods was on duty on the night of June 12-13 at Observer Post Mike 3, high on the Kent Downs at Lyminge. Just after 4 am he received a message from Maidstone ROC Centre telling him there was something happening near Boulogne. Mr Wood, through his binoculars, saw a "fighter on fire" but it was just outside his sector. He gave a reading to Maidstone and handed over to his colleagues at Observer Post Mike 2 at Dymchurch.

Mike 2, a Martello Tower built at the time when Britain faced invasion from Napoleon, was now useful as a lookout for anything the Hun might throw across the Channel. On watch were Mr E.E. Woodland and Mr A.M. Wraight, a greengrocer and builder respectively.   At 4.08 am they spotted the approach of an object spurting red flames from its rear end, the engine making a noise like " a Model-T-Ford going up a hill". The first flying bomb to be released against England was rattling towards them and the two spotters on top of the tower instinctively knew that the new Battle of Britain had commenced.

The men followed the strange object in the sky with their binoculars. When it had approached to within five miles of Mike 2, Mr Woodland seized the telephone and passed the warning to Maidstone ROC Centre. "Mike 2, Diver, Diver, Diver — on four, north-west one-o-one." The plotter at the Group Centre reacted instantly. "Diver, Diver, Diver", he called across the Operations Room. The sirens sounded, the message was relayed to No 11 Fighter Group at Uxbridge and within minutes it had spread to Fighter Command HQ and then on to the highest reaches of Whitehall and Washington.

More reports came in from Observer Posts in Kent as the missile made its progress on a dead straight course towards London. It crossed the coast at Dymchurch, flew across Shipfield, now a housing estate, and clattered over the marshes, disturbing a few sheep. There were not many to disturb; 125,000 had already been evacuated in order to preserve a nucleus of the Romney Marsh breed. The robot flew on towards the county town of Maidstone, bisecting Ashford and Tenterden. Many heard the alert and went to their table shelters; others slept, unaware that their lives were soon to be in turmoil.

The Royal Observer Corps now knew that pilotless aircraft were about to invade southern England and their members were on duty that night, as usual. From the 1,500 Observer Posts, where the overcast June skies were being studied with extra vigilance, there was a telephone link to the Control Rooms where officers were waiting to pass vital information down the line to Fighter Command headquarters. Photograph shows the ARP Control Centre at Maidstone. Outside, the men on the Posts, working in pairs, watched and waited...

The Observers who reported the first Flying Bomb, making a "noise like a Model-T-Ford going up a hill" were Mr A.M. Wraight (with the binoculars) and Mr E.E. Woodland. The time was 4.08 am on June 13, 1944. The Dymchurch Observer Post in the Martello Tower was destined to be one of the busiest in the Diver belt for it is estimated that 2,000 passed by, or were shot down on land or sea. When the anti-aircraft guns were eventually moved (see page 83) there were eight batteries at the back of the tower and, at the height of the battle, the noise was so intense that the observers had difficulty in hearing each other speak. The first pair of V1's was also logged by one of the auxiliary coastguards at Folkestone Harbour, Frederick C. Marsh who recorded them as "two aircraft with lighted cockpits coming from the French coast in a north-westerly direction".

This map shows the firing lines of the launching sites in France which were identified on photographs. Sites aimed at Plymouth and Bristol were captured before the Germans could use them.

The new Battle of London begins

IN France, Colonel Max Wachtel was experiencing great difficulty in meeting the Führer's demands of 500 flying bombs a day. He had already withdrawn his men from the ski sites where they had been filling in craters after heavy Allied bombing. Now he hoped that the first modified launching sites in the Pas de Calais would be ready by the evening of June 12 but the invasion of Normandy had seriously affected his progress. The French railway system was in total disarray. Trains had been held up and many catapults had failed to arrive. However, Wachtel and Flakregiment 155 (W) were making frantic efforts to complete the last minute assembly of the few ramps they had managed to drag out of the storage depots. To mark the new Battle of Britain the Colonel spoke to his men:

"Soldiers! Führer and Fatherland look to us, they expect our crusade to be an overwhelming success. As our attacks begin, our thoughts linger fondly and faithfully upon our native soil........."

By 11.15 pm on June 12, when the opening salvo was due to be fired, only 18 of 64 sites in the Pas de Calais were operational and even on these essential equipment was missing. The attack was delayed until 3.30 am when battery commanders were told to open fire. Ten flying bombs were dragged on to their catapults and launched into the darkness, towards London. Five crashed immediately, one came down in the sea and four droned on across the Channel towards Dymchurch.

The first flying bomb, the one spotted by Observer Post Mike 2, was carefully plotted in its journey, north-west across Kent. Dymchurch handed over to post Fox-Three at Pluckley, near Ashford which passed it to Easy-Three at Lenham, near Maidstone. The missile droned on its unerringly straight flight towards Gravesend where it suddenly dived to earth and exploded on open farmland, at Swanscombe. The time was 4.13 am.

By now not everyone was asleep for the air raid sirens had sounded. Among them was George Darling. "There were three air raids in quick succession, with some gunfire in the first two at least. In the second I heard a bomb drop but was puzzled that I could no longer hear the sound of the plane. It turned out to be Hitler's first V1. It came down in a potato field a few miles from where I was living

The first LNER train crosses the temporary Grove Road bridge at Bethnal Green only 36 hours after it had been extensively damaged in the first V1 attack. Civil Defence were quickly on the scene that night, including, of course the WVS. Mrs Eileen Kelsey, who now lives in Folkestone has written: "I lived in Bethnal Green throughout the war years and remember the first V1. My mother who was with the WVS went to Grove Road that night and stayed on the next day, making tea for Mr Morrison and various other VIP's (ministry officials collecting evidence that this was, indeed a flying bomb). It was all very strange — no arms or legs — yet a lot of people had seen a plane come down".

in the Rosherville area of Northfleet."

Seven minutes later, the second flying bomb landed in a field behind Mizbrooks Farm, Cuckfield in Sussex. The blast blew open the door of a pig-sty in a nearby smallholding belonging to Mrs Phyl Bowring and pigs were running everywhere. The third clattered on towards London and the fourth flying bomb came down at Platt, near Borough Green. It crashed in the back garden of a very large house and "made a terrible mess of two rows of greenhouses".

It was the third bomb, however, which caused the first V1 fatalities. It landed at 4.25 am on the railway bridge over Grove Road, Bethnal Green — the main line from Liverpool Street to the

north-east via Chelmsford. Two tracks were torn up, the parapet partly collapsed, two houses were demolished and several others badly damaged. The blast injured 30 people and six were killed. They were: Mrs Ellen Woodcraft, aged 19 and her eight-month old baby, Tom, Lennie Sherman, aged 12, Dora Cohen, aged 55, Willie Rogers, aged 50 and Connie Day, aged 32.

The first of the terror weapons had caused some damage and loss of life — not the kind of opening salvo planned by the Germans, or expected by official circles in Whitehall. Dr Jones met Lord Cherwell that morning and Cherwell said: "The mountain hath groaned and brought forth a mouse".

Defence of London

Flying Bomb Sites in Pas de Calais

Diver Gun Belt

Balloon Barrage

LONDON

● ROCHESTER

● MAIDSTONE

● CANTERBURY

GUILDFORD
●

SEVENOAKS
●

● DOVER

● TUNBRIDGE WELLS

● FOLKESTONE

● DUNKIRK

● CALAIS

●● WATTEN

●● WIZERNES

●● SIBACOURT

●● DOMELEGER

●● ABBEVILLE

● TOCOQUEVILLE

● HOUPEVILLE

V1 Launching Areas

● LE HAVRE

This drawing shows the anti-Diver defence measures. Fighters were the first line of defence, patrolling the Channel and the Kent and Sussex coast. They were backed by a concentrated belt of guns in front of a balloon barrage that grew thicker as the campaign progressed. The shaded area in France shows the V1 launching areas.

Falling like flies

AFTER many delays and frustrations caused by the Allied advance through Normandy, the Luftwaffe units responsible for launching the next wave of flying bombs finally got their act together and, in the 24 hours from midday on Thursday June 15, more than 200 missiles were fired. Several crashed directly after launch, killing 10 French civilians, but more than 60 got through to London.

The men on the anti-aircraft batteries in Kent and Greater London could hardly believe their luck as wave after wave of enticing targets came rattling over, all flying a straight course and all trailing a flaring exhaust. The gunners greeted the monsters with more enthusiasm than accuracy and aimed wildly into the air, cheering madly when the sudden cut-out by the engine seemed to indicate yet another score. "Look", shouted one man, "they are shooting the bastards down like flies."

It did not take long for the people of Kent and the men on the surburban batteries to realise that they were now under attack from the first of Hitler's "secret weapons". Mrs Greta Flanders of Tunbridge Wells was 13 years old when she heard her father say to her mother: "Quick Ada, get the children up and come and see this lot. The bloody Huns are sending over planes on fire."

"We looked out from a back bedroom window across the valley from Forest Road over to Pembury. In the dark night sky the bright sinister lights shone out over the heavens. I remember the noise, the dreaded drone of the engine like nothing I had heard before. Three or four flew low over Tunbridge Wells and faded away into the distance. We shuddered and clung together as yet more of the horrors flared their way up from the coast. Come the morning — in the grey dawn the world looked forbidding as I walked to the bus stop to go to school. The planes were still coming over, the droning thud, thud of the engines was so frightening. I just felt sick and frozen with fear. The regulars waited for the bus into town, everyone chattering about Hitler's new secret weapon. I remember thinking, why aren't they all scared like me, but then looking back it was like the Battle of Britain all over again."

33

It is the noise I remember best

When the sirens in North Kent made their familiar wailing noise in the early hours of Tuesday June 13, 1944, I was already starved of sleep but somehow made the effort to put on my dressing gown and slippers and rush downstairs and into the garden. Overhead, a plane was in trouble, flames were shooting from the rear; it was obviously an enemy bomber which had fallen victim to our defences. I watched it plunge to earth and there was a shattering explosion as it hit the ground somewhere near Swanscombe.

Two or three nights later more planes came over with flaming tails but I now knew they were Hitler's much-vaunted secret weapon. As I watched them rattle overhead, greeted by an overwhelming ferocity from the suburban battery, dogs began to howl, cats ran around in abject terror and small children cried. This was The People's War once again.

It is the noise I remember best. The distant hum, getting louder and louder, growing into a roar and then a deafening rattle as it passed overhead. Sometimes the rattle would diminish as the flying bomb continued on its dead-straight flaming course towards London. But sometimes it would stop abruptly as the engine "cut out". I would hold my breath and count — one, two, three, four, five. Somewhere there was an explosion...somewhere there was tragedy.

Cyril Oakley,
Croydon (formerly of Gravesend)

A sort of stuttering, rattling, deep-throated growl

In 1944 I was 18 and working in the "test house" in Woolwich Arsenal. On the first night of the V1's a group of us watched what we thought were enemy planes coming over and many seemed to be on fire. We cheered as the first one was shot down (we thought) and crashed somewhere north of the river. We could not believe how the anti-aircraft fire from our guns had suddenly become so effective.

Before dawn we realised that something different was going on and I hypothesised a radio-controlled aircraft (not a bad guess). Dawn came with a layer of low cloud obscuring our view of these objects. I was very curious to see them. When one approached and we heard the engine stop, instead of taking cover I ran up the steel ladder to the roof. I was just in time to see a black object come vertically out of the cloud layer and dive straight into Woolwich. I believe the bomb hit one of the barracks. My mother says it was Red Barracks, where she worked as a civil servant. Though other sources say this was hit at 4.30 on June 21, I'm not sure.

V.P. Creek,
Eltham, S.E.9.

I lived in Ashford until March, 1945 and during the "day of the doodlebugs" was a student draughtsman and a sergeant in "A" Troop (Light Anti-Aircraft), part of the 28th Battalion Kent Home Guards. Three days before the first sighting we were briefed under the strictest secrecy that in a few days an attack against this country would commence by "pilotless aircraft". They would, we were told, fly straight and level at 1,000 to 3,000 feet at a high speed possibly up to 400 mph, which turned out to be a remarkably accurate assessment.

At around 4.30 am on June 13, 1944 our family was awakened by a strangely menacing sound, once heard never forgotten, but difficult to describe — a sort of stuttering, rattling, deep-throated growl. A plume of fire stretched low across the sky and I told my somewhat disbelieving parents that it was probably a pilotless plane. By its direction of travel it was almost certainly the last of the four doodlebugs to cross the coast just before dawn, the one which exploded at Crouch (Platt), near Sevenoaks.

R.A.Barham,
Chellaston, Derby

This photograph shows a V1 diving onto London, somewhere in the region of Piccadilly station, on one of the first days of the campaign. Londoners would hear the noise of the engine, followed by that terrifying moment when it stopped. The 15-second silence, described by many as a "deafening silence" was the hardest to bear. Then came the explosion and the mushroom of rubble and dust thrown high in the air.

CHAPTER 3: THE DEFENCES

"At the beginning of the battle the London guns had joined in the shooting, but the mere act of hitting it was of little use, for all they succeeded in doing was to bring the missile down on to the very target at which it was aimed. For this reason the London guns were restricted and all that Londoners, who had got used to the comforting roar of the defences, saw was the flying bombs arriving and crashing and spreading devastation while all around there was a depressing silence."

General Sir Frederick Pile - from his book "Ack-Ack"

Sir Frederick Pile, on the telephone in his office, head of Anti-Aircraft Command, deployed initially 376 heavy guns and 576 40-mm guns in a belt stretching from Maidstone to East Grinstead, a total which did not include 560 light anti-aircraft weapons manned by the RAF along the south coast. Defending London, however, was a big problem and the guns in the capital were withdrawn.

Battersea battered

Mouse begins to roar

Balloon barrage

The Guards' Chapel

RAF Biggin Hill

Pile's Mattress

News from France

Tempests at Newchurch

Tipping the balance

Kent's blackest day

Tragedy at Benenden

The Aldwych massacre

22 children killed

Hitler's secret weapon, for so long a music hall joke, was no longer amusing. "If you hear one of these things, keep under cover", advised the Ministry of Home Security. "When the engine of the pilotless aircraft stops and the light at the end of the machine is seen to go out it may mean that explosion will soon follow - perhaps in five to 15 seconds." In that first weekend of the new menace, South-East Londoners were soon heeding this advice for the missiles were arriving with alarming regularity. At 4pm on Saturday afternoon, June 17, rescue parties were rushed to St John's Hill, Battersea where a V1 had landed in the road, damaging the Surrey Hounds public house, two passing trolley buses and a row of shops. The death toll was 24. By Sunday night, Flakregiment 155(W) had fired its 500th missile.

ONE of the victims of the Battersea bomb was Sylvia Willie, aged 14, who lived with her parents in Speke Road. That morning she was shopping with her mother when the air raid siren started. Sylvia (now Sinclair) writes to say that they decided to get their precious meat ration from Dean's the butcher, and bread from the baker's shop next door to the Surrey Hounds pub, before returning home.

"I was making my way out of Dean's when a man standing in the doorway said 'there's one of them funny things up there and they're firing at it. It might come down'. He gave me a shove back into the shelter of the shop.

The next thing I remember is regaining consciousness in complete blackness, my mother shaking me like a terrier and slapping my face and her voice shouting 'wake up, wake up, for God's sake, wake up'. Then I became conscious of other voices calling out saying they knew we were there and they would soon get us out.

The bomb had fallen on the baker's and the pub on the other side of the road and the blast had blown in the front door of the butcher's shop and brought down part of the first floor. Thanks to the stranger in the shop doorway I am still alive to tell the tale.

When the rescue services had dug us out we were taken to the Granada cinema which was being used as a casualty clearing station. We were than taken to Bolingbroke Hospital to have our wounds dressed and to be given certificates to say we were official war casualties."

On June 18, at 8.25 pm a doodlebug, damaged by anti-aircraft fire, crashed in the triangle of Charleston Road, Milton Road and Mountney Road, Eastbourne. This was the first flying bomb to fall on the borough and it caused extensive damage. Fortunately no-one was killed but 41 people were injured. The incident attracted visits from Government and military personnel, including American army officers. Photograph shows a policeman examining a section of the bomb.

Mouse begins to roar

A FEW days after Lord Cherwell had likened the flying bomb campaign to a mouse, the missiles began to fall on London and its suburbs with unremitting frequency. Many were crashing on take-off but Flakregiment 155(W) maintained steady fire on Friday and Saturday, June 16 and 17, causing great damage in Lewisham and Westminster. However, it was the south-eastern boroughs, especially Croydon, Wandsworth and Battersea which were taking the brunt of this early assault.

Although the target was Greater London many bombs were flying well off course. One exploded at Billericay in Essex and the first fatal incident in Kent occurred on Saturday June 17 when one fell on a house in Benenden and killed a couple and their married daughter. This missile had been shot down. It narrowly missed the sanatorium where ceilings and walls were brought down by the blast. Many crashed in Surrey and Sussex and by 6 am on June 17 total casualties reported were 18 killed, 166 seriously and 83 slightly hurt. Seven V1's had been destroyed by night fighters and 22 by Anti-Aircraft guns.

After analysing the blast damage, Herbert Morrison advised the Cabinet that the effect was no greater than a parachute mine. Although this helped to allay fears about the massive destructive powers of the new weapon, there were reports of terrible casualties coming in every day. The photograph shows a little girl who was rescued from a badly damaged house in Buckingham Gate on June 16. Within one week of this new form of warfare, civilian casualties totalled 756 killed and 2,697 badly injured. 12 hospitals, 12 schools and four churches were already destroyed or damaged.

From the Croydon Advertiser: June 17, 1944

Dodging the Dingbats is becoming an acquired art in Southern England today. Before people began to know the habits of the brute there was a certain amount of very natural uneasiness. No-one quite knew what to expect. But now everyone goes about his or her normal business and when one is heard approaching, most people take appropriate evasive action.

In one district they seem to be generally named "dingbats". This word apparently comes from an expressive phrase of the RAF men who, when they wish to describe something very fast, say it goes like a dingbat.

One dingbat received a hearty cheer at the opening of Salute the Soldier Week. A politician had been speaking for 35 minutes and was obviously well set for another half an hour when the roar of the dingbat was heard approaching. The speaker said that under the circumstances he thought he had better cut his speech short, which he did. The applause was as much for the subsequent appearance of the dingbat as for the orator.

Seven hospitals in one week

The worst incident on Saturday June 17 was the flying bomb which struck St Mary Abbotts Hospital in Kensington at 4.05 am, destroying the children's isolation block, the main nurses' home and four wards. Thirteen patients, mostly children, and five staff were killed. The hospital had to be closed with the loss of 832 beds. St Mary Abbotts was the first of seven hospitals to be hit during the first week of the campaign. In all, the London County Council hospitals were damaged on more than 138 occasions and the strain on nurses, doctors and patients was intolerable.

London's goalkeepers

FOUR months before the first doodlebug fell at Swanscombe, the senior sector fighter station at Biggin Hill received a visit from 25 officers and senior NCO's representing Balloon Command. The men, who were quickly christened "gasbag types" by the Canadian pilots stationed at Biggin Hill, were looking for ideal sites for balloon emplacements. In two days they covered many miles along the crest of the North Downs, selected the sites and sent for the Airfield Construction Wing who built access roads, hard standings, central anchorages, huts and hydrogen depots — everything necessary for a balloon barrage to combat Hitler's proposed assault with "secret weapons".

Once it was certain that the enemy meant business, the balloons went up. Biggin Hill became the Balloon Centre and the first squadron to arrive came from Glasgow. They had driven all night with a convoy of trucks and a special police escort. Each day, from June 16, more and more balloon squadrons arrived in Kent. They came from Manchester, Liverpool, South Wales and even Scapa Flow. They were given only a few hours' notice to pack and board a train while their winches and equipment travelled by road. In his book *Front Line County*, Andrew Rootes describes the scene:

"They arrived in Kent in massive convoys; they could sometimes be seen stretching along the A2 as far as the eye could see. The men and vehicles parked along the verges of the road outside the old Laughing Water, near Shorne to refuel and collect their rations. The men had a hot meal before going on to

The people of Kent were delighted when the "balloon boys" arrived and did all they could to assist. At Meopham Green, the crew were supplied with cakes and pies and here at Biggin Hill, Miss Sheila Wedgewood cooks and serves the meals. The three leading airmen in the picture are J. McGowen S.Telford and J.Janp from Glasgow.

unload their balloons and inflate them. Hundreds of lorries were loaded up at Gravesend airfield with cylinders of gas — 30 of which were needed to fill one balloon. There were sites at Sole Street, Longfield, Cobham, Idleigh Court, Meopham Green and Fawkham Green. Local families were often willing to help the men...some providing tea and coffee, some filling sandbags and others putting rooms at their disposal".

The actual handling of the balloons was done by airmen but the WAAFs managed the transport, collected the heavy cylinders of hydrogen and delivered the water supplies

and food rations to the sites. By the middle of July a formidable barrier of 1,750 balloons was floating over the North Downs. With later extensions they stretched almost from Redhill to Chatham and covered 260 square miles of countryside — 31 miles long and 11 miles deep.

It was on June 20 that Biggin Hill Balloon Centre chalked up its first doodlebug victory, the missile crashing into an orchard. Two more were quickly brought down and then, tragically, a Mosquito fighter whose pilot, intent on destroying the robot, flew too close to the steel cables.

A balloon lorry arrives in Kent, complete with crew, winch and team bicycle. These airmen came from London and Burnham-on-Crouch.

THE balloons were the only materially beautiful thing produced in the whole campaign....up to 2,000 of them glowing in the southern sun, smooth and silver against the blue sky. They were at their most beautiful by moonlight and many people in "balloon alley" recall the whistling noise they heard as 6,000 cables stirred in the night breeze.

There were a few balloon tragedies. At Brasted, one airman and three WAAFs were killed when a V1 "ran down the cable". At Biggin Hill, a flying bomb exploded on top of a Nissen hut standing on the airfield. The three men sleeping inside the hut all died. Mr John Ivens, of Otford, recalls how the south boundary of the Biggin Hill balloon detachment ran along Telston Lane and fighters had to wheel away over Otford to avoid them. He said: "I remember chatting to some balloon men when suddenly they disappeared. The reason was clear. A V1 had snagged their cable and was spinning round and round while sliding down".

One balloon flew from the cricket ground at Farningham. No games were played in the summer of 1944 but Farningham maintained its wonderful cricketing tradition by catching four flying bombs in just over two weeks.

Women at work in a large hangar, sewing together the fabric for barrage balloon envelopes

Tragedy on a Sunday morning

IF Colonel Wachtel and his Flakregiment were hoping for a military target, then they achieved the bull's eye on Sunday morning with a flying bomb that may well have been the 500th launched on London. It was first seen just before 11.20 am on Sunday June 18 flying over Queen Anne's Gate before crashing onto the chapel at Wellington Barracks, home of the Brigade of Guards in Birdcage Walk.

The missile arrived in the middle of the morning service and was heard by the congregation. The dull buzz became a roar and the Guards Chapel collapsed in a billowing cloud of bricks mortar and dust . One of the first on the scene was the Chief Warden of Westminster. "The whole floor was covered by debris which blocked the portico entrance, rising on both sides to a depth of 10 feet, lessening in the centre. Apart from some movement at the east end there was a ghostly stillness over the whole scene."

When the final death toll was compiled, 58 civilians and 63 Service personnel had been killed — some had died later from their injuries. They included the Commanding Officer of the Scots Guards, Lt-Col John Cobbold, Lt-Col The Lord Edward Hay of the Grenadier Guards and the Director of Music, Major James Causley-Windram. It was the worst incident of the whole flying bomb campaign.

Heavy and Light Rescue Parties with ambulances and cranes worked without a break for 48 hours to remove the bodies and take the injured to hospital. One of those lying beneath the debris was Elizabeth Sheppard-Jones who later wrote: "I was suddenly aware that somewhere far above me, above the black emptiness, there were people, living helpful people whose voices reached me, dim and disembodied, as if in a dream....Someone frantically scraped the rubble from around my head...My eyes rested with horror on a blood-stained body that, had my hands been free, I could have touched...the body of a young soldier whose eyes stared unseeingly at the sky....I turned towards a Guardsman who was helping with the rescue work...'How do I look ? 'Madam', he said. 'You look wonderful to me!' Miss Sheppard-Jones later learned that she had a fractured spine and was paralysed from the waist down. She never walked again.

Three days into the main thrust of Hitler's assault with "secret weapons" and the situation looked grim. More than 500 people killed, a figure that was rising as Civil Defence recovered more and more bodies, 2,051 seriously injured and many more wounded. Already 647 bombs had crossed the coast and the damage they had caused was vast. Everyone from the Cabinet to those in the bleakest corner of Kent was under a great strain — a strain that was growing hourly.

On the evening of Monday June 19, Churchill held a Cabinet Meeting. He told his ministers that gun, searchlight and balloon defences were already being redistributed to mass their strength against the approach route of the bombs across Kent. The Number 11 Group Operations Room was fully engaged in controlling operations over France, so overall control of all "Diver" defences was given to RAF Biggin Hill where Operations was situated in a large house, called Towerfields, two miles north of the airfield.

With its Balloon Centre almost fully established, Biggin Hill was once again a front line station in the defence of London. The 519 airmen and 177 WAAFs living on the station, and those who worked in the Ops Room at Towerfields and another nearby mansion The Rookery, were now learning to live with the threat of annihilation, 24 hours a day.

This is Towerfields which was given overall control of Diver Defences. The actual Ops Room was located in the ground floor lounge

In the front line again

THE three cheerful WAAFs pictured here in their underclothes hadn't any uniforms to wear for a doodlebug had crashed into their billet, near Biggin Hill and reduced everything to rubble. The WAAF in the centre, Joy Caldwell, said they also lost their bicycles and slept in the hedges of the garden in a rolled-up blanket, rather than in the bombed house with plaster still falling down.

The girls worked for Biggin Hill "Ops" from a house called The Rookery and Joy was the N.C.O in charge of signals. She remembers the graphic warnings of what a "doodle" would look like but it was a great shock to see one "in the flesh", especially as she had not been prepared for it to cut-out.

She writes: "There was even a greater shock for us girls. Sixteen gum-chewing, medal-bedecked Yanks arrived in the middle of the night when we were on watch. They couldn't believe that we worked under such conditions. There were no windows left and the woman in charge didn't seem to notice all the chaos around."

On one occasion, Joy recalls, ice cream was delivered to the Americans while they were on night duty. "We waited for a "doodle" to cut out. The Yanks disappeared rapidly and we grabbed the container and enjoyed our first ice cream for many years."

By the end of June the deployment had swollen to 376 heavy guns and 576 light guns On the South Coast the RAF Regiment manned 560 light anti-aircraft weapons. Photograph shows a Mount machine gun, twin Cal. .50inch, M.33inch. The weapons mounted are .50 Browning M2HB models. The people watching this demonstration are local dignitaries from Hythe.

General Pile's Mattress

WHEN the flying bombs were first identified, General Pile, Commander-in-Chief of Anti-Aircraft Command had a mammoth task. His plan, prepared weeks earlier, was to instal 400 heavy anti-aircraft guns on the seaward side of the North Downs, stretching from East Grinstead, across Kent to Gravesend in a belt about five miles deep, with searchlights to assist the fighters at night. At first AA.Command acted cautiously to the attack but when the bombs started coming over in big salvoes, General Pile knew he had to work quickly.

He thought it would take him about 18 days to redeploy his defences — an estimate that had not gone unchallenged. Commanders of five American A.A. battalions placed at his disposal boasted that they would manage it in four days. They were wrong. The first guns were installed in their new locations in less than 24 hours in a military manoeuvre that was an outstanding success.

Experience had shown that the mobile 3.7 inch gun which had to be traversed by hand was "no match for the flying bomb". On Monday June 19, General Pile decided that all AA Command mobile 3.7 inch guns should be replaced by the static, power-controlled equipment. Instead of constructing a solid concrete base for the guns, which would have taken many months, the command's engineers devised the "Pile Mattress" — a movable lattice-work of steel rails and sleepers, filled with ballast.

Static guns were uprooted from all parts of England and sent south. More than 700 "Pile mattresses" were eventually made, requiring 35 miles of railway lines and 22,500 sleepers.

ATS girls look on with some apprehension as an ROC spotter points to the characteristic shape of a flying bomb rattling towards their post. Their next duty was to call the operations room with exact information on the direction from which the plotter would calculate the possible height. Reports followed from other Observer Posts and the position of the bomb was traced on the main table, with the information being related to Fighter Control. If the noise of the motor suddenly stopped an observer would give his call-sign over the field telephone and add "Diver-cut". The plotter at the table would shout the information across the operations room, adding the identification number "Diver 167-cut". A crash counter was placed beside the last reported position of the missile. Somewhere outside there would be an explosion and a plume of smoke.

The Daily Telegraph

and Morning Post

No. 27,775   LONDON, WEDNESDAY, JUNE 21, 1944

Printed in LONDON and MANCHESTER   PRICE 1½d.

ALLIES 3½ MILES FROM CHERBOURG

NAZIS REPORT LAND, SEA, AIR ATTACK

FLEET CUTS OFF ALL ESCAPE BY SEA

BRITISH HOLD PANZERS EAST OF TILLY

Advanced American patrols were reported last night to have infiltrated through the outer defences of Cherbourg and reached to within 3½ miles of the great port.

The main forces are believed to be four to five miles away, which would mean they had broken into the first of the three defensive zones in an advance of 15 miles in 24 hours.

This news came soon after Rennes radio had announced an all-out attack by land, sea and air against the fortress, which, it stated, Rundstedt had ordered must be defended to the last man.

The radio, quoting "last-minute reports," declared that Allied heavy naval guns shelled Cherbourg throughout yesterday, while four-engined bombers pounded the fortifications.

Despatches from correspondents with the Americans closing in on an 18-mile front from the south and south-east stated that a battle

PILOTLESS PLANE SHOT DOWN OVER ENGLAND BY R.A.F. FIGHTERS

One of the pilotless planes, which has been shot down by R.A.F. fighter aircraft over Southern England, lying with its tail in the foreground. Fighter pilots from a neighbouring airfield examine the wreckage to discover, if possible, more about its vulnerability.

TILLY TAKEN AFTER SEE-SAW BATTLE

NAZIS LEAVE TOWN A WRECK

From CHRISTOPHER BUCKLEY,
Daily Telegraph Special Correspondent

WITH THE BRITISH FORCES IN NORMANDY,
Tuesday Morning.

Tilly is ours. This little village, which cost us 10 days of repeated fighting, has been the scene of a see-saw struggle grimly reminiscent of the last war.

Again and again it has seemed nearly cleared: again and again German infantry units and

WOMEN WATCH BATTLE FOR CHERBOURG

ALLIED GUNS CHEERED

From RICHARD McMILLAN

BEFORE CHERBOURG, Tuesday.
Chasing the last tired remnants of two German divisions into Cherbourg, the Americans have begun the last battle for the port at its gates.

The attack opened at 5 p.m. today. Our artillery barrage began its shattering blows to break what may be the last line guarding the port.

I watched thousands of United States infantrymen trudging down the highways or cutting through the country lanes towards the battle line.

Many bridges which should have

RUSSIANS TAKE VIIPURI : BREAK 2 DEFENCE RINGS

1940 FRONTIER REACHED

The Russians have captured Viipuri, the fortress and port at the northern end of the Karelian Isthmus and the southern gateway to Finland.

This important success—gained 10 days after the opening of the Soviet offensive in the Karelian Isthmus, in which three defence zones were reduced—was announced last night by Marshal Stalin in an Order of

SAW ROBOT RUNWAY DESTROYED BY BOMBS

FIRST EYE-WITNESS ACCOUNT OF PAS DE CALAIS RAID

From CORNELIUS RYAN
Daily Telegraph Special Correspondent

AT A U.S. 9TH AIR FORCE MARAUDER BASE, Tuesday.

This evening I looked down on one of Hitler's pilotless plane launching platforms in the Pas de Calais area and saw bombs from this group march right across it.

The target was so cunningly hidden that the formation made no less than four bombing runs before it was definitely located and destroyed.

It lay at the intersection of a cross-roads and the actual launching platform was practically invisible from the air because it ran along the road, its white concrete structure merging with the colour of the roadway.

Through binoculars the platform appeared to be a long, shallow affair, about 200ft long, and 25ft wide, rising steeply at one end, and just behind it stood a small, square concrete building—apparently the control point.

From our height it was just a mere pinpoint, and on measuring it I found it to be about the length o the point of my pencil—about one sixteenth of an inch.

At the briefing, the importance of destroying the target was impressed upon the pilots and crews. Three senior officers of this group personally led squadrons in the formation. They were Lt.-Col. C. W. Lockhart, Lt.-Col. D. L. Weiss, and Lt.-Col. H. G. Hankey, with whom I flew.

The whole formation was led by the Air Executive Officer at this station, Lt.-Col. Sherman Beaty.

We crossed the French coast a 12,000ft and began the "hunt" to the launching platform.

I could see the terrific effects the large-scale bombing by For tresses, Liberators and the R.A.F. the past few days. All over the are the ground was pitted with bom

FEWER ROBOTS GET ACROSS CHANNEL

By Our Air Correspondent

Fewer of the pilotless planes reached Southern England yesterday than on previous days of the Nazi "meteor" bombing. Two main reasons for this seem to be:

1.—Hour-by-hour plastering of the runways in the Pas de Calais region of Northern France from which the robots are launched [details P6];

2.—The gale which raged over the Straits in a north-easterly direction, reaching at times a force of 60 m.p.h.

Many hundreds of tons of bombs rained down on the robot bases, for the first time defined as situated between Calais and Abbeville. Although cunningly camouflaged in densely wooded areas, the installations were identified and repeatedly hit in the most devastating assault yet made on these targets. [Picture, P.5.]

All types of Allied aircraft were

"AMERICAN troops are on the Cherbourg peninsula and the US Ninth Air Force Marauders are dropping their bombs on the 'robot runways' near Calais." British people, reading this news on Wednesday June 21, 1944, had every reason to believe that the sites would soon be obliterated or overrun, and the flying bomb campaign would fizzle out before it had really started.

In fact a few sites were captured by the Americans, advancing towards Cherbourg. These were situated in the Cotentin peninsula and aligned on Plymouth or Bristol but the Germans were still building their modified sites, and it was from these that the V1 bombardment was coming. For the bomber crews it was not too

difficult to find the sites, thanks to photographic intelligence, but to destroy them was another matter, despite the enthusiasm of the Daily Telegraph reporter.

By June 18, about 70 modified sites had been located and thousands of bombs dropped in heavy daylight raids. By mid-July more than 3,000 sorties were flown but, according to Colonel Wachtel's war diary, only four sites were silenced and about 38 badly damaged. In fact he was never short of bombs to fire, or ramps to fire them on; his problem was that trains, trucks, roads and railway lines were being destroyed, hampering the transportation of missiles to the sites.

Tempests of Newchurch

LIKE the bombers in France, the fighters in Kent and Sussex were not having things all their own way. The Spitfire, the Mustang and the Thunderbolts were experiencing some difficulty in matching the speed of the flying bombs and it was discovered that the Tempest V, which could reach speeds of 416 mph at low level, was the only aircraft capable of consistently intercepting and overtaking its robot prey. In view of this No 3 Tempest Squadron, one of three which formed 150 Wing, found itself in the front line of "Diver" missions and, from Newchurch on Romney Marsh, led the battle in the sky against the flying bomb.

Wing Commander Roland Beamont, commanding 150 Wing, with Sergeant Bob Cole of No 3 Squadron as his No 2 went into action just after dawn on June 16 and overtook his first Vl over Folkestone. It was flying at 370 mph. In his book *My Part of The Sky*, Beamont writes: "I missed completely with my first burst. Another short burst hit its port outer wing; and then with all the remaining ammunition a long burst hit it first on the fuselage, without immediate effect, and finally on the engine which stopped and it began to go down. The Vl slowed rapidly but remained on an even keel and, as I overtook it on the port side, I was able to get a quick look at its slim, pointed fuselage, high-mounted ram-jet engine at the back, and short stubby wings. It was painted dull grey overall and the jet pipe at the back was smoke-blacked. I called in Bob Cole to finish it off, which he did with a well-aimed burst and it rolled over on its back and dived into a field south of Maidstone, exploding with a lot of flame and black smoke".

On that first day, reports were coming in of more successes and by nightfall 150 Wing had shot down eight flying bombs. Back at Newchurch, Beamont and Cole learnt that their Vl was not the first to be shot down by a fighter; they had been beaten to it by one hour by a Mosquito night fighter flown by Flight Lieutenant Musgrave.

Beamont and his Wing learned a lot in those first few hours about the flying bomb and how to destroy it. They found that opening fire at 200 yards was the best range for effectiveness but there was great danger in exploding the warhead. This was duly confirmed the next day when a Vl was exploded by cannon fire and the aircraft went straight through the fireball, returning safely but streaked with smoke. The pilot was burned on the forearm.

Wing Commander Roly Beamont, who commanded the 150 Newchurch Wing was the pilot responsible for developing the tactics to be used against the V1. He recommended to Fighter Command that only the Tempest, Spitfire X1V and boosted Mustang should be involved in Diver operations and that the freelancing Thunderbolts and all other units should be banned from the main attack area between Dover and Eastbourne. He also suggested that the Observer Corps should be deployed round the coastline armed with distress rockets which could be fired in any required direction. This would enable the fighter pilot —already under radar control — to see the point of convergence of the rockets as an indication to where the missile might be. The recommendations were accepted and Beamont and his Tempest marksmen went on to become Britain's first well-known fly-bomb aces.

The pilot who tipped the balance

WEST Malling, on the doodlebug path to London, was another airfield earmarked for anti-diver operations and when the night-fighters moved out in mid-June they left 91 and 96 Squadrons as the squadrons in residence to combat the new onslaught and uphold the traditions of this famous fighter station.

The two squadrons swung vigorously into action, their pilots bagging a number of VI's, but it was 91 Squadron, flying the new Spitfire XIV, now fitted with the powerful Griffon engine, who became West Malling's best-known doodlebug destroyers. On Friday June 23, one of their ace pilots, a tall Australian, Flying Officer Ken Collier, discovered a method of VI destruction which is now part of aviation folklore.

On that Friday evening, Collier and his colleagues were scrambled at 9.50 pm to intercept Divers approaching from the Channel. Collier sighted his quarry from a few miles distance. It was flying on its steady course at 2,500 feet so Collier dived down to intercept, closed in and pressed the trigger. The burst was accurate but it had no effect. The bomb continued to spit fire, so Collier closed in and fired again. He was out of ammunition.

Flying at 330 mph, he glanced down to find a place without any buildings around, overtook the missile and flew alongside it. With the tip of his wing, Collier attempted to throw the doodlebug on its back. It failed so he tried again and with great satisfaction watched it spin down, crash in a field and explode.

The Australian pilot, delighted with his success, reported to the intelligence officer when he landed but his story was greeted with considerable scepticism. His colleagues, seasoned pilots, could not quite believe that anyone could have the audacity to fly alongside 120 kg of dynamite, moving at 330 miles an hour and perform a "circus trick". A shout from the mechanics ended all their doubts; they had discovered fresh black paint on the wing tip of Collier's Spitfire. It was, of course, the signal for a party in the mess.

The following week the story of Collier's daring act appeared in the Kent Messenger. "Quick thinking and cool courage on the part of a fighter pilot probably saved serious casualties from a flying bomb in Southern England on Friday evening......the pursuing pilot manoeuvered his plane close to it and diverted it from its course by tipping the wing. As a result the bomb dropped in some gardens at the rear of an old people's home."

The name of the Squadron was not given, nor the name of the pilot but it became the most talked about technique and soon many

Flying Officer Ken Collier (right), the Australian who tipped the balance, with Jean Maridor.

airmen were employing the same method. Sadly, up until now, Collier's feat has never been officially recognised, for he was shot down and killed in December 1944 and had little time to reflect on his "doodlebug days". Then, after the war, 91 Squadron's record book went missing, coming to light only recently after many exhaustive searches. The book is now in the hands of Peter Hall, the Squadron's historian, who made the historic rediscovery.

The official RAF history states that the first time a flying bomb was toppled over to fall prematurely out of control took place on June 23 by a Spitfire pilot. All enquiries in squadron records to find the pilot drew a blank.

A Tempest V of the 150 Wing from Newchurch chases a flying bomb at low level over Kent. The black and white stripes of the Tempest, introduced for easy identification during the invasion period, can be seen. Wing Commander Beamont had the guns on his Tempests altered to converge at 300 yards. This increased the effect of the firepower against the V1 and No 3 Squadron became the top-scoring doodlebug Squadron with more than 300 kills.

Frenchman was a hero of Kent

Jean and Jean pictured on the July day she introduced him to her parents. It was the only time they were to meet him.

A photograph of Jean Holme in 1992, living at the time with her husband in Sevenoaks.

ANOTHER pilot of 91 Squadron with a particular anger towards the doodlebug and the way it indiscriminately killed civilians was the Frenchman, Captain Jean Maridor. In April, 1944 he joined the West Malling wing under Wing Commander Bobby Oxspring and, with his colleagues, lived in a tent on the airfield.

On his arrival at West Malling, Maridor met and fell in love with a pretty WAAF, Section Officer Jean Lambourn. The couple, in the tradition of the pace of life which existed at the time, planned a wedding in August at Oxford where Mr and Mrs Lambourne lived. Jean Maridor's life was hectic. In the few months he was at West Malling, the handsome Frenchman courted his bride-to-be, helped with the arrangements for the wedding and shot down doodlebugs in numerous day-time patrols of mid-Kent.

Maridor knew his zone well. He had flown on many operational sorties in the south-east and on the other side of the Channel and had recently been involved in fighter sweeps and shipping reconnaissance operations. On one occasion he was returning alone from such a mission when he spotted a number of Focke Wulfes that were on a bombing mission to Folkestone. Summoning help from other members of his squadron he went into the attack and spectators below cheered as they watched the harassed Germans drop their bombs in the sea and flee back to the Continent. Maridor was a superb pilot and his almost fanatical hatred of the pilotless projectile was a feature of many late-night conversations in the Mess at West Malling.

Towards the end of July, at the height of the campaign, 91 Squadron was transferred to Deanland, near Lewes, where they continued with their anti-Diver duties, hoping that Saturday August 10 — the day of Jean's wedding to Jean — would be sufficiently free of robots to allow some of them to attend the service.

There was to be no service. On August 3, one week before the big day, Jean Maridor attacked his last flying bomb. Chasing the missile from the direction of Rolvenden, he pressed the trigger and hit the bomb but it had no effect. Maridor knew the danger of getting too near to his prey, but it was not in his nature to allow it to escape so he closed in again. Realising he was rather too close to some buildings below he held fire but, as a result, moved even nearer to the missile. He fired, the warhead exploded, but a wing was blown off the Spitfire and the two crashed into the Kentish countryside near Benenden. A number of cottages close to Walkhurst Farm were damaged by the blast. Jean Maridor was killed. He was 23.

Medway House,
Benenden,
Kent.

11. 11. 44.

Dear Mr Lambourn,

I wish I could tell you more about the terrible accident to Captain Maridor. As you can imagine it all happened so quickly we had no time to see much.

We were told here that in trying to save the hospital and the school where we live he shot at the flying bomb rather too close. The plane was cut in half and flew over the school.

Will you tell your daughter from us all here that his gallant deed saved the lives of soldiers in Hospital and many small children. I feel this is not much help to you all but it is all I can tell you. I am sending you one of the shells that we picked up in the grounds, it may be a little comfort to your daughter to have one of the shells shot from Capt. Maridor's plane.

Yours sincerely

(signed) Barbara Sharp

Flight Lieutenant J.C.Musgrave, of South Lincs and Flight Sergeant F.W.Somwell, Observer of Leeds who were flying a No. 605 Squadron Mosquito over the Channel, in the early hours of Friday June 16, when they encountered a "pilotless plane" coming from the Continent. The Mosquito turned, pursued it and opened fire. It exploded with a tremendous flash and dived into the sea giving Flight Lt. Musgrave the distinction of being the first RAF pilot to shoot down a V1.

His funeral was held at Brookwood, Surrey attended by many mourners, including General Valin, head of the Free French Air Force. Of the many wreaths, his fiancée, who later married and became Jean Holme, remembers one in particular. It came from the town clerk of Folkestone and contained a simple message which read: "To Jean Maridor, with grateful thanks from the people of Folkestone".

A doodlebug, brought down by a fighter on Saturday June 24, crashed onto Bartley Poultry Farm, Smarden. Six people died.

Kent's blackest day

WHEN the guns of London fell silent and the doodlebugs clattered along without a single shot apparently being fired, many people living in the capital felt they had been abandoned and, as the tragedies mounted, they called upon General Pile to resign. Why should the flying bombs get through just as they liked, they asked. Isn't it time you went? Little did they know that the General was actually rewriting his part of the original Diver plan.

Across the middle of Kent and Sussex it was a different story. The noise of the guns blasted away hour after hour at these infuriatingly small targets and shrapnel rained down on towns and villages, causing considerable damage. Fighters were learning new and effective ways of dealing with the robot and were anxious to bring them down in open country. However, they were not always successful.

The first two to be shot down (one by Wing Commander Beamont), crashed at Lamberhurst on June 16. More were to follow later in the day and those who lived in Frittenden, Goudhurst, Rodmersham, Cowden, Brookland, Gillingham, Queenborough, Mereworth and Snodland were the first to experience that ear-splitting explosion as a "mystery aircraft" hit the ground. At 10.40 on that same morning, anti-aircraft guns at Folkestone claimed their first Vl. For a time all seemed well.

It was a very different story on June 17 when a flying bomb which had been shot down killed three people at Benenden. The next day, another Vl was blasted out of the sky, only to crash on Lullingstone Castle. No-one was hurt but the windows were blown out of St Botolphs Church. Some days later one crashed into the garden of an old folks' home at Tonbridge and 60 elderly people had to be evacuated. There were 23 casualties.

The blackest day of June, and the worst incident of all for Kent in terms of fatalities, came on Saturday June 24 when a Vl, shot down by a fighter, hit the Newlands Military Camp at Charing at 6.18 am. 47 men were killed and 28 seriously injured. Just four minutes later another one was shot down over Smarden and wrecked a bungalow. Four died instantly and two in hospital on the same day.

THE first Polish fighter squadron to join the battle was No 316 "City of Warsaw" who were transferred from Coltishall to West Malling to "enjoy some good shooting!" Commanded by Squadron Leader Bohdan Arct, 316 Squadron flew south on July 1, beat the 'drome to show how the Poles fly, landed with perfect precision and immediately saw a black silhouette whizz past the airfield with lightning speed. Guns roared, the bomb cackled and disappeared in the direction of London. They were then greeted by the station commander who told them: "You'll find yourselves bloody busy, mark my word. The bomb chase has high priority. Good hunting". Photograph shows Squadron Leader Arct with his pilots just before their hunting season began.

The Aldwych massacre

The scene of the Aldwych massacre soon after the bomb had fallen. There were two explosions in the West End on this day. The first, just after midday, hit the roof of the annexe to the Regent Palace Hotel in Brewer Street, killing a chambermaid.

THE office girls were sunbathing on the roof of the Air Ministry building, Adastral House, in the Aldwych and the street below was crowded with lunchtime shoppers. It was a glorious midsummer day and, above the chatter of the people and the noise of London's traffic, few heard the approach of a flying bomb. High above The Strand the engine cut out and the missile glided down silently. It struck the road 40 feet in front of Adastral House and turned a peaceful summer scene into one of dreadful carnage. Forty eight people were killed on this Friday lunchtime. Casualties amounted to more than 200.

One of the injured was Miss Cecille Daly who worked for the Foreign Office in Ingersoll House, opposite the Air Ministry and next door to Bush House, home of the BBC External Services. Part of her job was top secret — to prepare leaflets for dropping over France and Belgium and propaganda speeches to answer the words of William Joyce (Lord Haw Haw). On Friday June 30 she reported for duty early after lunch. It was 1.50pm.

"I like fresh air and, as it was a sunny day, I opened my office window, when suddenly there was a terrible explosion. The bomb impacted on a row of buses and, when the dust lifted, there was a scene of terrible slaughter — pavements were littered with the dead and wounded and, on the road were the twisted, unrecognisable frames of a line of buses. The sunbathing girls had been blown to eternity. My secret papers had been scattered far and wide and I was lucky to be suffering only cuts and bruises. The blast damaged the face of Bush House and the two statues over the door had their arms blown off. I was taken to hospital in one of the many ambulances which arrived and, on the way, the ambulance crew asked me to help give injections to the badly wounded. After being bandaged up I went to see my mother, herself an ambulance driver, and my father, a Civil Defence warden, to tell them that I was OK."

The Aldwych injured are carried away on stretchers.

Nursery evacuated to a "safe haven", then....

THE official evacuation had not yet begun but already more than 200 boys and girls under the age of 16 had been killed, and the majority lived in London. Some children had been moved into thinly populated country areas where the chances of a flying bomb hitting a building was less likely. Among them were 30 children from a London County Council nursery school which had earlier been destroyed by incendiary bombs. The children had not been at school at the time, but the officials were taking no more risks and moved the little ones — all under five — to a safer haven in the Kentish village of Crockham Hill.   Weald House, requisitioned by the Ministry of Health as a short-stay nursery, was completely isolated, three miles from the small town of Westerham and less than a mile from Chartwell, the Prime Minister's country home. A staff of 11 women was appointed by the LCC to care for them.

 At 3.37 am on the morning of Friday June 30, 1944 a V1 was shot down by an anti-aircraft gun battery stationed on the North Downs. The missile crashed directly onto Weald House while the children and most of the staff were sleeping. The whole building collapsed leaving just a crazy chimney stack and the shell of a gardener's cottage still standing.

The garden itself was full of twisted metal cots, baby shoes, sheets and small blue blankets. The *News Chronicle* reported: "One by one the tiny victims were recovered. A dark haired baby boy in a knitted bed jacket, a fair-haired girl in pink, others just as they had been dressed and tucked in for the night. They were identified by little labels tied to their ankles.

Rescuers from Westerham, Edenbridge and Crockham Hill arrived on the scene and the emergency services quickly followed. In the avenue of lime trees leading up to the house they found white dust from pulverised plaster. In the surrounding woods and fields they found items of clothing and toys. Where the building had stood they found the most appalling tragedy.

Twenty two of the 30 children aged five or less, were killed or died later in hospital. Eight of the 11 nurses or domestic staff were also killed and the others were seriously injured. Many of those in the building were trapped by debris and only a few adults had been found by the afternoon. It was several days later — July 2 — before all the bodies were recovered.

Weald House, Crockham Hill which was taken over by the LCC as a nursery school. One of the domestic staff who was killed by the flying bomb was 30-year-old Catherine Inwood, whose two-year-old son, Peter was living in another nearby nursery called Little Mariners and mercifully missed the explosion. Peter was adopted by a family in Gateshead and grew up knowing nothing about the incident at Weald House until, at the age of 50, he decided to find out how his mother died. His investigations brought him to Crockham Hill, where he visited the re-built house, met a lady, Emma Norris who worked at Little Mariners in 1944 and gradually pieced together the full story of the tragedy.

Rooftop height

A photograph taken on June 30, 1944 while rescue work at Weald House, Crockham Hill was still in operation. The chimney stack is all that remains of the nursery and the damaged building in the background is the gardener's cottage. Beneath the debris lie the bodies of many more victims. The two ironies of this tragedy lie in the fact that the little ones had come from a London nursery school which had already been badly damaged by incendiary bombs and they were now in a house surrounded by woods, open fields and some way from a big town. The rescuers, many from the village of Crockham Hill, who had the grim task of extracting bodies from the rubble were never able to forget their anguish of that midsummer Friday morning.

In the early hours of June 26, 1944 a missile crashed on to the shops and houses in the London Road and Park End area of Bromley. Around one pm, I was standing in a back garden in Farwig Lane and saw a second flying bomb following the same course. The engine had cut out and it came along with just the sound of air passing over it. It was hardly rooftop height and I noticed the cone was painted red. I was rooted to the spot, fascinated by what I saw. The bomb landed on exactly the same place as the earlier missile. Builders were effecting repairs at the time and several of them were injured. Following the explosion my ear drums rang for an hour.

R. De'Ath, Mosul Way, Bromley

I remember a flying bomb falling on Stewarts Road, Battersea. Many people were killed and some were injured. I was one of them. I was taken unconscious to Battersea General Hospital along with the other victims. My teeth had practically been blown out in the explosion and the inside of my mouth was full of pieces of skin. I was lucky. I survived.

John Carter, Union Grove, London S.W.8.

I was eight years old during the doodlebug terror and I lived with my family at Folkestone, near the foot of the North Downs. One Sunday afternoon we were eating our tea, picnic style in the back garden, when there was a familiar buzz in the distance. The noise increased and a pilotless plane came into view, making its way right overhead. We all looked and listened intently. Our fears were confirmed. The engine stopped and there was an eerie silence. "Get to the front door", shouted my mother. With one accord we ran up to the front door where we fell in a heap on top of one another. There was a thud and the place was shaken. So were we. On the hillside were the remains of the smouldering doodlebug. We picked up what was left of our picnic, knowing the story could have ended in a very different way.

Mrs Enid Hills, Park Road, Tunbridge Wells

CHAPTER 4: THE FEARS

"The invisible battle has now crashed into the open. We shall now be able to watch its progress at fairly close quarters. Between 100 and 150 flying bombs, each weighing about one ton, are being discharged daily, and have been discharged for the last fortnight or so.....A very high proportion of the casualties have fallen upon London, which presents to the enemy a target 18 miles wide by 20 miles deep...The flying bomb is a weapon literally and essentially indiscriminate in its nature, purpose and effect....London will never be conquered and we will never fail."

Winston S. Churchill in the House of Commons — July 6, 1944

Part of the text of Winston Churchill's famous speech to the House in which he also said that the firing points in France were being continually attacked and the total weight of bombs already dropped on these and rocket targets in France and Germany had reached 50,000 tons. Here we see him with General Smuts on a visit to Dover.

The evacuation

Courageous Croydon

Worst week of all

Open country

One for Beckenham

To the underground

Raid on the caves

Crashes in Hastings

Women in Green

Churchill's statement

London on the edge of breaking

"LONDON will never be conquered." Churchill's words were of little comfort to those who were once again living under fire. The nightmare of the Blitz came flooding back and mothers felt that even if their children did not suffer injury, they might be mentally scarred by this new atmosphere of fear. By the beginning of July there was still no official pronouncement from the Ministry about the steps being taken to counter the bombardment, so many people decided for themselves on the best course of action. They packed their bags and left.

Tony Ruff of Willesborough, Ashford was 18 when he was summoned to attend a War Office Selection Board at Winchester for a possible commission into the Royal Engineers. On this early July day he caught the train to London.

"I got out at Waterloo East and crossed to the main Waterloo. I heard a flying bomb in the distance and I scurried into the station concourse. The ticket hall was one mass of people queueing for tickets. Men and women were fighting to get to the windows, police looking on quite hopeless to get order into the crowds, children crying, dogs barking and, overall a smell of panic and fear. I pushed my way through the crowd and found a porter. I enquired, "Where is everyone going?" He replied, "Anywhere, mate, anywhere" and I suddenly realised how afraid Londoners were. They had had enough of bombs, just as it seemed that the bombers were no longer a threat and the end of the war was in sight, a new terror was on them. Nothing in the newspapers had prepared me for this. 'Londoners can take it', were the reports, but London was on the edge of breaking.

Eventually I managed to get on the train and I stood in the corridor with some ATS girls. When the train finally pulled out, one could feel the fear evaporating. As we got further out into Surrey, people began to talk....there was now almost a party atmosphere. I spent three days in Winchester where they had never heard of a flying bomb."

On July 1, London County Council began to register mothers with young children who wished to be sent away. On July 3, the first parties were dispatched. By July 17 it was estimated that 170,000 official and 530 "private" evacuees had left London and the numbers grew daily until they reached 1,450,000. Escorted by the WVS and other volunteers, they went to the Midlands, the North, where Blackpool was a big favourite, Scotland, Wales and the West Country.

Mrs P.M. Surridge of Gibson's Hill, SW16 clearly remembers the reason for the evacuation to Wales as a child of 11. "One day I was playing on top of an Anderson Shelter near St Judes Church, Herne Hill with other children when we heard a rustling above the trees. Looking up we saw the horrifying sight of a buzz bomb brushing the leaves. It appeared to dive immediately beyond the church but in fact it had glided the length of Dulwich Road and landed in Trelawn Road, killing my friend, Nancy Moore and her two little sisters. Their mother was terribly injured but survived.

After the war the mother and her husband had three more little girls and each were given their sisters' names, which my own mother found very bizarre.

After the doodlebug incident another one landed in the field behind our house. That was enough. We were spirited away to my aunt's house in a village in South Wales."

Back on the Diver Belt, the combined defence of fighters, guns and balloons had achieved a kill rate of 40 per cent of all bombs launched. It was a great improvement but still no comfort to the thousands of Londoners and south Londoners who had stayed behind and mustered the courage to face the new Blitz. Not all of them were worried. Joan Strange, later of Worthing, kept a War Diary which she had published under the title *Despatches from the Home Front*. One entry reads:

July 8, 1944. Everybody's still talking about V1 flying bombs. On the wireless tonight was an old cockney talking about them. "Do these bombs frighten me ? Oh no, look at it this way. When it's got to England, it's got to find London. When it's found London, it's got to find Bethnal Green. When it's found Bethnal Green, it's got to find Widow's Walk. Then it's got to find Number Five and the chances are that I'll be at the pub anyway!"

TWENTY THOUSAND EVACUEES LEAVE CROYDON

Cordial Reception at most Towns

Croydon Times: July 16, 1944

Evacuees waiting at Maidstone West station for trains to take them away from "doodlebug alley". When they eventually arrived at their destination they received an enthusiastic reception, the north-country welcome in particular was superb. However, there were exceptions and the methods adopted during the first evacuation in 1939 were practiced again. The evacuees were often lined up against a wall, waiting to be chosen by their new families. They said they felt like cattle waiting to be sold. It was quite humiliating.

Children, evacuated from the Marian Vian School, Bromley, are pictured here with a WVS party leader. One leader, a Mrs Slingsby in a letter to the Bromley Times wrote: "All you parents who have parted with your little ones for the time being can rest assured that, apart from your own, they could not be in better hands". And of the little Welsh town: "Pengenmawr we salute you. You have done your part. Now it's up to your guests to do theirs". By the end of June, before the official evacuation began, 231 boys or girls under the age of 16 had already been killed by flying bombs and 493 taken to hospital. The children were by no means happy to be taken away from their families and many were indignant at missing all the excitement at home. Although the weather was rather wet and miserable in the summer of 1944 this did not stop the London children enjoying the hills and valleys of Wales and the rolling moors of Yorkshire and Lancashire.

THE borough of Croydon received its first flying bomb on the night of Thursday June 15, when one fell at the junction of Avenue and Warminster Roads. On that night several people were killed or injured. But this was only the forerunner of a bombardment which was to last, unbroken, for nearly three months. Croydon, it seemed, had been singled out for the special attention of robot aircraft.

There was scarcely a road in the town which escaped damage and during one exceptional weekend as many as 15 flying bombs crashed in residential areas. The record number to fall in one night was eight. This was a night of grief and terror with hundreds made homeless. Thousands of properties were damaged and the emergency services were strained to the limit.

In the first full week of the attack, 22 flying bombs landed in the borough, which included Norwood and Thornton Heath. There were 24 in the second week and 27 in the third. By the end of the campaign 142 missiles had landed in Croydon's streets. It was the V1's greatest battlefield.

Few people in Croydon enjoyed a full night's sleep during the flying bomb campaign. They took it in snatches and declined to go into the shelters when an attack was imminent. It was safer to listen for the familiar spluttering noise, wait for the jet engine to "shut off", gauge its possible target and then look around for any convenient cover from the blast. The "cut-out" was the danger signal that Croydon came to know all too well; for this meant that a home, school, factory, shop, church or hospital would almost certainly be hit. Few fell in open ground. Those that continued on their lethal, predetermined course were destined to create the same chaos and heartbreak in Streatham, Mitcham, Wandsworth, Penge and Sydenham.

In all, 58,968 houses in Croydon were damaged — more than the total number of houses in the town, explained by the fact that many homes sustained further damage after being repaired.

To help carry out repairs, 1,500 workers were brought in from other parts of the country and accommodated in schools, halls and temporary huts. A party of men from Scotland and Ireland arrived and were billeted in huts in Aurelia Road, West Croydon. A few hours later a V1 crashed on top of the huts and 11 of the newcomers were killed.

Courageous Croydon

(142 flying bombs)

The black dots on this map show where the 142 flying bombs crashed in Croydon. Nineteen others fell on the fringes of the borough. The bombs killed 211 people, seriously injured 697 and slightly injured 1,277. Nearly 59,000 houses were damaged — and of these 1,400 were completely destroyed. This map was on sale in Croydon in 1944 with proceeds going to the National Fire Service Benevolent Fund and the Croydon Civil Defence Fund.

This is Moffatt Road, Thornton Heath where 14 people died on the evening of July 4. Mrs A.E.Adams, a resident of Moffatt Road told the Croydon Advertiser: "It was 9 pm and my mother and I had just switched on the wireless when we heard it coming over. It was so low it seemed on the roof itself. I managed to pull the plug from the wall so the wireless was off and we just had time to get behind the dining room door in the corner of the room. The noise I shall never forget. It was the roof being blown off and the front of the house took the worst of the blast. The next thing we knew was a kind ARP Warden telling us to leave immediately and take our valuables with us." Photograph shows the scene in Moffatt Road the next day.

Dejection and defiance in the "bravest town of all"

WHEN the censor allowed the Croydon Times to publish this photograph the caption read: *"Pictures of dejected refugees driven from bombed German towns by the advance of the Allies were often published in 1944 but they did not exceed the misery and pathos of the story told by this photograph. Whatever the German families had to suffer was only retribution for the kind of thing which became an everyday scene during the fly-bomb attacks."*

During this period life went on in Croydon very much as usual. Thousands, of course, had been evacuated but those who remained maintained a tremendous calmness in the face of such adversity. The women in their homes went on with their housework — and their part-time jobs in the factories. When windows were smashed and ceilings brought down they just patched everything up as best they could.

Cinemas in the town remained open, with the exception of two that were closed for repairs. Trams and buses did not stop unless the driver happened to see a bomb approaching. Then the bus would stop and there would be a scramble for the floor.

Ten people died when a newsagent's shop opposite The Windsor Castle pub in Brighton Road, South Croydon was hit on July 18. Those killed were either walking along the street on their way to work, or calling in the shop for their morning papers.

Tea is served to repair workers from a YMCA canteen outside the bomb-wrecked Mission Hall at Old Town, Croydon. The bomb fell onto Cranmer Road during the night of July 26-27.

Worst week of the campaign

THE first week of July saw the flying bomb attack reach its zenith. In seven days more than 800 missiles were launched and, although many got through to cause death and destruction in London, the county of Kent suffered badly from those which either stalled and fell, or were shot down by the guns or fighters.

The popular term for a bomb crashing in Kent was "open country". But "open country" as Alderman E.S.Oak-Rhind, chairman of Kent's Civil Defence Committee, pointed out at the time, was dotted with villages, cottages, farms and houses with, here and there, a big town. "A flying bomb exploding in the air, let alone on the ground, will strip the roofs, bring down the ceilings, shatter the windows of all beneath. A flying bomb will often take somebody's life — in order to save London."

The worst day of all was Sunday July 2 when 161 VI's crossed the coast. They were attacked by the Spitfires and Tempests of the RAF. They were hindered by a vast, concentrated belt of guns and they faced a balloon barrage that had been growing thicker by the day. Scores came down in Kent but many got through to their target.

During the week that followed, flying bombs were shot down on Folkestone, East Peckham, Maidstone, Ruckinge and Higham. A total of seven people were killed and 68 injured.

This V1 fell into an orchard at Bobbing, near Sittingbourne. No-one was hurt. Trevor Horton, now of Folkestone, remembers two Spitfires chasing this flying bomb and one of them tipping it over. It exploded in the orchard and he found hundreds of unripe apples lying on the ground.

This was "open country"

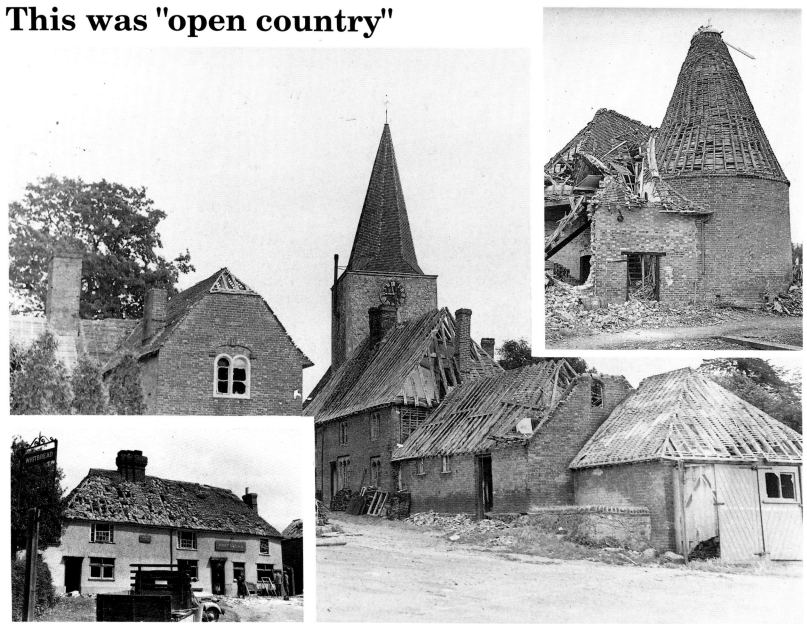

The village centre at Pluckley, near Ashford, the Horseshoe Inn at East Farleigh, near Maidstone, an oast house (normally used for drying hops) at Tudeley, near Tonbridge — all visited by doodlebugs in the summer of 1944. This, according to the War Ministry, was open country.

In the early hours of July 2, a flying bomb fell in Albemarle Road, Beckenham near the junction with the High Street. Three died, 30 were injured and 11 shops were destroyed. The incident happened in the early hours of the morning. Civil Defence personnel and rescue equipment were soon on the scene and, before it was light, an emergency food van was handing out refreshments to both the homeless and the rescuers.

It was quite uncanny how the flying bombs were landing on or near military targets. The Air Ministry building in the Aldwych, the Guards Barracks at Wellington Square and the Newlands Military Camp at Charing in Kent were three such sites. The worst of all came at breakfast time on Monday July 3 when the US Army billets at Sloane Court, Chelsea received a direct hit, killing 64 soldiers and 10 civilians.

By early July there was a rapid increase in the number of people sleeping in the London Underground — the numbers were estimated to be in excess of 70,000.

Raid on the caves

IN France, Bomber Command hammered away night after night at the launch sites and what were thought to be the supply depots but it had little effect on the frequency of the attacks on London and the south-east. Dr Jones began to think that the bombs were being distributed from other sites, so he set his agents to work. Back came the answer; there were three underground fly-bomb storage depots. The largest of these was at St Leu d'Esserent, in caves in the Oise valley, just north of Paris. The second was at Nucourt, north-west of Paris and the third at Rilly-la-Montagne, south of Rheims, in a railway tunnel.

Dr Jones recommended that the storage sites be attacked and, in the last week of June, the Eighth Army Air Force dropped so many bombs that two of the three were obliterated. At Nucourt, 241 V1's were buried beyond recovery by the collapse of the roof of the caves and at Rilly, the cavern entrance collapsed rendering it useless.

St Leu, however, was less vulnerable, owing to the greater thickness of the limestone roof. For the Germans it was the perfect home for their flying bomb supply and they had adapted the caves with great efficiency, building railway tracks, living quarters, canteens with water and electricity supplies. There were hundreds of men employed in the building work and, among these, were members of the French Resistance who sent back detailed plans of the storage galleries. It appeared that as many as 37 train loads of flying bombs were entering the caves on a single day and thousands of missiles were stored there. Orders were given to attack the sites again.

Heavier bombs were needed for St Leu and Dr Jones recommended "Tallboy", the big streamlined bomb developed by Barnes Wallis, which had already ruptured the Ruhr Dams. On the night of July 4 — 5, 1944, Wing Commander Leonard Cheshire, led his famous 617 Squadron on a raid of the caves at St Leu d'Esserent. The 12,000 pound

This was the entrance to one of Germany's secret flying bomb factories. The rail track led directly to the caves, which were almost two miles underground. The site was heavily bombed by the Allied Air Force and the photograph, taken later in the campaign, shows American soldiers on guard at the entrance.

bombs were dropped. They blocked the main tunnel and several others collapsed. The approach road was rendered impassable. The railway, the branch tracks, the blockhouses and the gantries were blown to pieces. It was an awesome demonstration of air power which had an immediate effect, for the average number of flying bombs launched against London dropped, from 100 a day, to fewer than 70.

According to Dr Jones, the reduction in the rate of the bombardment meant the defences were less saturated and the gunners and fighters were able to achieve a higher rate of success. Before the attack on the caves, 40 per cent of the bombs entering the defences were being shot down. This rose to well over 50 per cent after St Leu had been bombed. "The original Wachtel plan", said Dr Jones, "had been to fire the bombs in salvoes, so that while one was being engaged several others would get through."

Fortunately Colonel Wachtel never achieved the necessary synchronisation.

The destruction caused by the flying bomb which fell at Hollington, Hastings on Friday afternoon, July 16. Pursued by fighters, the robot was hit and dived among small houses in Old Church Road and Hollington Old Lane. Three people lost their lives and 47 were injured. Many were rendered homeless and accommodated at the Castleham rest centre.

Above: When a doodlebug fell at Westfield in July, an inventive resident placed a union jack next to the remains of the bomb, which was lodged in a hedge, and a notice inviting passers-by to make a donation. A substantial amount was collected and donated to the Red Cross.

Left: One of the worst incidents in Sussex occurred at Shortgate, Laughton on August 4 when a flying bomb fell on three cottages, which included a sub-post office, and completely demolished them. The postmistress, Mrs F.Tobitt and four others were killed. Picture shows the Bell Inn, on the opposite side of the road, which was also severely damaged.

"Well, that's one less for London"

ALONGSIDE the ARP wardens, the firemen and all those in the front line of rescue work during this hectic period of doodlebuggery, there was always a group of smiling, caring, hard working people quietly helping — members of the Women's Voluntary Service. They cooked, they washed-up, they gave comfort and they set up inquiry points at every incident. They acted as nurses, messengers and escorts. They ran mobile canteens where they dispensed hundreds of thousands of cups of tea. In the much-bombed borough of Beckenham alone, the WVS served 101,407 cups of tea, an average of 1,500 per flying bomb.

In Uckfield, the WVS Centre Organiser was Miss V.M.Porter who lived in Crowborough below three doodlebug lanes to London. More than 150 crashed in her area, many of them shot down by fighters, and her abiding memory today is the way that those people whose homes were destroyed frequently said — "well, that's one less for London".

On one occasion Miss Porter saw a Spitfire chasing a V1. The pilot waited until he was past the village of Wadhurst, then opened fire. The shots hit the giro mechanism, the doodlebug turned full circle and dived onto Green Square, Wadhurst. Miss Porter remembers when the children of Uckfield were evacuated. She was standing with them on Uckfield station when they saw a V1 overhead and then suddenly the engine stopped. There was pandemonium but all was well. The missile glided on before crashing in open countryside.

WVS members have many memorable stories. One concerns a toothless old man who was sitting outside a bombed house in West Ewell. They gave him a cup of tea, and offered him a bun, which he refused. The old boy then returned to the debris of his home, scrabbled around for some time and then came back. "I'll have a bun, now", he said, "I've found my false teeth." On another occasion an elderly couple were rescued from under a table in a blitzed building. Arriving at the WVS incident point, the lady turned to her husband and said: "Now, dad, was it worth buying, or not ? I told you it was a bloody good table, didn't I".

When the alert sounded one day at Clapham, a man quickly grabbed his small children, popped them into the Anderson shelter and turned to look for his wife. V1's were approaching and she was upstairs. He told her to hurry up and she yelled: "Wait a moment. I've got to find my dentures". "Listen you", came the reply. "They're dropping doodlebugs — not sandwiches."

Miss V.M.Porter, WVS Centre Organiser for Uckfield — a photograph taken in 1944.

Intertwined with humour there was always tragedy. One of the most tragic tasks for the WVS was tracing missing people and, on numerous occasions, breaking the news that a friend or relative was dead. The effect of blast from flying bombs was horrifying and on various occasions, men and women had all their clothes blown off. In his book *Women in Green, the story of the WVS*, Charles Graves writes that a policeman asked a member of the WVS if she could find a blanket for his colleague who, at that moment, was hiding behind a wall clad only in his boots. On another occasion, an elderly woman from Yorkshire was having a bath when the house collapsed. Six hours afterwards when the rescue squads were getting near her, she called out. "Ee, you'll get a surprise lads. I've nowt on."

The Anderson shelter, which was like a small bicycle shed partly buried underground, really came into its own during the flying bomb campaign. It offered wonderful protection against falling masonry and blast as this photograph clearly shows. Two people emerge unharmed from their Anderson after a bomb had completely destroyed their home.

One bomb, one fatality

THE toll of death, injury and damage to property from the flying bomb attacks was far greater than anyone had imagined and Londoners, in particular, wrote irate letters to their MP's demanding to have more details of the campaign and asking what the Government intended to do about it. As it was now impossible to apply the censorship policy any longer, Churchill agreed to make a statement in the House on July 6.

"Up to 6 am today 2,752 people have been killed by flying bombs and about 8,000 have been injured and detained in hospital. The number of flying bombs launched up to 6 am today was 2,754.

"The firing points in France have been continually attacked for several months and the total weight of bombs so far dropped on these and rocket targets in France and Germany, including Peenemunde, has now reached about 50,000 tons.

"The invisible battle has now crashed into the open. We shall now be able to watch its progress at fairly close quarters. Between 100 and 150 flying bombs, each weighing about one ton, are being discharged daily, and have been discharged for the last fortnight or so.

"Considering the modest weight and small penetrative power the damage done by blast effect has been extensive. It cannot be compared with the terrific destruction by fire and high explosive with which we have been assaulting Berlin, Hamburg, Cologne, and scores of other German cities and war manufacturing points...

"A very high proportion of the casualties have fallen upon London, which presents to the enemy a target 18 miles wide by 20 miles deep. It offers the unique target of the world for the use of a weapon of such inaccuracy. The flying bomb is a weapon literally and essentially indiscriminate in its nature, purpose and effect.

"The House will ask. What of the future? Is this attack going to get worse? Will the rocket-bomb come? Will more destructive explosions come? Will there be greater ranges ? I can give no guarantee that any of these evils will be finally prevented before the time comes when the soil from which these attacks come has been fully liberated.

"I must make it perfectly plain. I don't want any misunderstandings. We shall not allow the battle operations in Normandy, nor the attacks we are making against specific targets in Germany, to suffer. They come first. We must fit in our own domestic arrangements in the general scheme. There is no questioning of the slightest weakening of the battle. It may be a comfort to some that they are sharing in no small way the burdens of our soldiers overseas.

The brick surface shelters also saved many lives in the days of the doodlebug. Blast caused this street in Islington to collapse in a horrifyingly spectacular way but the surface shelters remained intact.. This type was most unpopular during the London air raids in 1940.

"London will never be conquered and we will never fail and that her renown, triumphing over every ordeal, will long shine among men."

Churchill told the House that he had visited various scenes of bomb explosions and spoken to a number of the injured of which there were now about 8,000 in hospital. He said that penicillin, which had only been available to the military, would now be given in the treatment of flying bomb casualties. It was a magnificent, robust Churchillian speech which cleared the air, answered a lot of questions and gave the chief censor a clearer picture of his future duties. Flying bombs were now officially landing in London!

Doodlebuglers

When the doodlebugs were coming over thick and furious the alert would go off but sometimes it was hours, or even days, before we heard the All Clear. I was living in Crayford and realised that someone had to warn people of the approach of a doodlebug, and of the short lulls before the next batch came over. It would at least give housewives a chance to do their chores.

My brother and I had in our house a bugle taken from a dead German in the first world war by my Uncle Fred and it was just what we needed in our plan for a doodlebug alert system. Paul and I decided to take turns "on duty" on the roof of our shed. We had one distinctive blast for the approach of a V1 and a clear signal when it exploded, or flew on.

We lived at Lower Station Road, and when the campaign was over there was a street collection. For our efforts in "doodlebug bugling" we were awarded the princely sum of £3.

Peter Fender, Greatstone, New Romney, Kent

Pilot waved a warning

On a beautiful sunny day in July, 1944 my friend and I and my baby girl were taking a walk in open farmland near Newhaven when we heard a doodlebug* flying over Mount Pleasant. Having nowhere to shelter we crouched down over the pram and just hoped for the best.

At this point a fighter aircraft suddenly appeared out of the blue and fired at the doodlebug which exploded in mid air. The plane then turned in a semi-circle, dipped its wings and appeared to do a Victory Roll. We could see the pilot waving to us and we were so excited we cheered and waved madly.

Then, to our horror the plane passed over our heads, came down like a stone in the adjoining field and burst into flames, less than 100 yards away. The pilot had not been waving to us. He was trying to warn us to get out of the way. His crash, as we later learned, had been caused by the impact of the doodlebug exploding. He was a Polish airman and his remains were buried in the local cemetery.

Gwen Chadwick, Newhaven, East Sussex

*This incident occurred on July 6 at 1.04 pm. Two people living at Mount Pleasant were seriously injured.

Peter Fender and his brother, Paul of Lower Station Road, Crayford who gave their neighbours the doodlebug warning.

A photograph which sums up a typical early-morning situation in a London street which had been "fly-bombed overnight". No letterbox for the postman but a housewife waiting to collect her mail, showing a determination that was such a remarkable feature of those grim days. The disclosure by Winston Churchill that London was bearing the brunt of the attacks came as a complete surprise to many living in other parts of England. The Americans, too, were amazed because the heavily-censored reports had given the impression that the missiles were landing harmlessly in rural areas. The news that 2,752 persons had been killed in three weeks, and that the impact was greater than the Blitz of 1940/41 made headline news in both countries.

CHAPTER 5: HEIGHT OF THE BATTLE

"The efficiency of my pupils is amazing. They have never failed to give a warning, and what is more they do not let it interfere with their lessons. The spotters on duty have a desk just outside the classroom door so they can hear the lesson, do their work and listen for the doodlebugs at the same time."

Miss Amy Barkley, headmistress, Otham School, near Maidstone

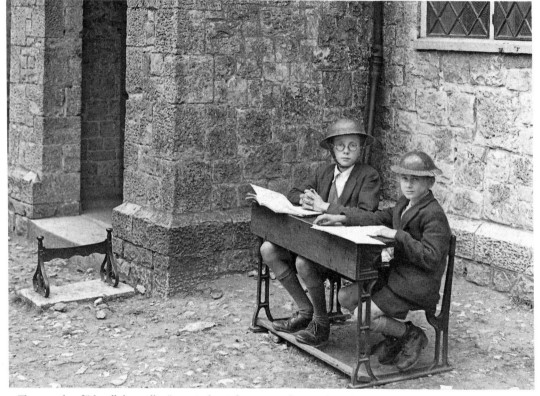

The people of "doodlebug alley" went about their everyday work with their eyes trained on the skies and their ears tuned in to that ghastly low-level roar. Offices, shops, factories and all public buildings posted "spotters" and at Otham Church of England primary school, the headmistress asked for volunteers to sit in the playground, wearing their tin hats and shout "doodlebug" whenever one approached. The class would then troop obediently into the shelter. This photograph, taken by the Kent Messenger in July, 1944, shows Gordon Spendly, aged 10 and Alan Chapman, eight, doing their spell of doodlebug spotting.

Bombs, landmines, incendiaries, cross channel shelling, machine gun bullets from enemy aircraft, anti-aircraft shells from "friendly" guns and now doodlebugs -- little wonder the people of Dover took to the shelters so often. This photograph shows some of the ladies of Kent's most-bombed town casually playing whist during a V1 alert. The tables were set out in one of the series of tunnels which runs under the White Cliffs. During the war, 199 civilians from Dover town were killed and 727 injured. More than 10,000 properties were damaged. Although many flying bombs came over only three crashed in the town and six flew slap bang into the cliffs between Folkestone and Dover. Hundreds came down on the beaches.

THE children of Otham became such proficient doodlebug spotters that other schools in Kent and Sussex adopted the same method, rather than trust the more official "alert" warning. At night, however, it was a different story. Thousands upon thousands of people lay in their beds listening for that tell-tale noise. They listened to the sound of the night fighters and they listened for the worst sound of all — silence. They knew then they had 15 seconds in which to find cover before an explosion could rip their home apart.

The people of London had their own spotters and alarm systems. At some factories a bell was rung and others had flashing red lights. At Ford's of Dagenham, there was a "six-pip" alert indicating imminent danger. Others just relied on their ears and then dived for the sturdiest desk.

There was a rapid increase in the number of people using the Underground — more than 70,000 by the middle of July. Some just slept there. Many Londoners, however, remained underground all day and went home just now and again to fetch food. There was a demand that the Government open up the deep shelters, which had been completed too late for the 1940-41 Blitz. The first to be opened was at Stockwell on Sunday July 9 when 4,000 people spent a happier night 130 feet below ground. A second shelter was opened four days later.

Photograph shows the guns being towed along the road over the marshes on their way to Rye in July 1944. It was between Rye Harbour and Camber that the biggest concentration of artillery in the country was established.

Goodbye Rye

SUSSEX'S first flying bomb fell in a field behind Mizbrooks Farm, Cuckfield at 4.20 am on Thursday June 13 — the second to land on British soil. Two days later, on Saturday June 15, anti-aircraft guns on the Sussex coast hit a second diver which crashed on the embankment of the Hastings railway line, the blast stripping tiles from the houses in nearby Bexhill Road. This was the prelude to a hectic two months in which East Sussex was rarely out of the action.

Altogether 775 doodlebugs were to fall in the county and many hundreds more fell in the sea around the coast. The AA gunbelt which stretched to Beachy Head was responsible for many of these "kills" and, as in Kent, they also caused considerable damage to property. In Portslade, Brighton, for example, 81 homes were hit by AA shells.

Sixteen flying bombs fell on Bexhill and although many properties were destroyed there were no civilian deaths. The first came down in Richmond Road in late June where it made a 30 foot crater in the middle of the road. It was in Bexhill that a missile, tracked all the

way from France, was seen heading straight for the town, flying exceptionally low. Two miles off the coast it turned westwards, passed over Beachy Head and then, inexplicably, turned again, flew south-east and crashed onto Boulogne from whence it came. Hastings and St Leonards received 14 doodlebugs, including one in Pevensey Road on June 23 which injured five people, one in Amherst Road on July 1 which caused two casualties and a third in Conqueror Road two days later in which there were 10 serious and 18 slight injuries.

Although only five missiles fell on Rye, the flying bomb period was the noisiest of the war for its inhabitants. The biggest concentration of artillery in the country, 1,300 gunners, was massed between Camber and Rye Harbour and the bulk of the population was moved to "safe quarters". The Grammar School was evacuated to Bedford and other children went to Blackpool and Monmouthshire. The rest were scattered throughout Cornwall, Somerset and Gloucestershire. Left in the town were the old people who refused to be driven out by Hitler, and those in business and factories of importance to the war effort.

Moving the guns

BY the beginning of July, the three groups of defenders — gunners, airmen and balloon crews — were so frequently getting in each other's way in their bid to shoot, tip or blast the VIs out of the sky that something had to be done, and quickly. Trigger-happy Americans and undisciplined AA batteries were blamed for illicit, freelance firing that destroyed not only flying bombs but RAF fighters. The Polish squadrons complained that the wings of their Mustangs were so perforated from "friendly fire" that they could be used as sieves and Roland Beamont, CO of the two squadrons of Tempests flying from Newchurch said his pilots spent much of their time trying to dodge the shell bursts of ack-ack.

Two Tempests were shot down by anti-aircraft guns in the first week of the battle but Wing Commander Beamont was able to retaliate in a rather bizarre fashion. A Tempest pilot shot down a flying bomb which crashed into the grounds of a country house used as a mess by the gunners. The explosion blew out all the windows in the mess as the gunners were having their breakfast. "No-one was hurt", said Beamont, "but the pilots came back from this particular sortie holding their sides."

Air Chief Marshal Hill, Commander-in-Chief of the Air Defence of Great Britain, himself flew on a number of sorties to assess the situation and decided that it was wrong to maintain the gun batteries inland; they should be redeployed to the coast. General Pile endorsed the plan and, on July 13, the greatest and most important decision in the battle against the flying bomb was made. The guns were to be moved to the coast, leaving the balloons where they were and creating two new areas for fighters alone, one between the balloons and the new gun belt and the other in front of the gun belt, over the sea.

Hundreds of guns and great reserves of ammunition were in position on the North Downs, thousands of miles of telephone cables had been laid and accommodation had been found for the gunners. "In short", said General Pile, "a small city was spread out between Redhill and the Thames and the proposal was that we should pick it up and transport it 30 or 40 miles south."

Only five days later another great military operation was completed. The guns were moved and resited between St Margaret's Bay and Cuckmere Haven. There were many batteries involved — 376 heavy and 572 light guns from General Pile's command, 16 90 mm guns from the US Army, 560 light guns manned by the RAF Regiment for

The New Defences July 1944

LEGEND
VI LAUNCHING AREAS
DIVER GUN BELT
BALLOON BARRAGE

airfield defence and 28 from the Royal Armoured Corps. The new "Diver" zone stretched 10,000 yards into the sea and 5,000 yards inland. The balloon barrage was increased, to 1,000 by July 21 and to 1,750 by the end of the month, and fighters had their own freedom of action between the guns and balloons and over the sea.

It was an enormous success. From their new position the gunners shot down 17 per cent of all flying bombs entering the gun belt in the first week. The score mounted from 24 per cent in the second week to 74 per cent in the last week of August. By then, those that escaped the fighters over the sea and the now-brilliant shooting of the gunners, met the fighters again inland. Hundreds of doodlebugs were again falling in "open countryside". As the weeks went by Kent was to suffer badly and so, to a lesser extent was Sussex but London, thanks to the co-operation that existed between the AA Command, Balloon Command and the RAF, could see, at last, a glimmer of hope on the horizon.

A 3.7 inch heavy battery takes up position on the Kent coast in a move that turned out to be an extraordinary success. Of the new compact gun belt, General Pile said at the time that it would give the fighters plenty of room for interception over the Channel and plenty of room for interception behind the guns where they would be acting as wicket-keepers, with the balloons away in the distance as long stops. There was also more chance, he said, of bringing the flying bombs harmlessly down into the sea.

The "Brocks Benefit" over the skies of south Kent from one of the batteries of guns on Romney Marsh. Hundreds of gunners, both British and American, contributed to the barrage which brought down so many V1s. Now the great danger was not only from falling doodlebugs but shrapnel, for everything that went up had to come down.

Their Majesties, the King and Queen at East Grinstead a few hours after a flying bomb had crashed on the town.

East Grinstead tragedy

BOMBS, incendiaries and even sea mines had fallen in or around East Grinstead during the course of the war, but the town's greatest tragedy and certainly the worst incident in Sussex occurred on Friday July 9, 1943 when a single raider picked out a convoy of Army trucks and dropped a string of bombs which demolished the Whitehall Cinema and many shops in London Road and the High Street. 108 people were killed and 235 injured. Fire added to the horror for it spread rapidly through the town and a score of premises was reduced to rubble. It was one of the great civilian disasters of the entire war.

A year later, on July 12, 1944, with East Grinstead still suffering from the scars of this tragic day, a flying bomb was shot down onto the rubble of the London Road. On this occasion three were killed, 41 injured and more than 400 houses, shops and offices damaged by blast. Several shops were completely obliterated but as the incident occurred just after 7.30 am there were few people about.

Within a few hours the King and Queen visited the scene of the disaster to give some words of comfort to the people of this stricken town. They remained for some time talking with the Civil Defence workers.

A few miles away, on the ridge which runs through the Ashdown Forest lay the Crowborough Golf Course, requisitioned by the Army for a military camp. On July 5, at 6.20 pm, just one week before the East Grinstead incident, a fighter spotted a doodlebug high above the forest — perfect countryside for some evening shooting. Diving from behind, he closed in and pressed his finger on the trigger of the control stick. Cannon shells spat out, the missile exploded and dived steeply to earth. It fell on top of the camp, killing eight Canadian soldiers and wounding 17. It was the county's worst doodlebug incident.

The row of thatched cottages in the tiny Hampshire village of Goodworth Clatford are seen here, gaily decorated for the Diamond Jubilee of 1897. On July 15, 1944 they were all destroyed by a flying bomb which hit a telegraph pole and crashed into the village centre. Six people were killed and several injured. The explosion and blast damaged many other houses including the village forge, the school and an inn, The Royal Oak. It was the furthest point west in the country that a V1 landed and it is believed that the missile was interrupted in its flight by a Spitfire pilot who, according to local legend, was attempting to turn it around and send it back to Germany!

Attack switches to Hampshire

FOR several nights during the second week in July no flying bombs were plotted over London; in fact the capital enjoyed a welcome rest from the constant barrage of the first 10 days of the month. Had the Germans run out of VIs? Had the Allies finally overrun the launching sites in Pas de Calais? No. Colonel Wachtel and his Flakregiment had redirected their point of attack and were now aiming at the great ports of Southampton and Portsmouth. On July 11, 29 VIs fell in Hampshire and they were delivered by a squadron of Heinkels, specially equipped to launch them from the air.

This new method of attack had actually been introduced on July 7 when a Heinkel flying over the North Sea had released a flying bomb on London without any resistance from the coastal defences. It is believed to have landed in Canterbury Road, Croydon. A few days later came the switch to Southampton with 29 fired on July 11 and 27 on July 14-15. Only two actually hit the city, the remainder being scattered so far and wide that one travelled as far inland as Winchester. During this period the Isle of Wight had a taste of what London and

the Home Counties had been experiencing for more than a month.

On the night of July 15, a V1 landed on Newcomen Road, Portsmouth and caused terrible damage. Fifteen people were killed, including several children, 63 injured and scores of homes destroyed by blast. After July 15 more VIs were launched on Southampton and Portsmouth and by the end of August almost 100 had been aimed at the Hampshire ports, most of them landing harmlessly in rural areas.

The Andover Advertiser wrote: "The thatched houses caught fire in the explosion lighting up the street and the village school stood windowless with some of its brickwork shattered and contents destroyed. The only other building to suffer was the licensed house which had several occupants but fortunately the only casualty was the landlord, Mr Fred Welham."

Ironically, the people who were killed were all Londoners seeking refuge in the village from flying bombs. They had arrived only that day.

Edna, Gladys, Molly and Marian of the 490 H.A.A Battery

The searchlight radar which helped Marian and her colleagues to improve the "kill" rate against the flying bomb.

Looking for love nests

AMONG the anti-aircraft batteries sent to the coast in mid-July was the 490th Heavy, which encamped at Lympne on the cliff above Romney Marsh in hurriedly erected tented accommodation. Like other batteries, there were plenty of women on the gun sites, including Marian (now Mills), a radar operator who recalls her days in the front line.

"On our arrival at Lympne, new American radar sets replaced our cumbersome Mark 2's and 3's, the cabins of which had to be rotated by hand in order to line up the aerial with the target. The American 584's had dish aerials rotating on a static cabin. It was much easier to get and stay on target even when the missile passed overhead. I can still feel the tension and thrill of those seconds when each operator called in turn — "on range", "on bearing", "on angle" and the No 1 called "on target" to the command post, the information being electrically passed to the gun positions. The speed of the flying bombs made our speed imperative."

Marian remembers the feeling of comradeship which was so strong that many took comfort in each others' arms. "I saw the battery sergeant major, a tough little regular, with his ATS counterpart, searching the camp and surroundings with torches for love nests. Here there was a large number of Americans, and no doubt strictures came down from on high that the protection of British maidenhood required extra vigilance."

Who are we to act as God ?

BACK in London, a dilemma faced the Air Ministry and MI5. The Germans were telling their supposed agents, whom they thought were freely operating in Britain, to report the times and places of flying bomb incidents in London. Truthful information, it was decided, would aid the enemy but false information could be checked by German photographic reconnaissance, in which case the agents would be "blown". The man in charge of scientific intelligence, Dr R.V.Jones takes up the story.

"I had noticed that in the Peenemunde trials the bombs tended to fall short of the target, and now knew that......the operational bombs were also tending to fall short, the centre of gravity being in south-east London, near Dulwich. In a flash I saw that we might be able to keep the bombs falling short, which would mean fewer casualties in London, and at the same time avoid arousing any suspicion regarding...our agents.

"We could give correct points of impact for bombs that tended to have a longer range than usual, but couple these with times of bombs which had fallen short....Therefore, if they made any correction at all, it would be to reduce the average range."

Dr Jones recommended this course of action to "George", with whom he had been involved in supplying misleading information to the Germans but in doing so he realised he was keeping the mean point of impact in Dulwich, where his own parents lived and where he went to school. But he knew that neither his parents nor school would have it otherwise. "George" adopted the plan.

The idea reached political level and both Mr Sandys and Lord Cherwell supported it, but Home Secretary, Herbert Morrison, whose constituency was in Lambeth, thought

Temporary accommodation was found for the patients while the nurses of Lewisham Hospital continued with the task of clearing rubble and debris from the ward which was blasted by the flying bomb of July 26. It was a familiar scenario that summer, for 76 London hospitals were damaged, involving the loss of some 8,200 beds. Altogether 138 patients were killed in hospitals and 1,155 injured — many of them casualties from earlier incidents. The St Helier Hospital at Carshalton was struck twice. The first V1 landed on the morning of Thursday June 21 and injured many nurses who became patients in their own hospital. Six days later it was struck again, killing two people.

the attempt to keep the aiming point short was an effort by Government officials and others in Westminster, Belgravia and Mayfair to "keep the bombs off themselves at the expense of the proletariat in south London".

Dr Jones said: "I was not present at the meeting at which the deception policy was discussed but Herbert Morrison was in the chair and he ruled that it would be an interference with Providence if we were to supply the Germans with misleading information, because this might mean that some people would be killed through our action who might otherwise have survived — overlooking the fact that what we were hoping

to do, would also enable more to survive who might otherwise have been killed."

"George" told Dr Jones of the ruling and asked what he should do. The scientist said he was not at the meeting and until he received instructions in writing, he must continue as they had started.

The deception worked brilliantly but Morrison still went to some lengths to denounce the idea and said that if it had come out into the open there might have been the most serious political circumstances. Later he wrote: "Who are we to act as God?"

"We were soon at work with our jet which I was directing down into what looked like a little bit of hell. Beneath me was swirling, curling smoke, black, brown and other colours and, like all smoke, dirty and stinking. Flames were leaping everywhere and seemed to be doing their best to reach me on the ladder. Intermittently a drum of paint or spirit would explode and shower coloured flames everywhere."

London fireman describing the fire, caused by a doodlebug crashing onto a factory at Great Eastern Street, near Liverpool Street station

West Ham Borough Council's Electricity Department on the junction of Romford Road and Vicarage Lane was hit in the early hours of July 2, completely destroying the southern end of the building. Two weeks later, on July 19, a flying bomb landed on exactly the same spot — again in the early hours of the morning. In each case more than 100 houses were damaged.

THE 55,000 members of the London Fire Brigade, with memories of the Blitz still very clear, found the doodlebug days difficult, unpleasant and exhausting but less of a problem than the "firing" of London in December, 1940.

Even so there were thousands of incidents to attend to and many fires; spectacular fires like the burning of the South Metropolitan Gas Company in east Greenwich and the OK Sauce factory in Wandsworth, terrifying fires like those at the docks where ammunition and petrol cans were stored, repulsive fires where charred limbs had to be removed in sacks and fires at paintworks, schools, churches, factories, workshops, and garages.

Outside London, especially in Kent, the flying bombs caused more destruction than conflagrations. The National Fire Service had excellent communications, great mobility, good equipment and a dogged determination that had served so well during the period of high explosive and incendiary raids. Wherever flying bombs fell they joined civil defence workers in digging out trapped people, covering damaged homes with tarpaulins and making safe potential fire risks. The firefighters often risked their own lives in shattered buildings to assist the victims.

Elmers End bus garage after its direct hit on July 17. Altogether there were more than 250 separate incidents affecting London Transport, with many lives lost. On one occasion, at Waterloo, two double-deckers had their tops sliced off and, near the Oval, two trams and two buses crowded with people going home from work, were blown to pieces. By the end of August, few London buses had windows, for what had not been blown out by blast, had been removed to save passengers from being showered with glass splinters. Travelling by bus in the summer of 1944 was not popular — but, for many Londoners, it was the only way to get to work.

Petrol tanks exploded

THE photograph on page 91 shows the remains of the Elmers End bus garage, near Beckenham, after it had received a direct hit on the evening of July 17. About a dozen London Transport staff were in the entrance of the garage when they heard a doodlebug cut out. Everyone scattered. The bomb exploded near the entrance, wrecking the ticket office, canteen, ARP stores and mess room. Six people who went to the kit room were killed instantly and a woman conductor died in another area.

After the explosion, which occurred about 8.30 pm a furious blaze broke out among the debris of the bus garage and the petrol tank of a parked bus exploded. Within minutes the fire had spread and other petrol tanks were blowing up, one by one. The London Fire Brigade appeared quickly on the scene, in time for more explosions. Tyres smouldered, debris was scattered everywhere and bodies were strewn across the kit room.

In all there were 18 fatalities at Elmers End, including the London Transport employees who died instantly in the blast, two members of the Home Guard, a heavy rescue worker, a 74-year-old woman in the street and another woman in a nearby street shelter. There were also more than 40 injuries. The firemen had a particularly hazardous time. With tanks exploding and a fierce fire raging, they had to remove stored petrol and Home Guard ammunition from the garage. A number of firemen were badly injured.

Urgent telephone calls to other garages enabled Elmers End to borrow buses and tickets and next morning the service was resumed as normal, except that some buses had no windows or destination blinds. It was a remarkable achievement in the face of such appalling havoc, for 27 double-deckers, two single deckers and ten ambulances had been destroyed.

There were many other bus incidents. In Battersea, a V1 hit a lorry on Lavender Hill and killed 14 people on a No 77 that was passing at the time. The Battersea garage was damaged three times in two weeks, Camberwell tram depot received four flying bombs and the West Ham depot was hit twice. The first was on July 23 when a large number of trolley buses was damaged but, within 13 hours of the incident, services were operating as normal. In Snaresbrook Road, Wanstead 15 buses were destroyed and on July 27, at Forest Gate, a trolley bus was destroyed and both driver and conductor killed.

A Mustang pilot on constant Diver duty in July was Warrant Officer Tadeusz Szymanski, whose doodlebug heroics with 316 Squadron included a frantic chase above the Kent countryside on the evening of July 12. Szymanski, out of ammunition, flew alongside to get a close look. "The thing was jerking along and the elevator was flapping with each vibration of the crude jet motor", he said. "I noticed that on the front of the bomb was a silly little propeller. It looked ridiculous. I decided to tip it off balance." Wing under wing, stick to starboard but, alas, his adversary proved to be stubborn as a mule. Szymanski was more stubborn. He repeated the manoeuvre eleven times but still they flew on in total harmony until a balloon barrage loomed right in front. "I tried a different manoeuvre, hitting very hard with my wing tip as I went into a loop. When I recovered I found to my dismay it was still flying but I had turned it upside down." Suddenly it plunged to earth in a steep spin and the Polish ace, contented at last, set course for West Malling. Szymanski went on to intercept many more V1s and his heroics earned him the admiration of Polish leader General Sikorski. Tadeusz Szymanski's Mustang (pictured above) bore the name of his daughter, Halinka and shows the number of his successes. Later in life, Tadek (as he was known) and his family settled in Norwich and he became a printer with Jarrolds. He died in February 1992.

The witch hunt

THE July phase of the anti-Diver battle was the most intense. The strain on the airmen who spearheaded it was shown by the rapid turn-round in squadrons. There were bases at Deanland, Ford, Holmesby, Middle Wallop and Brenzett but it was West Malling and Newchurch which were to gain recognition as the foremost airfields on doodlebug duty. The greatest number of bombs crossed the coast at Dungeness, so the emphasis on air defence was placed there with 150 Tempest Wing at Newchurch, the Mustangs of 129 Squadron and 315 (Polish) Squadron operating from Brenzett and the night-fighting Mosquitoes of 96 Squadron at Ford. Further inland, at West Malling, 316 (City of Warsaw) Squadron flew the Mustang alongside 322, 157, 274, 85 and 80, who came and went on brief, but hectic courses of duty.

Squadron Leader Bohdan Arct, leader of 316 (City of Warsaw) Squadron had another name for the V1's. "As they crackled overhead", he said, "they seemed to laugh at us. We called them witches." He recalled how the repulsive sound of passing missiles was accompanied by the roar of the guns and quite often shell splinters rained on their heads. An order was issued to wear steel helmets but the Poles were reluctant to obey it. "The anti-aircraft batteries disturbed us considerably", he said. "The gunners knew very well the silhouettes of flying bombs and our own fighter planes but sometimes they lost their heads. Often we would fly into a cloud of our own artillery bursts and, on one occasion, a medium calibre battery fired so accurately that my wings became perforated and resembled a hunk of Swiss cheese."

Squadron Leader Arct remembers how he was preparing for a patrol when his mechanic said: "Look, sir, here comes a flying witch". Said Arct: "Before I could taxi to the runway it was already overhead. It spluttered its horrid laughter as if saying — 'go on catch me now, you idiot'. When I was at last in the air all I could see was a microscopic dot on the horizon".

The Poles had the last laugh. By the end of July, 316 Squadron had claimed 50 destroyed and moved to a coastal airfield at Friston to chase and "break the bloody backs of more flying witches".

Meanwhile at Newchurch, under the fearless leadership of Roland Beamont, the Tempest V was having even greater success. Up to 50 sorties a day were flown by each of the two Tempest squadrons and pilots' individual scores of two or three V1's in a day were becoming frequent. In mid-July, with 150 Wing approaching its 500th V1 destroyed, the fighter controllers based at Maidstone and Horsham threw a party at Bexhill in honour of Beamont and his men. 150 returned the compliment on July 20, with a "doodlebug dance" at Folkestone. On August 23, Roland Beamont shot down his 30th and last V1, the 632nd to be destroyed by his Wing.

One of the greatest hazards which faced the pilots at Newchurch was the night patrol against the flying bomb. One man, however, enjoyed the challenge so much that he became the greatest doodlebug ace of them all. Squadron Leader Joseph Berry shot down seven in a hectic night of non-stop action on July 23, and by the end of August he had destroyed more than 60. After the campaign was over, Berry was shot down by AA fire over the Dutch coast and killed.

Two airmen who flew on night sorties from Cambridge had a special reason for wanting to stop the V1's from reaching England. One was a pilot whose wife and children had nearly been killed when one fell on their house and the other was a navigator whose mother lived directly beneath the regular flight path.

In the early hours of July 26, 1944, flying over the English Channel in their Mosquito, they were informed that a V1 had been spotted and they were to destroy it. Their progress was followed on the radar screen at operational headquarters — a tiny blob of light which flashed, faded slowly and flashed again. Then, with the Mosquito flying at a height of 7,000 feet and some 25 miles north-east of Margate, the flashing light suddenly disappeared from the screen. No-one really knew what happened but it was assumed that they had collided with their target.

The navigator who died was 20-year-old James Farrar and few people realised just how great a loss England and the world of literature had suffered by the death of this young man. Had he lived he would certainly have become famous as a poet and novelist. A notebook in which he recorded his personal thoughts and experiences, sprinkled with stories and verse was published in 1950 under the title *The Unreturning Spring*.

The Tempest

A Tempest V at Newchurch, on Romney Marsh during the flying bomb campaign. In 1944 the Tempest Vs were the fastest propeller-driven fighters below 20,000 feet in operational service on either side. The smaller picture shows a Tempest closing in on its prey but Wing Commander Roland Beamont said there was a danger in getting too close. "On one occasion a flying bomb was exploded by cannon fire from 200 yards away. The Tempest concerned went straight through the fireball and returned safely but streaked with smoke and evidence of charring on the elevators and on the rudder."

THE GENIUS OF JAMES FARRAR

James Farrar, the young navigator who was killed while attempting to destroy a flying bomb, was only 20 when he died, but he left behind poems, stories and sketches which show him to have been one of the most promising writers of his generation. These were published in 1950 in a book titled *The Unreturning Spring*. The editor, Henry Wilkinson in an introduction about James Farrar wrote: "In his letters burns the many coloured flame of genius, now tender, now fierce, sometimes meditative, sometimes light-hearted, but always the master of beautiful language."

AFTER NIGHT OFFENSIVE

*Glowed through the violet petal of the
sky
Like a death's-head the calm summer
moon
And all the distance echoed with owl-cry*

*Hissing the white waves of grass
unsealed
Peer of moon on metal, hidden men,
As the wind foamed deeply through the
field.*

*Rooted to soil, remote and faint as stars,
Looking to neither side, they lay all night
Sunken in the murmurous seas of grass.*

*No flare burned upwards: never sound
was shed
But lulling cries of owls beyond the world
As wind and moon played softly with the
dead.*

James Farrar, who disappeared over the Channel, chasing a V1.

THE DAILY MAIL, Tuesday July 25, 1944

Beamont—first fly-bomb ace

By Daily Mail Reporter

Britain's first ace flying bomb killer has won another award, it is announced today.

He is acting Wing Commander Roland Beamont and he wins a Bar to his D.S.O. He also holds the D.F.C. and Bar.

Although the citation makes no mention of his successes against flying bombs, it is known that Wing Commander Beamont, in recent weeks, has shot many of the bombs down into the sea.

Wing Commander Beamont is a former test pilot, and at 25, commands a station from which the Tempest, fastest aeroplane in the world, operates.

He comes from Chichester and is known as Britain's ace loco-buster.

Permanent duty

He is more or less on permanent duty against the flying bomb, I was told last night. He is never far from his fighter and volunteers to go up as soon as his station plotters locate the bomb.

"We have plenty of good marksmen here, hence our success", he told me.

"Some of us have had queer experiences with flying bombs. We've come back spattered with black oil all over our machines, with fuselage singed, and even with rudders burnt off.

"We do all sorts of things to them — blow their wings off, shoot their engines away, fire their fuel which sets their bombs off. During one period we knocked down four out of five."

The story which appeared in The Daily Mail on July 25, 1944 about Roland Beamont. After the war Beamont became a leading Test Pilot and an immensely respected figure in aviation circles.

This is the photograph which appeared in the Daily Mirror almost two weeks after the incident at Leytonstone. Eileen Clements was the then anonymous 11-year-old girl being carried to safety in the arms of a fireman from the wreckage of her home.

Carried to safety in the arms of a fireman

THE photograph on the left of a little girl being rescued from the wreckage of her home is one that has been used time and again to symbolise the days when the doodlebug was at its most menacing. It first appeared in the *Daily Mirror* and shows 11-year-old Eileen Clements being carried in the arms of a fireman from No 5 Arundel Road, a terraced house in Leytonstone.

Eileen, aged 11, was playing in the street on the evening of Monday July 24 when the flying bomb came over. She ran to the Anderson shelter and dived in just as there was a tremendous crash. The explosion flung her to the far end of the shelter. Her sister, Lily, aged 18, was in the bedroom, combing her hair in the wardrobe mirror. The house collapsed in the impact, the wardrobe fell over and Lily was trapped underneath, but shielded from falling plaster and debris. The view outside was horrific. The row of terraced houses had disintegrated and a massive pall of smoke and dust hung in the air.

In Leytonstone town centre, Eileen and Lily's parents, Alfred and Thirza, were at the cinema when the explosion occurred. The film stopped, the audience rushed out and the couple ran frantically home as fire engines approached. When they reached Arundel Road, they found it had been roped off, and the sight that greeted them was a massive pile of jagged timber and masonry; in fact the whole street had collapsed.

Rescue workers were already there. They had lifted a shocked and bruised Eileen from the shelter and joined the firemen from Leyton in digging Lily from the rubble. Leading Fireman Bill Sayers carried Eileen to safety for a tearful reunion with her parents, who minutes later learned that Lily was also alive.

The photograph was used in the *Daily Mirror* a few days later. There was no reference to the identity of the girl, or the locality but a story, accompanying the picture said that 17,000 homes had been destroyed and 800,000 damaged by flying bombs — and still they kept coming. "Where can the luckless, the threatened and the homeless go?", asked the Mirror. "Homes are wanted desperately."

Eileen Alexander (née Clements) has never forgotten the day she was carried from the debris of her home in Leytonstone. She still remembers the silence of the engine cutting out, the blast that followed, the smell of brick, dust and soot, the absolute despair of people emerging from their shelters and the bravery of the firemen, police and wardens.

Following her appearance on the BBC TV programme, London Plus some years ago, a viewer rang Eileen to give the name of the fireman, Bill Sayers, whom she had never met. Sadly he had died but she met his widow and that, she says, was a very moving experience. A painting of Eileen appears on the dust cover of the third volume of the magnificent trilogy on the Blitz, produced by "After The Battle". The editor, Winston G Ramsey, in dedicating this volume to the victims, also invited Eileen to write the foreword. In 1992, when her photograph (left) was taken, she was living at Wickford in Essex.

97

KENT MESSENGER FRIDAY JULY 21, 1944

GUN-FIRE BAPTISMS IN ATHOL TERRACE

Front-line kiddies have never slept in their own cots

Children are still being born and brought up in a row of houses, Athol Terrace, Dover, which faces across the Channel to enemy occupied France.

Nestling between the towering white cliffs, Athol Terrace is in all England the inhabited place which is nearest the enemy.

It is the hottest part of Hell's Corner !

And when the history of Dover's part in the war comes to be written a proud place will be given to the mothers of Athol Terrace. Five years of terror have failed to drive them from their homes. They are still rearing families of healthy and happy children.

Many of the children born in Athol Terrace since the war began have never known what it is to sleep in a bed in their own homes.

Each evening when bedtime comes the mothers, instead of taking the children upstairs and tucking them in their cots, take them along to the deep caves which honeycomb the cliffs.

Typical of the front-line mothers is Mrs Mary Culley, of 4 Athol Terrace. Up to the war she had one son, Bombardier Jack Culley who is with the Royal Artillery in Gibraltar.

After the birth of Jack she went 15 years without any more children. Then on April 23, 1941, a little boy, Michael was born. On March 20, 1942, Kathleen entered the world of explosions and now Mrs Culley has a baby in arms, Patricia, born on March 17 this year.

The children of Athol Terrace do not know what it is like to be afraid of the dark. They toddle around the dark caves as cheerfully as an ordinary child would run down the passage of a house.

This is the story which appeared on the front page of the County Edition of the Kent Messenger on July 21, 1944. The photograph shows Mr and Mrs Culley with their three children Patricia, Kathleen and Michael at the entrance to the caves above Athol Terrace, Dover. In the next column is a heavily-censored story of flying bombs which were shot down over "Southern England" watched by thousands of people. "Children, waiting in a queue, were among those killed by one which crashed in a street and struck a shop", said the newspaper.

Swanscombe's turn again

SWANSCOMBE'S place in the history of the flying bomb campaign was already assured with the first to crash on British soil in mid-June. Although that one fell harmlessly in a potato field it reminded villagers what might have been and they anxiously watched or listened every day and night, silently uttering the words that were on everyone's lips at the time — "keep going, you bugger, keep going".

On Sunday July 30 at 11.30 am, women came out of their kitchens and men, in their gardens or allotments looked up as the menacing drone was heard again. The engine cut out and the missile fell onto Taunton Road in the village centre with an earth-shattering explosion which echoed for many miles around. It was one of North Kent's most serious incidents; 13 people killed, 22 seriously injured and 69 slightly hurt. There was damage to almost 100 properties and, on this peaceful summer Sunday morning, Swanscombe was transformed into a scene of pandemonium. The serious cases were taken to Gravesend Hospital. The first-aid post at Northfleet paper mills dealt with the non-serious. Rest centres were opened at Lawn Road School in Northfleet and the Southfleet Road Central School at Southfleet.

Eight houses in the village were completely demolished and more than 150 people were made homeless. Among them were two Royal Marine sergeants, home on leave after taking part in the Normandy landings. They were blown from a window by the blast onto the street below. One regained consciousness to find himself in the street surrounded by rubble. His wife and two children had reached the shelter and were unhurt.

One eye-witness, a Mr Everdale, was standing in a field beyond the village when he saw a doodlebug being chased by fighters. "The flying bomb began to lose altitude and I thought it would crash in the fields but it hit the village", he recalled. Another to have a narrow escape was a local dairy farmer who was loading up his milk delivery van when he heard the missile cut-out. He dived under a haystack and escaped unhurt. His van was demolished.

Furniture is salvaged from damaged homes. This is Swanscombe village on July 30, 1944.

The children of St. John's School, Shirley had heard the air-raid warning and were in the shelter when the bomb fell. They were unhurt, as were the occupants of the cottages just 10 yards from where the missile impacted. They were said to have emerged hysterical and covered in dust.

Shirley school demolished

THE villages surrounding Croydon, and the town itself, were still in the centre of the bombardment and, by late July, flying bombs were falling with devastating regularity. Many were actually brought down by the balloon barrage near Sevenoaks, for those that got caught in the cables often limped on for a few miles, losing height and momentum, only to crash in the borough of Croydon.

The photograph above shows the ruins of the village school at Shirley which received a direct hit on July 26. The blast damaged many houses, including the two school cottages and took part of the roof off St John's parish church. The loss of the school involved numerous complications for the church and took ten years to resolve. The church was restored in 1947.

One who witnessed this, and many other incidents in Surrey is John Rawlings, now of Lewes, Sussex whose father was vicar of Shirley in 1944. John writes: "My youth was spent in Shirley vicarage in an area which provided a front-line view of the Battle of Britain, the blitz, doodlebugs and rockets. We suffered severe damage from bombs, incendiaries and, worst of all, flying bombs. Our church was damaged by these and the school demolished.

On one occasion, whilst helping the verger to dig a grave (one of my wartime activities) we counted 17 flying bombs approaching in line—abreast, some gliding, some diving and some under power. If hit, we thought at least we could save anyone the job of burying us.

As a member of the Home Guard I spent much time helping civilians to clear rubble and salvage belongings from destroyed homes. Nearly 4,000 doodlebugs were destroyed by AA guns and fighters but unfortunately the balloon barrage at Sevenoaks tended to merely interfere with the flight of these missiles so that they could just about reach the Croydon area."

Many flying bombs managed to slip between the balloon cables and chug on towards London; others, spitting furiously, struggled forward for a few miles and dived to earth near towns like Croydon. This one was splendidly caught by the balloon at Meopham, exploded on striking the cable and impacted in a nearby field, uncomfortably close to the balloon site at Shipley Hills Road. The balloon crew were quick to inspect their first victim.

101

Horrors of Lewisham

SOUTH-east London's worst flying bomb incident occurred on July 28 at 9.41 am when one landed on the market place at Lewisham. It was a Friday. The post office was full of old age pensioners and a department store crowded with shoppers. The market stalls, in a line outside Marks and Spencer's, Woolworth's and Sainbury's, caught the full force of the blast and two passing omnibuses were blown to pieces. The bomb actually exploded on the roof of a shelter, demolishing shops on both sides of the street. Ultimately it was established that 59 people were killed, 124 seriously injured and 178 slightly injured — many by shards of flying glass.

It was an appalling sight, for the dead and injured were spreadeagled everywhere. People with limbs torn from their bodies lay in the market place, where minutes before they had been shopping. Many of the dead and injured were discovered in the basement cafe of Woolworth's and several others were office workers who just happened to be passing by.

Less than 10 minutes after the explosion the first of the Civil Defence workers arrived and the WVS set up their incident inquiry point. There was no house with a telephone available so they borrowed a table from a coffee stall and planted it alongside the control van with debris all around.

Ambulances arrived quickly but they were unable to take the casualties to nearby Lewisham Hospital. That had been hit by a flying bomb two days previously and the patients had been evacuated to other hospitals, which were now overflowing with casualties. The ambulance drivers toured

Lewisham High Street in 1992. The missile exploded on the roof of the shelter, where the market stalls stand today.

south London to find a hospital with suitable accommodation for the injured.

In some instances the unfortunate people were booked into hospital, but not booked out which made accurate information about survivors very difficult to secure. The rescue work continued for many days but several bodies remained unidentified. Some of them were probably Irish labourers employed on near-by road repairs, whose surnames were unknown to the foreman.

Mrs J.Lemos of Bexley was a teenager at the time and still recalls the horrors of Lewisham. Her office was "bombed out" but she escaped unhurt. Her nightmare memory is seeing the sales girls from Marks and Spencer's running from the store with their clothes alight.

As with all incidents, serious or otherwise, the mobile laundries and the mobile baths were soon established in Lewisham while hundreds of people took advantage of the meal service canteens. A few months later another type of bomb was to land less than two miles away and cause even greater death and destruction.

The scene of the Lewisham carnage of July 28, 1944. Fifty nine people were killed.

A "magpie" called Hemingway

THE RAF Special Investigation Branch spent some weeks looking for a relatively intact flying bomb, one that had crashed without exploding, so they could unravel the mystery of its fusing system and timing device and then, perhaps, find some way of putting it off course.

Air Commodore Harold Shephard, then a Squadron Leader working with the Branch, was sent to Romney Marsh where a Vl had been brought down intact. On arrival he discovered that the control device had been removed, either by a German agent, or a souvenir hunter. Thwarted but certainly not defeated, Shephard and his colleague, Warrant Officer Henry Stuckey decided to hunt for the missing parts in the Romney area.

"We met with no lack of co-operation", he said. "Everyone, everywhere showered us with information. Curiouser and curiouser became the odd fragments of Vl pressed into our hands by conscience-stricken souvenir hunters, shocked to the sudden realisation that they might be concealing a vital clue."

With their car loaded up like a totter's barrow, half a wing, a tail section and a collection of other fragments, the couple took the bizarre gifts to ADI (K) at Harrow in the hope that the boffins might find "something vital". But no luck.

Then came a call from a local newspaper reporter who had heard of their quest and its urgency. At Dunsfold airfield in Surrey, not far from Gatwick, he had met a real magpie of an American named Ernest Hemingway, who had a remarkable collection of Vl bits and had been in Romney Marsh the previous week. They tracked down "Papa" Hemingway, not knowing that the famous American author, an avid souvenir hunter, was working as a war correspondent.

They met in a briefing room at Newchurch. "He was a big man in blue flying overalls, with a weather-scarred face and a lumpish bearlike look", said Shephard. They asked to see his Vl bits. "Sure", said Hemingway. "But I doubt if they are anything you're looking for." That evening Mr Hemingway was relieved of his "bits and pieces" and they were taken to Harrow and given to the intelligence officers. One jumped two feet in the air when he saw them. It turned out that Hemingway's souvenirs included two live, dangerously volatile detonators that could explode at the slightest jolt.

These Vl parts did not yield very much information of value but others certainly did and, thanks to the bravery of the bomb disposal men who risked their lives to defuse the warheads, many missiles were taken apart to reveal some remarkable German ingenuity.

On July 28, a flying bomb crashed onto a smallholding near Powdermill Lane, High Brooms, Tunbridge Wells. Two people, who were feeding chickens when they heard the machine coming, took cover but there was no explosion. They emerged from the shelter and found a large black doodlebug tangled up in the chicken wire.

Walter Clary, serving with the 20th Bomb Disposal Unit of the Royal Engineers, based at Oak Hill Road, Sevenoaks remembers his unit dealing with this one. The two officers sent to investigate the crash discovered that police had evacuated 1,500 people from their homes in the vicinity of Southborough and High Brooms. It was just as well — the warhead was likely to explode at any time causing widespread damage and the fuse had to be removed without delay.

The officers, almost holding their breath, found that an 80-amp fuse in one of three fuse pockets was jammed. This was withdrawn by remote control. The other two were carefully taken out and the leads severed. Thanks to the 20th Bomb Disposal Unit, officers and sappers who worked with them, the first complete unexploded flying bomb was immobilised without mishap.

Mr M.F.Vernall of Tunbridge Wells also remembers this incident. "It landed in an allotment, knocking down an apple tree just off Powdermill Lane where Mr Medhurst was feeding his chickens. Nearby residents were evacuated and schoolchildren spent the rest of the morning in the shelters. If I remember correctly small parts of the V1 were sold locally to raise money for the war effort."

> In 1944 I was teaching small children at Frant Primary School, and was responsible for a class of 40. The doodlebug raids had begun and I was aware that when the engine cut out, almost immediately there would be an explosion.
>
> On one particular morning we heard the blood-curdling sound of an oncoming doodlebug. We had no protection of any kind so I told my little ones to get under their tables and, as the engine cut out, I hurried under my desk. I peered at all the little white faces and said a prayer: "Dear God, if this is the end of us all, please let the parents know I did my best to save their children".
>
> We waited for the explosion but it never came. That doodlebug had made a perfect landing on allotments at Hawkenbury.
>
> **Dora E. Bassett, Wadhurst**

This is all that was left of Beechmont, Sevenouks, a long rambling building in the ownership of the Lambarde family for many years. By 1944 it had been requisitioned by the army and was used as a billet for the ATS girls who maintained the army vehicles stored in Knole Park. On July 12 at 8.57 am, a flying bomb landed square on the house, the blast destroying many hutments which had been built in the grounds. Two girls died and 44 were injured but, had the bomb struck a few minutes earlier the house would have been full — the majority had just left for Knole Park to care for the trucks.

Give them one for George !

In the summer of 1944 I was a 12-year-old living in London and enjoying the new excitement of doodlebugs. When the school holiday started in late July my dad suggested we should get out of London and take the opportunity of helping with the harvest in Benenden, Kent. A week later we caught the steam train to Headcorn and, on arrival at the station found the sky almost filled with Verey lights — signal flares, mostly red with some greens all in line across the sky. "What's that?", we asked the porter. Back came a rich Kentish accent. "They be doodlebugs." "What?" we said, "we've come down here to be away from them." "Well you 'ain't," he replied. "You've come right down in the middle of them."

The Verey lights, we discovered, were markers sent up by the Royal Observer Corps when a flying bomb passed over their observation point. A pilot could see the line of the flares, pick up the course of the missile and hopefully "down it". As a four-wheel cart took us to the farm three or four miles away we watched a Spitfire chase a V1 and then shoot it down in a field about a mile away.

That was the pattern for the next eight weeks. My shrapnel collection grew as we watched Spitfires, Typhoons and then Meteors join in the chase to down the V1s in Kent before they reached London. It was an idyllic summer for a 12-year-old. The delights of the farm, fishing, trees to climb, waving to the fighter pilots as we worked in the fields and the skies peppered with the flares of the Observer Corps.

My most vivid memory was the actions of a lady called Mag. She was a plump, round lady with greying hair in her mid-forties and had two children of my age working in the field with her. On one occasion we heard the staccato noise of a V1, looked up and saw it flying towards us pursued by two fighters. We threw ourselves into the ditch. All of us that was except for Mag. She stood on a slight rise in the ground in the turnip field, feet apart, holding her weeding hoe in her hands and waving it in huge circles above her head.

As the bomb and pilots approached, the pilots opened fire and the empty shell cases began to fall, but above the noise of the V1 and the aircraft and the guns we could hear the shouts of Mag. "Go on boys. Go on boys. Get the bastard. Give them one for George."

The aircraft and bomb came directly overhead but still Mag stood there shouting. "Give them one for George. Give them one for George." The pilots hit the bomb and it fell three fields away with a bang. We cheered and joined Mag in the turnip field. She had returned to her usual quiet self. I was working alongside a man called "Acid Drop Jack". I said "What did Mag mean by 'Give them one for George?' Was it St George of England, or King George?"

"St George or the King be beggared," he lisped. "That be her eldest boy, George. He was in the Navy and got killed in an air raid a few weeks ago. That'll make her feel better."

R.L.Ainsby, Oakley Drive, Bromley

These photographs, above and right, released by Associated Press on August 3 are among the most dramatic of the whole campaign. They show a flying bomb falling on London (the buildings in the foreground are the Law Courts) and, in the second picture, a huge pall of smoke from an area behind the Law Courts. No date is given for the incident, or incidents but it is believed they were taken in late June and may well have been of the bomb which caused the Aldwych tragedy. (see page 56)

The view from Fleet Street of the flying bomb which crashed behind the Law Courts. (See opposite page)

The Clock House pub which stands close to the site where many people were dining on that fateful day in 1944.

Beckenham Vl kills 44

AT lunchtime on August 2, a flying bomb crashed onto a restaurant in Beckenham Road, Beckenham between the railway line and Churchfields Road, killing 44 people and injuring many more. The restaurant was full of customers and many died instantly. Several shops on both sides of the road and 12 houses were demolished.

The blast extended many hundred yards in each direction. There was severe damage to 60 shops and houses, including the Prince Arthur pub. More than 140 shops and homes were slightly damaged and several fires broke out among the ruins.

For the Borough of Bromley it was the most tragic day of the entire war. Rescue workers were on the scene quickly but the road was blocked by great piles of rubble. For many hours they toiled, removing the bricks and debris, recovering the bodies and carrying out the injured. The dead included many shopkeepers, Sidney Hancock, the fishmonger, Albert Richards, husband of the woman who ran the restaurant and the wife and daughter of Philip Rust, the tailor.

The shops were never rebuilt. After the war the road was widened and a new public house, the Clock House was built on the site.

The remains of the old Norman church at Abinger.

"INTO the quiet beauty of a Southern England village, well known to thousands of visitors, there roared on Thursday last week one of Hitler's flying bombs. It struck the picturesque parish church which stood serenely apart across the green. When the noise and the dust of the shattering explosion had passed the ancient building presented a sorry spectacle. The spire and the whole of the west end had gone. So had half the roof, and the remaining walls were cracked. The bells had been flung forward beyond the church and great beams had crashed down from the roof and splintered the oaken pews below. All this happened in a flash before a service was due at the church."

This was the report in the *Surrey Advertiser* of the demise of the church of St. James at Abinger, near Dorking. It happened just before the 8 o'clock service on Thursday August 3 and the rector, the Rev L.G.Meade was actually leaving the rectory to walk to the church when the explosion occurred. He watched the tragedy unfold before his eyes and when the dust lifted he saw a distressing heap of rubble amidst the blasted trees and broken tombstones. Nearby houses and a hotel also suffered damage but there were no casualties.

The church was rebuilt after the war.

A shepherd's tale

In 1944 I lived in Hastings and worked on a farm owned by Sir Harry Newton. He was in charge of the Home Guard and, of course, I was in his platoon. On one occasion the guns at Hastings brought down 72 doodles in one day. Many fell in the sea but some landed in such places as Broad Oak, Brede Church, the Waterworks and the "Big House".

I remember the day I had to move sheep from the fields back to the farm — with great difficulty. They went everywhere but the right way and I said to them: "I hope a doodle lands on you". Almost as I spoke, I heard one coming, followed by the rattle of machine gun fire. The engine stopped but it was misty and I couldn't see it. I started running, then looked up and saw a doodlebug coming straight at me about 70 yards away. It was so low it went under the electric wires.

The next moment I saw my cap spinning towards the road and I was following it, spinning round and round. I don't remember an explosion but I heard a hissing sound and was thrown through a fence. I gathered two stunned rabbits which were blown out of their burrow, stood up with them in my hands to let the pilot of a plane circling above see that I was alright. There was red-hot shrapnel about two feet square where I stood.

A daily newspaper, I think it was the Mirror, wrote the next day that a shepherd was blown out of a field with his sheep when a flying bomb crashed nearby.

W.P.Winter, Tangmere. Chichester, West Sussex

She smiled and died

Mr Walter Hodder remembers the day on August 3, 1944 when he was helping his father, a builder, at work at Mark's Cross, Sussex. Mrs Hodder was at home in School House, Tidebrook and his younger brother Colin was at Tidebrook School, having not yet broken up for the summer holidays.

Hearing a fighter shooting at a doodlebug, they looked up and watched the pilotless aircraft crash. To their alarm it appeared to have landed near Tidebrook church in the vicinity of the school. Racing back, they found to their relief there had been no casualties. The older children had managed to reach the Anderson Shelter, while the younger ones, in the playground, had sheltered in a dug out. Mrs Hodder took cover under the stairs.

The bomb landed 25 yards from the school causing much damage. Pictured here before the event, the school was never rebuilt. School house the rear of which is shown after the bomb fell, was rebuilt as a private house.

THE Borough of Croydon was still receiving more than its fair share of doodlebugs and the only shred of comfort to battle-weary Croydonians was the knowledge that, across the Channel, Allied forces were still advancing towards the launching sites. During this time a borough policeman was involved in an incident that left him with a tragic memory.

"There was only one other police officer with me and that was the driver of my police car. Already on the scene were members of the local ARP team. These men and women were volunteers who willingly gave their time and efforts to serve the public during the air raids.

When I arrived I naturally took charge. We could hear cries for help coming from under the debris of the house which had been shattered by the blast from the bomb. The ARP members worked hard to clear away enough debris to make a hole through which it was possible to crawl down to the damaged shelter.

When I had managed to crawl down to the trapped people I found Mrs Wagstaff, the occupier of the house, nursing her baby, Nicola, another elderly lady whom I understood was the nanny, and a young girl, Elizabeth, buried up to her chest in debris.

Mrs Wagstaff pleaded to be allowed to stay with Elizabeth but I told her if she did not get out quickly we would probably all be buried and killed. At last she was persuaded to go and I promised her I would remain with Elizabeth until she was rescued. I started to clear away the debris but the concrete roof of the shelter began to slip down and I realised the more I took away the more chance there was of a total collapse.

I also realised that Elizabeth would not survive as it was obvious her chest was crushed and I had seen death too many times not to know that the end was very near. She opened her eyes once and I said: "It is all right love. I will keep the light of my torch on and we shall be all right".

She just smiled and closed her eyes. I did not consider myself a religious type but I could only repeat the Lord's Prayer out loud and hope for the best. I had one more go at clearing the debris from her but it was no good, and by then I knew Elizabeth was dead.

Eventually I managed to crawl out and I had the sad task of going to the Rescue Centre where Mrs Wagstaff and the other survivors had been taken. The only comfort I could give was to tell her that Elizabeth had not died in the dark and alone. I had remained with her until the end. For myself I was very upset at my failure to save the child and even today wonder if I could have done more."

This letter from William Holloway, of Gladeside, Shirley was published in the summer of 1984 by the Croydon Advertiser in a booklet called Courageous Croydon — as a tribute to danger, suffering and unity which existed in the borough in 1944.

Street baths like this were used frequently in Croydon. The public baths had been damaged by a flying bomb, thousands of homes were wrecked and people were living in shelters without washing facilities of any kind. They still managed a smile for the cameraman.

For a couple of memorable hours, flying bombs were forgotten among the workers at the Short's Aircraft factory in Rochester as the Lancashire lassie herself, Gracie Fields dropped in to sing "Sally" and a few other favourites. The factory was vital to the war effort for here they were producing the Stirling four-engine heavy bomber for attacks against the industrial centres of Germany and some of the launching sites. The factory, opened in 1938, had been badly damaged in 1940 when 18 Dorniers dropped hundreds of bombs, destroyed six aircraft and put production of the Stirling back by almost a year.

FIGHTERS WHICH HUNTED THE V1

Aircraft	Engine	Armament	Speed 2,000ft	Squadrons
Hawker Tempest V	2,400hp Napier Sabre 11 B	Four 20 mm cannon	420 mph	Nos 3, 486, 56, 274, 501 with NFDU
Vickers Supermarine Spitfire F-XIV	2,000 hp Rolls Royce Griffon 65	Two 20mm cannon and four 0.303inchMG	385mph	Nos 91, 322
North American Mustang 111 (P-51B/C)	1,380 hp Packard Merlin V-1650-3	Six 0.50in MG	375mph	The Polish Wing with 316
Gloster Meteor	Two 1,700lb st Rolls-Royce Welland 1	Four 20mm cannon	485mph	No 616
D.H.Mosquito Various marks	Two 1,390hp Rolls-Royce Merlin 23	Four 20mm cannon	365mph	Nos 25, 68, 85, 96 125, 157, 219, 409, 418 at various times

Meteor joins the fray

ON August 4, 1944, Flying Officer Dixie Dean of 616 Squadron took off from Manston on anti-Diver duty to patrol an inland area under Biggin Hill control. At 16.16 hours he sighted a flying bomb at 1,000 feet, dived down at a speed of 450 mph and attacked the missile from dead astern. His 20mm cannons failed to fire owing to a technical fault so Dean flew alongside, manoeuvered his wing tip a few inches under the wing of the flying bomb, pulled upwards sharply and sent the bomb diving to earth south of Tonbridge.

This report in Operations Record Book of 616 Squadron is part of aviation history. Dean was flying the twin-engine Gloster Meteor, the first high-performance jet fighter in RAF Fighter Command and had become the first jet pilot to destroy a flying bomb.

The Meteors had come into operational service at the end of July and 616 Squadron, based at Manston, had been given the honour of baptising them. It was the afternoon of August 4 that seven Meteors were scrambled and Dean's success was followed, at 16.40, by Flying Officer J.K.Rodger who fired two bursts at a flying bomb and saw it crash five miles north-west of Tenterden.

Tram queue in Lordship Lane

BY August some 50 per cent of the flying bombs were being destroyed before they could reach London but those that beat the defences continued to cause heavy casualties and damage. In the first week, 395 were killed in London and 57 elsewhere. There were big fires at West Ham on August 1 and Greenwich on the 3rd. On August 5, a bomb crashed onto the Royal Arsenal Co-operative Stores at Lordship Lane, Camberwell. The shop, crowded with customers, was demolished and a tram queue outside was cut to pieces. Twenty three people died and 43 were injured.

In the second week of August — the ninth of the campaign — 459 flying bombs were reported, a figure that increased to 700 in the third week and 550 in the fourth.

In Kent, during the month, there were flying bomb fatalities in Maidstone, Horsmonden, Littlebourne, Snodland, Tunbridge Wells, Dartford, Swanscombe(again), Boughton Monchelsea, Benenden, Ightham, Hythe, Appledore, Newington, Strood, Otford, Dover and Smarden. In Sussex, there were fatalities at Laughton, Pevensey, Bexhill and Hartfield.

In one incident, at Frinsted, near Hollingbourne, a flying bomb which exploded in a field contained cannisters carrying German propaganda leaflets. These showed gruesome pictures of victims of an Allied raid on Cologne. The cannisters were taken to Sittingbourne police station, and then on to London.

One of the worst incidents was on August 23 at East Barnet when the premises of the Standard Telephone and Cable Company were hit and 21 people died.

Maidstone misery: 3 in a day

Three flying bombs fell in, or near, Maidstone on Thursday August 3. The first dived onto the golf course in the early hours of the morning, seriously injuring three women, slightly hurting 11 other people and damaging 450 houses. The second, just before noon, exploded in the goods yard of Maidstone West railway station. Five men were killed, five women and five men seriously injured and 40 people slightly hurt. Gas supplies and telephone lines were wrecked and 1,180 homes damaged. On that same day a third bomb crashed at nearby Allington, causing more damage.

A flying bomb, shot down by a fighter, crashed in Malling Road, Snodland at 6.58 pm on Saturday August 5, demolishing ten houses and damaging many more. Twelve people were killed and 16 seriously injured. The Kent Messenger reported that two local doctors displayed great heroism despite being injured themselves. One, a Czech refugee, was holding his surgery when the bomb fell. He was badly cut in the face by glass splinters and bleeding heavily but he continued to do what he could for those who had been hurt. The other doctor, who was in the front room of his house, received the full force of the blast and was thrown against the man he was treating. Although his leg was broken he also continued to treat the injured.

Among those killed was a nine-year-old girl, who was a patient at the surgery, a police sergeant, his wife and two girls, who were staying with the doctor, and several neighbours.

Mr Derek Pantony, of Whitstable was crossing an open field at Coxheath, near Maidstone when he saw this flying bomb tipped over by a Tempest. It veered to port before crashing in Snodland. Mr Pantony writes: "The pilot was heavily criticised at the time for employing this well-known tactic but from my position it was clear that if he had opened fire it is highly likely that it would have crashed in the centre of Maidstone, where the casualty rate may have been much higher. I feel the pilot was unjustifiably pilloried."

One feature of the flying bomb campaign was that queues outside shops in London became thinner and long-forgotten goods suddenly appeared on the shelves. Why? Because many thousands of people had gone to the country and London was now the city of the brave and the few. In country towns, however, it was a different matter. Swollen by the evacuees and the desire to shop as early as possible, long queues formed outside most of the food stores. The photograph (left) was taken in Tonbridge High Street where the queue, waiting to buy bread and cakes at Carlton Cafe, stretched down to Lyons Crescent. On some occasions the alert would sound and the queue would quickly disperse, but this wasn't always the case. On one occasion the South London Press reported that "not a woman moved when danger klaxons sounded while there was a queue for cherries at a stall, though the queue did disperse in disorder a few minutes later. The cause of the panic? A mouse."

Summerhouse tragedy

TUNBRIDGE Wells, which lay below five or six regular doodlebug routes to London, somehow escaped the worst effects of the crashing bombs. Thousands passed over the town but only six fell in the borough, causing two fatalities — and one was a horse!

The man who died was George Gearing of Stanley Road. On Sunday afternoon, August 6 he was sitting in a small thatched summerhouse, then a feature of Tunbridge Wells Common, watching fighters overhead chase two doodlebugs. They were both shot down; one crashed to the rear of Pembury Road, causing damage to 37 properties and the other exploded on the Common between the Higher Ground and the Spa Hotel. George Gearing was injured by the blast and died in hospital.

In his history of the Civil Defence in Tunbridge Wells, Mr F.C.

Squirrell writes: "It is estimated that 2,000 of these missiles passed over the town. It was, for all the world, like a Walt Disney nightmare to see the distant spark of the rapidly approaching flying bomb growing larger and larger till it passed overhead with a shattering roar. Surrounded by a ghastly greenish glow and spitting white flames from its tail, the long streams of red Bofors tracer shells curving gracefully, and apparently lazily upwards to the target, then the sharp golden bursts spangling the dark sky and the slender white beams of searchlights, directing a wing-lit night fighter into action."

It was on Sunday August 6 that Dartford experienced its most tragic incident. At 5.10 pm a flying bomb came down in Carrington Road, East Hill, killing 10 people and seriously injuring 12. Twenty homes were wrecked and more than 700 damaged by blast. Soldiers, based in the town, helped with the rescue work.

In mid-August, a flying bomb fell on waste ground at the rear of Genesta Road and Eglinton Hill, Woolwich causing blast damage and slight casualties. It was one of 77 doodlebugs to fall on a borough in which homes were damaged over and over again. This was one of three incidents from enemy action which occurred in the area covered by this aerial photograph. The other two were in October, 1940 when a landmine fell in Barnfield Gardens at the rear of Wrattersley Road, killing 14, and in June, 1944 when a flying bomb landed in the Genesta Road, Wrottersley Road area, killing two.

Ack Ack shells rained down

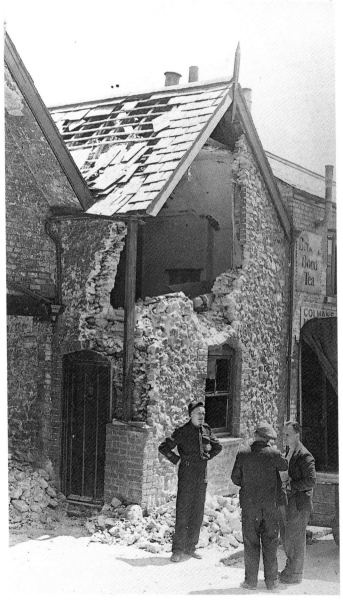

TO those who lived in Kent and Sussex, the Ack-Ack guns were to become almost as great a trial as the doodlebugs themselves. It was possible to stand outside in open country and watch a bomb in perfect safety, so long as the engine was running but nobody in their senses would risk being peppered with the jagged fragments of shrapnel which rained down on rich and poor alike as the doodlebugs came within range of the guns. Between Hythe and Rye, where the greatest number of British and American guns were assembled, thousands of homes were damaged by falling shells, some of which hit their target, bounced off and caused more damage on land. The photograph shows a house in Bower Lane, Maidstone which was damaged by an Ack Ack shell. The owner of the house, Mr Savill, was fire watching at the time and when he returned home he found that a large chunk of roof and wall was missing.

THE CROOKE COTTAGE

The 16th-century Crooke Cottage, Brenchley was formerly home of artist Janet Chrisholme-Simpson. In the summer of 1944, a battalion, with approximately 20 anti-aircraft guns set up camp in a nearby field in a bid to shoot down doodlebugs. The effect of the guns on the cottage was devastating. Vibrations shook down nearly all the roof tiles and a couple of ceilings inside were brought to the floor. Miss Chrisholme-Simpson was so incensed that she demanded to know why they were "shooting at my house". The gunners were full of remorse. The next day the whole camp was transferred to Horsmonden.

Posthumous VC for pilot

A Lancaster pilot with 635 Squadron from Downham Market was with a marker force raiding a V1 storage depot at Trossy, St Maxim, France on August 4, when his aircraft was crippled by flak. Acting Squadron Leader L.W.Bazalgette lost two engines and the starboard wing and fuselage burst into flames. The bomb aimer was badly wounded and the mid-upper gunner overcome by fumes.

Bazalgette regained control, released the markers, then flew the burning Lancaster on for another 30 miles, before ordering the crew to bale out at 1,000 feet. He then attempted to land in a field but his aircraft exploded as it touched down and Bazalgette was killed. A year later, on August 17, 1945, he was awarded a Posthumous Victoria Cross.

Peaceful Eastbourne which earned an unenviable wartime reputation as the most raided town in the south-east, received its final act of hostility at 11.16 pm on August 7 when a doodlebug crossed the coast near Holywell and crashed in Baldwin Avenue behind St Elisabeth Church. Many houses were damaged over a wide area, but fortunately no-one was killed. Compared with the 671 high explosives, the 28 oil incendiaries and the 4,000 Thermite incendiaries to fall on Eastbourne, let alone the 112 raids by heavy bombers, the doodlebug days were not the most serious and the town escaped comparatively lightly. The most serious incident occurred on July 27 when six houses were demolished at Brassey Avenue, Hampden Park and 34 people were injured. The picture above shows what happened to one of the homes.

The mayor of Hythe. Councillor G.Few and members of Hythe council inspect a Bofors 40mm on their visit to the gun belt in August 1944. The visitors also saw the 3.7 which had shells fitted with the new VT proximity fuse. This had been developed in the United States and was designed to "detect" the presence of its target before exploding. The fuses were so secret that they were placed under a 24-hour guard and were called "bonzo" by the gun battalions.

One shell and one doodlebug

THE people of Dover, Folkestone, Hythe, Romney and all the villages in this beleaguered part of "Hell's Corner" had emerged as a courageous, united band who showed cheerfulness and sheer tenacity when life was at its grimmest. Thanks to Anti-Aircraft Command, they now had a reason to smile, for all along the coast the gunners were enjoying their finest hours. Few doodlebugs managed to escape the shooting gallery and those that did met the fastest fighters in their territory above Tenterden and Ashford.

On August 16, 39 flying bombs were destroyed and the next day it was 29. By August 23 the percentage of "kills" had risen in a week from 55 to 60 per cent, and in the last week of this phase of the battle it rose to 74 per cent. On one night the total actually reached 84 per

cent. Those who were used to the German bombers and fighters and the crunching, ear-splitting explosion of shells fired from over the Channel, were enjoying this new kind of action. At night, children and their parents sat at open windows and watched in fascination at the combined spectacle of searchlights, tracer shells and robots with fiery tails. They cheered when one was downed, waited for the explosion and saw everything lit up for miles around.

No-one could fail to be impressed with the army of weapons assembled along the coast of south Kent and east Sussex, or the noise they made. There were thousands of Ack-Acks, light and heavy; American 88s, British 3.7s and a line of Bofors on high ground behind the road between Dover and Folkestone. There were

(continued)

rocket guns in the valley behind the Downs, between Dymchurch and St Mary in the Marsh and close to the Sussex coast.

The men were more accurate thanks to consistent practice, the new radar equipment and the introduction of the proximity fuse, code-named Bonzo, which increased the performance of all types of guns so dramatically that at times it was "one shell, one doodlebug". The young, heroic fighter pilots were still chasing those that slipped the net but the gunners were, by now, easily the top scorers and on one occasion shot down 68 in a single day.

General Pile said at the time: "The strain on these men was enormous; troops had to be at constant readiness, each site needed several spotters and training had to be carried out when there was no action going on. Sleep was difficult until the troops got used to the fearful noise but their morale was colossal......There was no doubt in my mind which needed the greater courage — to stand on a gun site and fire at a directly approaching flying bomb with the knowledge that, if you hit it, you would bring it down, either on to or near to your own site or to fly an aircraft at a suitable distance behind the bomb and shoot it down."

To the General, the dazzling array of medals won by the fighter pilots compared to the lack of medals for his gunners, remained a very sore point.

From their vantage point on The Leas, the people of Folkestone looked out to see the action over the Channel. One of the most extraordinary days was Thursday August 31 — for it was hot in more ways than one. While bathers took to the sea off the East Coast Sands a doodlebug exploded directly over their heads but no-one was hurt. Another flying bomb was shot down and exploded on houses in Claremont Road. It was catastrophic. Four houses were demolished, four partially demolished and more than 400 damaged. While the Civil Defence units attempted to reach those buried under mounds of bricks, tiles and masonry, more bombs droned menacingly over the town.

ONE of the American anti-aircraft units who "dug themselves in" at Dymchurch, named their camp "Doodle Bug Villas" and got on with the job of shooting Hitler's "buzz bombs" out of the sky. They soon proved their worth. The 20 American batteries operated their 90-mm equipment so effectively that they contributed 138 bombs to the total score and shared in the destruction of a further 309.

One of the American battalions was the 127th AAA who arrived in Dover in early August and enjoyed six weeks of "first rate shooting". In this time they fired 5,614 rounds of high explosive ammunition at 188 targets, claimed 89 destroyed but accepted 56 definite "kills".

General Pile said: "General Eisenhower always took a personal interest in the state of the battle, for England was as much a base for American troops as for the English. The US contribution to the Diver defences, and the interest that the Americans showed in them, had a very real bearing on the ultimate victory over the flying bomb."

Civil Defence personnel are pictured searching among the debris after a bomb wrecked these homes in Twiss Road, Hythe on August 15. The doodlebug had been shot down by anti-aircraft fire at 2.10 pm and five people near the Royal Military Canal were killed, five seriously injured and 12 slightly hurt. Many homes were wrecked.

No immunity for the churches

The remains of Little Chart Church, near Charing in Kent — a symbol of the county's ordeal. (See page 207).

THE terrible tragedy at the Guards Chapel in June, one of the great disasters of the campaign, was certainly not an isolated incident as far as churches were concerned. They enjoyed no special immunity; on the contrary their height made them more vulnerable than many other buildings. In London, 111 churches were damaged by flying bombs, some more than once. St George's Roman Catholic Cathedral at Southwark suffered blast damage on three occasions and St Michael's Paternoster Royal in College Street — the church rebuilt by Wren after the Great Fire — was totally demolished. Many stories are told of preachers pausing for agonising seconds after a V1 engine had cut out, and then continuing with the service upon hearing the explosion.

In Kent, the church of St Mary of the Holy Rood at Little Chart, two miles south of Charing, which had been built by the Normans in 1240 was destroyed on August 15. According to witnesses it occurred at 8 pm when a bomb, destroyed by a fighter, continued for half a mile and ended its flight on top of the church tower. The impact brought the walls of the church crashing down. No-one was hurt.

A new church was consecrated in 1958 on a new site, but the gutted remains of the Norman church, now covered in ivy, still stand as a symbol of Kent's ordeal in the summer of 1944.

Germans evacuate flying bomb sites

One of the V1 launching sites in Pas de Calais which were being located daily by the advancing armies. This one was discovered on September 2 but very little material had been left behind by the retreating Germans. It had been bombed by the RAF.

THE rapid advance of the Allied armies in France was a severe blow to Col Wachtel and his men. Paris was liberated on August 23 and by the end of the month the British and Canadian armies were sweeping on towards Pas de Calais. The Germans began to evacuate their modified sites and retreat further to the east into Holland, but in doing so they lost the chance of attacking London which was now practically out of reach.

The German retreat was rapid and the Allies' only fear was the possibility of flying bombs being launched from the air but this seemed unlikely in view of the Allied ascendancy over what was left of the Luftwaffe. Churchill sent a message from Italy to General Pile: "Many congratulations on the brilliant work of the anti-aircraft batteries which has more than borne out what we did hope for them". The gunners had destroyed more than 1,500 flying bombs and the searchlight crews had played their part. 142 missiles destroyed by fighters at night had been picked out and illuminated by searchlights.

The battle was nearing its close.....

Rescuers at the scene of the crash on Wednesday August 18, 1944

The railway bridge at Oak Lane, Newington in April, 1992.

Express train derailed by flying bomb

WHEN a group of women, picking damsons on a fruit farm just off the A2 near Sittingbourne, heard the familiar sound of a fighter chasing a flying bomb, they looked up and saw the wounded missile coming straight at them over Hartlip Hill. To their great relief the bomb suddenly turned right and dived into the ground with an enormous explosion. Large clumps of bricks and concrete rained down for several seconds but not one woman or child, standing in this open field was hurt. As the dust settled, they witnessed a most horrifying sight.

The doodlebug had crashed under the Oak Lane railway bridge at Newington and had blown it up. As they watched, the London to Margate express came into sight and hurtled into the wreckage of the bridge. The engine and tender jumped the gap and turned sideways. The first two carriages plunged into the chasm and were burnt by the fuel from the doodlebug. The whole train arched its back and slithered to a juddering halt on the buckled rails. More than 600 people were on the train, many of them servicemen and women. Eight were killed, 33 seriously injured and 28 slightly hurt. Amazingly, the driver and fireman at the front escaped with minor injuries.

Philip Tapp, now of Milstead, near Sittingbourne, whose first job on leaving school was helping to move ladders for the damson pickers, rushed to the scene and helped to get many people off the train and down the embankment. "The noise at the time of the incident is hard to explain", he said. "The explosion of the doodlebug was followed seconds later by the fury of the crash and then the sound of steam escaping when somebody opened the whistle. It was like a nightmare."

Ambulances from Sittingbourne were the first to arrive and the casualties were taken to Medway and Maidstone hospitals. Among those killed were a naval officer from Chatham Barracks, a soldier in the Queen's Royal Regiment, returning to Faversham and an Able Seaman serving on HMS Queen of Kent.

Shelling returns

OF the last two flying bombs to be launched from Pas de Calais, the first crashed at Church Road, Lyminge on August 31 at 5.46 am damaging 150 houses; the ensuing fire destroyed the Methodist Chapel. Nine were hurt. The second landed in Folkestone at 12.14 am on September 1.

For the people of East Kent there was a new ordeal to face as September dawned — the return of cross-Channel shelling from the long-range German batteries at Cap Griz Nez and Calais. From early morning on Friday September 1 and then almost daily for the next two weeks, there was no let-up in the bombardment. There were fatalities in Ramsgate, Folkestone and Hythe but it was Dover which bore the brunt of the attack. Thirty nine shells fell in the town or harbour on that first day. Four people were killed when one hit the entrance to the shelter at the Lagoon Cave in the High Street, two died when shells fell between Anderson shelters in Tower Hamlets, there was a direct hit on the back of Woolworth's, gas and water mains were fractured, telephone wires brought down and 50 business premises damaged.

As the days progressed, the Allied troops moved nearer to Cap Griz Nez and the RAF bombed cross-Channel gun sites. But the attacks intensified and the shell warning in Folkestone on Wednesday September 11 lasted 11 hours — the longest period in more than four years of suffering from that form of attack. During this time the town was almost deserted. Bus companies ran restricted services, only a few hardy people braved the cinema, business fell to a trickle. Amazingly, some visitors — determined that Hitler should not spoil their holiday — continued to "enjoy" picnics on the beach.

By the end of the ordeal on September 26, 40 people had been killed in Dover and 60 seriously injured. Eleven died in Folkestone, two in Ramsgate and one in Hythe.

On Saturday September 23, a shell exploded on the Salvation Army Red Shield canteen and hostel in Snargate Street, Dover. Seven were killed and the rescuers spent more than 36 hours and turned over 100 tons of rubble before the injured were rescued.

Through these powerful field glasses on the ramparts of Dover Castle, H.R.H. The Duchess of Kent could see the cross Channel shelling .

Front Line Anglia

"EXCEPT possibly for a few last shots, the Battle of London is over." With these words Mr Duncan Sandys spoke with great confidence about the immediate future to a crowded press conference on September 7. He said that during the 80 days of the bombardment the Germans had sent over some 8,000 flying bombs of which 2,300 had got through to London. "The understanding and restraint of the people living in Kent, Sussex and Surrey are deserving of great praise. By their readiness to accept their share of London's dangers, the people of Bomb Alley played a notable part in keeping down overall casualties."

Mr Sandys had a special word of praise for the Americans. "They have thrown themselves into the job of beating the bomb with just as much determination as if New York or Washington had been the victim of the attack."

He mentioned the possibility that the missiles might now be launched from aircraft. Mr Sandys had firm evidence that a new attack from the east was being organised from Heinkel 111s or Junkers 88s. but he knew there were considerable fears among German officers about the inaccuracy of air-launched Vls — a fear that was to prove well founded.

On September 14 after an interval of some days, the air-launched attacks were renewed in a line over East Anglia to the north of the small anti-aircraft 'Diver box' which had covered the approaches to the capital from the east. In consultation with Fighter Command, AA Command decided to redeploy all the available defences from the South Coast in a strip 5,000 yards wide extending from the Thames Estuary to Great Yarmouth. It was another mammoth operation in which great convoys of 10 ton lorries moved guns and gunners to their new positions. By the middle of October, 300 static guns, 542 heavy guns, 503 40-mm guns and 18 searchlight batteries were achieving further high successes.

The gunners had to learn a new technique for destroying low-flying air launched Vl's but, despite the autumn weather which was particularly wet, morale was high and the percentage of "kills" rose eventually to 82. During this period 13 flying bombs landed in Norfolk, injuring 11 people. No-one was killed.

On the day that Duncan Sandys held his press conference and mentioned the possibility of air-launched V1s being aimed at London, one was actually spotted, chased and shot down by a fighter over Kent. It landed in Hawkhurst churchyard, uprooting tombstones and causing great damage to the church .

Duck-boards across the mud

ALTHOUGH winter had not yet begun, conditions on the new gun sites in Essex and East Anglia were appalling. One visitor, concerned about the conditions under which men and women were living and fighting was the Speaker of the House of Commons. In his report he said:

"It reminded me of Flanders in the last war, but the mud was not quite so sticky. The gun crews were living in tents, the men were on the alert all night, so little could be done by day. But they had erected duck-board passages across the mud which I thought was highly creditable."   The Speaker explained how, in ten minutes, he saw two doodlebugs out of three shot down over the coast and the third probably winged. "Not bad shooting under such conditions."

By now there was great controversy over the plight that faced the ATS girls, who, nevertheless, were proud that they were allowed to "rough it" with the men. One mixed battery at Burnham lived in tents surrounded by quagmires. Even hardened gunners complained, so the brigadier offered to transfer the 1,000 girls of the brigade to other, more comfortable sites.

He received nine applications — all from clerks. The ATS girls in the front line of the anti-aircraft campaign all volunteered to remain on the unwelcoming marshes of Essex, and fight the battle with the men.

The Battle of London is over! This welcome news, far too premature as events turned out, spread like wildfire across England and within days of the announcement evacuees came flooding back gleefully, many to their deaths — for soon to arrive from the east was Hitler's deadliest weapon of all, the V2. The photograph here shows a group of children who had been as far away as possible from the flying bombs. They landed at Southampton on September 11 after a long sea voyage from Australia on RMS Andes.

Every home damaged

THIS *Evening News* map shows where the flying bombs fell in the boroughs and districts of Beckenham, Bromley, Orpington, Bexley, Crayford, Erith, Chislehurst and Sidcup and Penge. The latter had the reputation of receiving more flying bombs per yard than any other spot in the United Kingdom. From the first attack on June 18 when a missile plunged into the High Street and killed 11 people, 18 landed in Penge in two months.

The High Street was hit again on June 29 and worse followed at breakfast time three days later when an explosion demolished 21 houses in Trenholme Road. Thirteen people died including a boy of eight and his parents and a 16-year-old girl.

Seven died on July 10, two in hospital the following day and nine the day after that. On this occasion the missile hit a public air raid shelter, causing more than 100 casualties. Multiple deaths occurred again on July 21, including five members of the Carter family, of 7 Blenheim Road. As their bodies were being recovered, another V1 fell in Penge High Street and the day ended with more than 300 shops destroyed or damaged in the town centre.

The final attack occurred on August 24 when seven members of a Home Guard AA unit were killed. The bomb fell in an orchard in the grounds of Anerley Residential School; the part-time soldiers were sheltering in a building which received the full effects of the blast.

When the campaign ended there was not one single house or building in Penge (770 acres) entirely undamaged, a fact that prompted an *Evening News* reporter to comment that the town, quite involuntarily, was likely to go down in the history of the war with a title — the most fly-bombed town in the country.

One of the last flying bombs to hit south-east London came down silently from an overcast sky at 2.04 pm on August 29. The wing of the missile collided with the steeple of the parish church at Eltham and sent the top section crashing to the ground. The bomb then impacted into some workshops beyond the churchyard and close to the town centre. Two people were killed and 50 injured.

Great and glorious

THIS is the front page of the *Kent Messenger*, published on Friday September 15, 1944, containing the "official story" of the county's ordeal. The main article was an interview with Alderman E.S.Oak-Rhind, Chairman of Kent's Civil Defence Committee who explained how the people of Kent had helped to save England's capital city.

He said: "Dr Goebbels, the dear doctor, wrote 'Life in Southern England is at a standstill'. Well do I remember stepping out into Maidstone's High Street on the first morning to come up to County Hall, as the flying bombs still rattled overhead. Would the buses run ? What would I see?

What I did see was a very brave people, a little strained and very sleepless, carrying on, just as they had carried on throughout the Battle of Britain. So throughout the county, from coast, through villages and countryside, up to the London boundary, the same grand and determined spirit.

During those early weeks it was the boys of the Royal Air Force who saved London, for it was they who shot down an overwhelming percentage. Often I have watched from the Pilgrim's Way, near Hollingbourne the RAF shooting down the bombs over the heads of the land girls and other farm workers. Their work never ceased but I have seen one of them cry as a bomb escaped and sped London-wards.

It would be around the middle of July that the AA guns were massed on the coast in a great arc, and here came into their own until they were the greatest "killers" of all our defences. Fully 1,000 flying bombs were shot down within and seaward of this arc but Folkestone, Hythe and the other towns down there suffered hell.

Police, National Fire Service, Civil Defence, Local Government officers, WVS — all and every service has given of its very best but over and above all it has been the people themselves — the great and glorious people — whether a bus driver, a waitress or a housewife at home — who beat the V1."

Where the doodlebugs landed in Kent

Of all the south-eastern counties, Kent had the most V1s to endure with 1,444 crashing on land and a further 1,000 shot down in the sea. This was 100 more than London had received. Altogether 448 communities reported damage and some suffered time and again.

During the first week of the campaign, 101 were shot down in Kent and the incidents after that occurred, on average, at the rate of 20 a day. Deaths in Kent attributable to the flying bombs totalled 152 with 1,716 injured. The material damage was vast.

Tenterden	238
Ashford	184
New Romney	149
SevenoaksRD	137
Malling RD	97
Tonbridge RD	95
Hollingbourne	81
Dartford RD	76
Elham RD	64
Maidstone RD	63
Strood RD	35
Folkestone	29
Dover	21
Sittingbourne	19
Faversham `	15
Dartford MB	14
Bridge-Blean	13
Tonbridge UD	11
Hythe	11
Swanscombe	10
Eastry	8
TunbridgeWells	6
Maidstone RD	6
Rochester	5
Sheppey RD	5
Southborough	5
Northfleet	4
Gillingham	3
Gravesend	3
Broadstairs	3
Dover MB	3
Whitstable	2
Canterbury	1
Herne Bay	1

Chatham, Deal, Margate, Ramsgate, Sandwich and Sheerness did not receive a single flying bomb.

EACH OF THESE SMALL DOTS
REPRESENTS A FLYING BOMB
BROUGHT DOWN INTO THE SEA

This map, published by the *Kent Messenger* on September 15, 1944, shows where every V1 in the county had landed up to the beginning of September*. It was accompanied by a front page story indicating that Kent had more flying bombs than London.

This issue of the *Kent Messenger* sold out within hours of the newspaper arriving in the shops. The demand was so great that newsagents became tired of explaining that they had no copies left, and one actually hung a notice around her neck to this effect.

The following week, the *Kent Messenger* published the map again, this time offering it for individual sale, with proceeds going to the county's Civil Defence fund. Within days they had received orders for 100,000 copies and again ran out of supplies. More were printed but the strict rationing on newsprint made it impossible for the newspaper to meet all enquiries received.

Today, the "Doodlebug Map" is part of the county's history and a treasured relic in thousands of homes. It hangs in workshops, offices and pubs. In researching this book the author was reminded, on countless occasions, that a map existed showing where every V1 had fallen in the county. Such is the intense interest among the people of Kent in their great ordeal of 1944, that the *Kent Messenger* still receives orders for the map.

Several more V1s were destined to land in Kent between September 1944 and March 1945, including those launched in the air.

Casualties and damage in Kent

THIS list consists of most of the known V1 incidents in Kent involving injury or extensive damage and is taken from the Civil Defence War Diaries held by the County Archivist at Maidstone. There are some discrepancies because not all military incidents were listed and there were some cases where people died later of their injuries after the diary entry had been made. We have listed below the date and time of each incident, the location in the town or village and then a figure for those who died, were seriously injured and slightly injured. The last figures relate to the overall damage and, where known, what caused the missile to crash. For example:

August 3 (11.30am) Maidstone West Station 5/7/40. Damage to 1,180 houses and shops. Shot down by fighter.

June 1944

16th (03.53) **Dartford**, jctn Shepherds Lane & Princes Road. 0/4/10.
Extensive damage to 14 houses.
17th (05.25) **Benenden** 3 killed. One house demolished, extensive damage to Sanatorium.
24th (06.18) **Charing** 47/28/0. Shot down by fighter.
(06.22) Bartley Poultry Farm, **Smarden** 5/1/0. Bungalow damaged. Shot down by fighter.
30th (03.37) Weald House, **Crockham Hill** 30/8/0. House demolished.

July

3rd (02.51) **Marden** 11/8/8. Shot down by AA fire.
(15.30) Denmark Street, **Folkestone** 3/8/44 9 houses & pub demolished. Shot down by AA fire.
12th (09.13) **Tonbridge** 0/3/20. Extensive damage to shops & houses.
(08.57) Beechmont, **Sevenoaks** 2/44/0
19th (13.51) **Rolvenden** 2/1/1
22nd (20.20) **Chartham** 0/4/12. 15 cottages damaged

23rd (15.15) Stone Street, **Lympne** 1/9/15 Shot down by AA fire. Extensive damage
26th (07.55) **Old Romney** 1/5/0
(04.20) **Aylesford** 0/0/12. Extensive damage to 100 houses including Friars Building
27th (16.50) Lattice Farm, **Capel** 1/1/2. Extensive damage to surrounding property.
(22.45) **Brookland** RAF Camp 0/3/7.
(15.25) **Maidstone**, Lancet Lane & Loose Road 0/0/14. Extensive damage to houses.
(22.45) **Folkestone**, Shorncliffe Rd 0/3/6.
28th (22.37) **Tenterden** 0/2/10.
(13.27) **E.Brabourne** 1/3/1. 2 bungalows demolished.
29th (22.45) **Appledore** 0/4/2.
30th (23.17) Stone, **Dartford** 0/0/3.
(23.47) **Swanscombe**, Taunton Road 13/22/69.
(13.50) **Smarden**, Malt House Farm 0/2/4.

August

3rd (13.50) **Shorne**, near Strood 6/0/0. Exploded on Nissan hut.
(11.50) **Maidstone** West Station 5/10/40. Damage to approx 1,180 houses & shops.
4th (02.27) **Leybourne** 0/2/6
(03.08) **Littlebourne** 1/3/25. 8 houses to be demolished.
(19.03) **Ashford** 0/3/21. Damage to 2 schools, houses, flour mills & bakery.
5th (18.58) **Snodland**, Malling Rd 12/16/17. 10 houses demolished.
6th (17.05) **Tunbridge Wells** Common 1/0/5.
(17.05) **Pembury**, south of Blackhurst 1/0/7.
(17.10) **Sellindge**, Stonehill 0/3/3. 2 houses partly demolished.
(17.10) **Dartford**, Carrington Road 10/12/95. Extensive damage to 20 houses.
7th (11.00)**Swanscombe** 2/18/29. 20 houses demolished and extensive damage in four streets.
(06.20) **Boughton Monchelsea** 1/0/3. Cliff cottages demolished.
8th (05.55) **Benenden** 1/13/20. Severe damage to 4 houses.
(05.35) **Staplehurst** 0/2/10. 50 houses

uninhabitable.
(06.10) **Folkestone**, Foreland Avenue 0/1/7. 12 houses demolished, 100 seriously damaged.
9th (06.41) **Ightham** 2/7/14. 5 houses beyond repair,13 seriously damaged.
10th (17.40) **Hythe** 1/0/8. 5 houses demolished, 500 damaged.
15th (15.40) **Dymchurch** 1/3/1. Considerable damage.
(14.10) **Hythe**, Earlsfield Road/Twiss Road 5/5/12. 5 houses demolished, extensive damage to over 500 others.
(14.15) **Hougham**, Fairview Terrace to rear of "The Three Horseshoes" 0/4/4. 6 cottages and inn partly demolished. 30 other houses and school damaged.
(16.45) **Rochester** 4/1/21. 1 house demolished,superficial damage to 600 others.
17th (20.35) **Folkestone**, Wear Bay Crescent 0/4/3. Widespread damage to houses, shops.
18th Newington (Upchurch) 8/33/28. Train derailed. Oak Lane bridge demolished.
19th (14.30) **Folkestone**, 30yards east of s.railway 0/1/4. Widespread blast damage.
21st (11.20) **Sevenoaks**, Knole Road 0/13/4. Many houses damaged.
28th (16.25) **Tenterden**, Newenden 0/0/2.
(14.10) **Frinsted**, Madames Court Farm 0/2/1. Extensive damage to Lords Hill Cottages. Fly bomb carrying leaflets in cannisters now at Sittingbourne Police HQ.
(13.26) **Chart Sutton** 0/0/3.
(17.31) **Smarden**. Road to Bethersden blocked 4/2/2.
30th (07.49) **Darenth** LCC Rural Training Colony 0/0/7. Extensive damage to buildings.
31st (05.53) **Whitstable** 0/1/3. Widespread damage to property.
(09.59) **Folkestone**, Brockman Road 0.6.49. 13 houses demolished, extensive damage to 500

houses. Area damaged covers 1 mile.
(05.46) **Lyminge**, Church Road 0/0/9. Approximately 150 houses damaged, Methodist Chapel destroyed by fire.

September

1st (12.14) **Folkestone** 0/1/11. 1 house demolished, 6 seriously damaged.
30th (04.39) **Meopham** 0/3/7. Extensive damage to cottages, farm buildings destroyed.

October

7th (20.45) **Sutton at Hone**, exploded in field 0/1/4. 6 houses badly damaged.
18th (06.30) **Chislet**, Nethergong Farm. Crater 40' across in marsh, debris scattered over 3 miles.
24th (01.31)**Hartlip**, Sittingbourne 2/0/1. Two houses demolished.
27th Sutton at Hone. Missile in field, damage to property in vicinity.

November

8th (20.45) **Rochester**,Grafton Avenue 8/17/31. 14 houses demolished, 575 damaged.
10th (20.02) **Ash** 1/0/0. 1 house demolished, several damaged.

December

11th (24.45) **Herne Bay**. Explosion out to sea 65 houses & 4 shops damaged.
23rd (07.10) **Ightham** 0/0/5. Damage to 70 houses.

March 1945

16th (05.35) **Dartford**, Moreland Avenue 4/4/23. Over 450 houses damaged.
23rd Elham. Serious damage to 2 houses, minor to approx 150 and railway station.

Where the flying bombs crashed in East Sussex

This map of East Sussex shows approximately the position of the 775 flying bombs which fell in the county. Like Kent, hundreds more fell into the sea round the coast, many of them close enough to the shore to damage property inland.

Battle rural district bore the brunt of the campaign with an incredible total of 374 doodlebugs, most of them crashing harmlessly in open country. Of this total, Ticehurst received 20, Burwash 19 and Camber 19, Brightling 16, Icklesham 14, Northiam 13, Westfield 12, Robertsbridge 10, Dallington 10 and Udimore 10.

Hailsham RD	159
Uckfield RD	146
Cuckfield RD	20
Chailey RD	16
Bexhill	16
Hastings	14
Eastbourne	14
Rye	6
East Grinstead	5
Seaford	2
Lewes	1
Newhaven	1
Cuckfield	1

No flying bombs were reported in Burgess Hill, Portslade or Brighton and Hove.

Casualties and damage in Sussex

Casualty figures and damage to property in East Sussex. These figures supplied by the County Records Office at Lewes, list the majority of the most serious cases.

June

13th (04.20) **Cuckfield**, Lizbrooks Farm. First PAC came from direction of London, circled between Plaw Hatch & Danehill then went SW over Lindfield, turned due W & exploded. Slight damage.

17th (22.20) **Waldron**, Possingworth Hotel 1/8/7. Damage to hotel & houses.

(23.58) **Mountfield**, Southover Estate 0/2/3. Cottage demolished.

19th (22.57) **Bexhill**, Richmond Road 0/10/10.

20th (04.45) **Herstmonceux** 0/0/2.

(18.45) **Hailsham**, Southlands Estate 0/1/13. Damage to over 250 houses.

21st (01.52) **Cadborough Cliff** 0/17/17. Slight damage to 174 homes.

(01.55) **Icklesham** 0/1/4. 8 properties damaged.

23rd (0500) **St. Leonards** 0/5/0

25th (03.45) **Willingdon**, Church Street 0/3/3. Slight damage 12 houses.

(21.05) **Staplecross**, Ewhurst 0/0/5. 17 houses damaged.

26th(15.52) **Sidley** 0/1/7. Extensive damage to Glovers Farm .

27th (20.36) **Robertsbridge**, Poppinghole Farm 2/0/1.

(18.50) **Rotherfield**, Danegate Farm 0/0/7.

29th (22.57) **Jevington** 1/0/0. Superficial damage to 20 houses.

(11.55) Military Road, **Playden** 1/1/2. Several houses seriously damaged.

(18.55) **Pevensey**, on beach 0/0/9. Extensive damage to 150 houses.

(21.00) Sandy Cross, **Heathfield** 0/6/6. Damage to approx 50 houses.

30th (03.10) Maynards Gate, **Crowborough** 0/2/4. Severe damage to houses.

(20.43) **Ticehurst** 0/5/0. Ticehurst infirmary severely damaged.

July

1st (01.50) **Hellingly**, Springham Wood 0/1/0. 12 houses damaged.

(19.30) **Northiam** 0/4/6. Serious damage to property.

3rd (00.53) **Rye** 1/0/3. 60 houses damaged.

15.20 **St Leonards**, Conqueror Road 0/10/18

(16.15) **Mayfield**, Park Farm 0/1/6. Damage to property.

(18.55) **Westfield**, Down Oak Farm 0/1/0. 2 houses demolished.

4th (10.00) **Udimore** 0/0/3. Cottages damaged.

(15.45)**Hailsham**, Northeath Farm 0/0/3. 60 houses damaged.

(19.30) **Heathfield**, West St Lane 1/8/7. Over 40 houses damaged.

5th(18.05) **Iden**, Elms Farm House 0/4/4.

(18.20) **Crowborough** Golf Course on military camp 8/17/0. Several Canadian soldiers killed and injured.

6th (13.04) **Newhaven**, Mount Pleasant 0/2/11. 30 houses damaged.

7th (23.48) **Battle**, Westfield 0/0/3. Extensive damage to property.

(16.15) **Polegate**, Southlands Estate 2/4/15. Extensive damage to 250 houses.

(16.30) **Arlington**, Plackets Corner 1/0/2. 1 house demolished.

(17.00) **Battle**, Prinkle Farm, Dallington 1/1/0. Farm and 50 houses & shops damaged..

9th (23.25) **Fairwarp**, Kings Standing 0/1/0.

(10.50) **Willingdon** 0/1/8. Blast damage to church, school, memorial hall & 50 houses.

(23.08) **Balcombe**, Woodlands Farm 1/2/1. Damage to farm house & buildings.

10th (10.55) **Warbleton**, Yew Tree Farm, Punnetts Town 0/0/6. 21 houses damaged.

(16.56) **Hailsham**, Millbrooks 2/2/1. 7 properties damaged.

12th (07.25) **East Grinstead**, London Rd 3/5/36. Damage to houses & shops.

(08.40) **Mayfield**, Sharnden 1/0/0. Damage to property.

(21.15) **Rushlake Green** 0/2/3. 71 houses damaged.

13th (14.50) Chapel Field, **Camber** 0/0/2., Damage to coastguard buildings and cottages, 31 houses extensively damaged.

14th (08.12) **Ticehurst** 0/2/6. 18 houses & farm buildings damaged.

(17.54) **Cowden**, Clanning Walk 0/1/1. 1 house demolished, considerable other damage.

16th (16.40) Hastings, Hollington 3/47/0

20th (10.20) **Burwash** 0/0/16. Damage to 23 properties.

21st (09.25) **Waldron**, Burnt Oak Farm 0/2/4.

22nd(01.10) **Crowborough**, Tinten Lane 1/1/5. Cottage demolished.

(16.35) **Bexhill**, Old Town 0/7/2-. 1 home seriously damaged, other damage to residential & business properties

23rd (06.30) **Northiam** 0/0/1. Serious damage.

(06.00) **Chiddingly** 2/3/2. Farmhouse demolished, 40 houses & farm damaged.

24th (15.05) Broad Oak, **Heathfield** 0/2/7. Many houses damaged.

(22.07) **Ewhurst** 0/0/4. 39 properties damaged.

(22.16) **Buxted** 0/1/1. Damage to property.

27th (00.05) **Ticehurst** 0/2/1. Damage to property.

(05.05) **Polegate**, Hailsham. 70 houses damaged.

29th (01.15) **Laughton**, Blackshaw. Damage to church vicarage.

(18.45) Green Square, **Wadhurst** 2/1/7. 8 houses uninhabitable.

(23.08) **Ewhurst** 0/2/6. 3 properties demolished, serious damage to 14 & 10 outbuildings.

30th (03.40) **Newhaven**. Damage to 34 houses in Gibbons Road, West Pier & South Road.

August

1st (07.00) **Sedlescombe** 0/0/1. 40 houses damaged.

(09.50) **Maresfield**, Nutley 0/1/3. 1 house extensively damaged, 8 slightly damaged..

2nd (12.45) Moat House Farm, Isfield, **Little Horsted** 0/1/0. Farmhouse & 2 cottages damaged

3rd (07.41) Dallingridge Farm, **Forest Row** 0/1/0. Damage to Dallingridge House & 14 houses.

(11.05) **Tidebrook**,Wadhurst 0/0/6. Extensive damage to school.

4th (15.46) **East Grinstead** 0/1/4. 20 houses slightly damaged.

(15.58) **Battle** 0/0/10. Serious damage to 4 properties, slight to 118.

(16.05) Shortgate, **Laughton** 5/1/1. 3 houses demolished, pub & 4 houses damaged.

5th (07.00) **Cross in Hand & Waldron** 0/0/1. 10 houses damaged.

(16.35) **Pevensey** 1/1/3. 50 houses damaged.

(18.55) Pumps Lane, **Framfield** 0/0/2. 1 house demolished..

6th (04.42) **Broomhill** 0/0/4. Coastguard station look out slightly damaged. Rocket station demolished

(17.35) Pickford Lane, **Ticehurst** 0/0/5. 4 homes seriously damaged, 116 slight.

8th (23.05) **Uckfield**-over Sub Central Office & Tinten Grange. 2 houses partly demolished, 56 houses & shops seriously damaged.

14th (04.28) **Rye** 0/0/2. Extensive damage to houses, chemical works & buildings.

17th(06.13) Rye Harbour, **Icklesham** 0/0/1. 5 houses & 1 shop damaged. Extensive damage to electrical equipment on gun site.

18th (07.05) **Cuckfield** 0/2/5. 4 houses demolished, 3 badly damaged.

29th (13.52) Marsh Green Camp, **Hartfield** 2/37/0. 20 civilian properties damaged.

November

5th(19.50) **Frant**, Clay's Wood 0/0/1. Extensive damage to Frant Place.

March

25th (07.58) **East Grinstead**, Lowdells Lane & Sackville Lane 0/2/6. 50 shops & houses damaged.

Some of the casualties and damage in Essex

June

16th (00.30) **Tilbury Marshes**, 0/4/0. Extensive blast damage in Seymour Road, Melbourne Road and Broadway.

(04.00) **S. Ockendon** 0/13/0. Extensive blast damage.

(10.20) **Lt Thurrock**, Rookery View 0/31/0. 2 houses uninhabitable.

(23.50) **Brentwood**, Hill Road 0/9/0. 3 houses demolished, 3 severely damaged.

(03.30) **Rush Green** Hospital 6/23/0. Considerable damage to property.

(02.40) **Billericay**, Ramsden Bellhouse 3/13/20. 4 cottages demolished, 12 severely damaged, 20 slight damage.

17th (05.27) **Romford**, Lodge Lane 1/6/16. 3 houses damaged.

(06.06) **Chelmsford**, Waterloo Lane 0/8/1. Considerable damage to property.

20th (05.00) **Romford** 3/18/21. 8 houses demolished, 100 shops & houses seriously damaged, 200 slightly damaged.

21st (14.55) **Hornchurch** Station 0/10/14. Approximately 1,000 houses damaged.

23rd (06.52) Central **Romford** 0/3/0. 100 houses affected.

(21.12) **Hornchurch**, Ascot Gardens 0/3/15. Widespread damage to houses.

24th (06.31) **Rainham**, Ferry Lane 0/1/7. Briggs Bodies and Salaman's factories 50% demolished, 2 houses demolished.

25th (21.50) **Romford**, Clockhouse Lane 1/27/0. Clockhouse Lane School & emergency rest centre seriously damaged & out of action, 5 houses demolished, 28 seriously damaged, 250 properties slight damage.

30th (20.15) **Romford**, Railway Bank, Eastern Road 0/5/29. 500 houses damaged.

July

1st (10.40) **Upminster**, The Grove 0/2/10. 10 houses seriously damaged, 190 superficial damage.

3rd (23.10) **Battersbridge**, LNER Goodsyard 0/5/0. Extensive damage to 2 houses, superficial damage to 30.

7th (23.55) **Hornchurch**, Rainham Road 0/13/0. 6 houses demolished, 300 damaged.

8th (00.27) **Romford** 0/5/0. 2 houses demolished, 20 seriously damaged, 250 slight damaged.

(23.15) **Thurrock**, Aveley, Dacre Drive 0/4/18. Extensive damage to property.

9th (12.15) **Rush Green**. Damage to 297 properties.

16th (00.20) **Margaretting**, Bearman's Farm 0/4/1. 1 house demolished, 2 seriously damaged.

20th (00.08) **Ingatestone**, The Hyde. Extensive damage to The Hyde (historic building). 20-25 houses superficial damage.

21st (21.40) Elmer Garden, **Rainham** 2/39/0.. Approx 200 houses superficially damaged.

22nd (01.43) **Upminster** 2/12/0. 6 properties seriously damaged, 300-400 others damaged.

(11.34) **Canvey Island** 4/7/19. 3 bungalows demolished, 6 partly .Extensive damage to over 100 houses and shops.

25th (20.00) **Purfleet**, Thurrock 0/4/12. Approx 100 houses badly damaged.

27th (18.21) **Aveley**, Thurrock 2/17/0. 7 houses destroyed, 16 damaged.

August

1st (09.55) **Rainham**, Danbury Rd 1/0/5. 6 houses demolished, 300 houses damaged.

6th (23.19) **Romford**, jnctn Hillfoot Rd & Collier Row Lane 1/4/19. 4 houses demolished, 50 seriously damaged, 400 others damaged.

7th (06.30) **Hornchurch**, S.E.Harold Wood Station 0/4/2. Chapel & 3 cottages demolished.

10th (04.26) **Billericay**, Laindon 0/0/17. Over 100 houses damaged.

11th (14.15) **Theydon Bois**, Lower Heath Drive 0/2/6. 30 houses seriously damaged.

September

19th (04.33) **Hornchurch**, Crystal Avenue 4/11/18. 6 houses demolished, 30 seriously damaged, extensive superficial damage.

(04.40) **Hornchurch**, nr Llewyns Lane 10/6/32. 6 houses demolished, 50 seriously damaged, 600 superficially damaged.

20th (01.45) **Little Baddow** 1/0/2. Dukes Orchard House partly demolished, widespread damage to 32 houses.

25th (23.00) **Great Denham**, Bacons Farm 0/0/2. 3 houses uninhabitable, 46 seriously damaged, 30 slightly damaged.

26th (03.50) **Ardleigh**, Redbury Farm 4/3/2.Nine houses demolished, 9 houses seriously damaged, 20 houses, 1 pub and 2 farms slightly damaged.

October

7th (08.55) **Pitsea**, Northlands Drive 0/6/43. Seven houses demolished, 24 seriously damaged,

35 slightly damaged.

8th (20.15) **Marks Tey**, Jays Lane 0/1/7. 30-40 houses seriously damaged.

18th (23.27) **Thorrington**, Glebe Farm. 20 houses seriously damaged, 40 slightly damaged.

21st (23.22) **Navestock** 4/9/20. 2 houses demolished, 30 seriously damaged.

23rd (19.45) **Grays**, Cromwell Road 2/15/54. Extensive damage.

November

8th (21.09) **Thurrock**, Mill Lane, Sth Stifford 1/23/15. 6 houses demolished, 30 seriously damaged, 500-600 superficially damaged.

9th (22.05) **Brentwood**, Mount Crescent 3/8/0 3 houses demolished, extensive damage.

13th (22.20) **Billericay**, Langdon Hills, Vowler Road 1/8/30. 4 houses demolished, 5 seriously damaged, extensive minor damage.

17th (19.21) **Thurrock**, Orsett Fen 1/11/5. Widespread damage to property.

A few flying bombs fell in Essex after November 1944 but they caused no loss of life and little significant structural damage.

The counties of Doodlebug Alley were Kent, with 1,444 and East Sussex with 775 flying bombs. Essex, which took over the role of Doodlebug Alley after September, received 412 and were the recipients of the most air-launched V1s. Although the maps and statistics on the last six pages reflect the bombardment which these three counties received we have not completely ignored the other counties, where the bombs were widely distributed. A map of England, showing the total number to fall in each county, appears on page 197 and a plan of the London Civil Defence Region, on page 196, lists the total for each borough during the main attack.

CHAPTER 6: THE ROCKET

"Ever since the attack of August 17/18, 1943 on Peenemunde, the long range rocket seemed to have been eclipsed by the flying bomb. Our ringside seat at the Baltic trials had shown us that, although there was the occasional attempt to plot the track of a rocket, they were almost entirely concerned with flying bombs. Now the question was: What happened to the rocket? In recommending the attack on Peenemunde I had offered: Intelligence would be prepared to take the risk of the work being restarted elsewhere."

Dr R.V.Jones - from his book 'Most Secret War'

Nazi leaders watch an A4 rocket trial in 1943. In the centre shielding his eyes is Josef Goebbels. Albert Speer, German Minister of Munitions, is on the right with the armband.

Rocket trials continue

WITH newspaper headlines declaring that the Battle of London was over, with the Nazis in retreat, with Brussels now liberated and with the flying bomb attacks seemingly over, a sense of euphoria gripped London and the south-east. On Tuesday September 5 reports that the Germans had surrendered and that Churchill was to broadcast in the evening spread like wildfire. People crowded the streets, many stopped work and flags appeared everywhere. It was just a rumour. The war was far from over; in fact the Germans were preparing to launch their most indiscriminate, terroristic and sadistic weapon of all — one that had no military or industrial objective. The A4 was designed to annihilate the civilian population of London.

Since the bombing of Peenemunde on August 17/18, 1943, the rocket programme seemed to have been abandoned. This was far from the case; an "out station" of Peenemunde had been set up at an SS Camp known as Heidelager at Blizna, some 170 miles south of Warsaw and out of reach of the British bombers. Peenemunde itself had also been rebuilt and experiments with missiles resumed. Hitler, enraged by the news of the bombing of Peenemunde, had demanded that all possible measures must be applied to produce the A4 as soon as possible. He had appointed SS-Gruppenführer Dr Hans Klammer, an expert on building gas chambers, as Commander of the restoration programme and ordered that the assembly of the rocket components, now in the hands of hundreds of small firms throughout Germany, be moved to a gigantic underground factory at Nordhausen in the Harz Mountains of Central Germany.

The Nazis had intended to launch the rocket from huge concrete firing bunkers. One built at Watten attracted the interest of the Allied Air Force and, on August 23, 1943, 185 B17 Flying Fortresses attempted to destroy it. It was then decided to launch the A4 rocket from a Meillerwagen — a mobile firing table. This was part of the rocket's towing trailer, the supporting cradle being designed to swivel the projectile upwards into its firing position. The big advantage, of course, was its mobility and the ability to evade detection.

Scientists struggled with numerous problems, for some of the rockets had a tendency to break up in the air from the stresses of flutter during the trials at Blizna. In fact the design required 65,000 modifications before it was ready for mass production and that went ahead so rapidly that between January and May, 1944 almost 1,000 missiles were completed and two fully-trained army units established. The rocket attack on England was on course to begin in July, 1944.

An A4 launched from inside the elliptical earthwork at Test site V11, Peenemunde.

'Swedish rocket'

ON June 13, 1944 — the day the first flying bombs fell in England — an A4 Test Rocket was fired from Peenemunde carrying a serial number and radio-controlled gear. It took off perfectly but went out of control, turned to the north and, some minutes later, crashed in a cornfield in south-west Sweden, causing a 13-foot crater.

The locality was quickly cordoned off, the remains carefully collected by the Swedish Air Force and taken to Stockholm. Souvenir hunters were instructed to hand over bits and pieces they had picked up some distance away.

Four days later, the Daily Express published photographs of a "German rocket bomb or Pilotless Plane" which had crashed near Kolmar, Sweden. This set off a flurry of activity behind the scenes and experts in the dissection of crashed aircraft were flown to Sweden where they took more than 100 photographs and arranged to ship the remains of the wreckage to England.

Dr Jones examined the Swedish rocket, looked again at Intelligence reports and re-assessed information gathered from talkative prisoners. He was now able to bring the A4 down to size, establishing that it was fuelled by liquid oxygen, that it carried a warhead of only one or two tons and that 1,000 at least had been manufactured. He also estimated that rocket bombardment of England could begin before September 1944.

4 EXTERNAL CONTROL VANES
COMBUSTION CHAMBER AND VENTURI
TURBINE AND PUMP ASSEMBLY
LIQUID OXYGEN TANK
ALCOHOL TANK
CONTROL COMPARTMENT
WARHEAD
4 INTERNAL CONTROL VANES
4 STABILISING FINS

V.2 GERMAN ROCKET

THE A4 was a rocket with a cylindrical body, its nose tapering to a sharp point, 46 feet in length, a diameter of five feet at the widest point with four stabilising fins. The nose section contained the fuses, the warhead and the control compartment; the centre section, alcohol and liquid-oxygen fuel tanks; and in the tail section, the turbine-pump, burner, venturi, exhaust-control-vanes and the four fins with control vanes. Electrical fuses of a new design were used so as to give it instantaneous detonation with maximum blast effect.

Fully loaded the weight was about 13.6 tons, which included nine tons of fuel and a ton of explosive. The rocket was placed vertically on a portable platform and then fed with the fuel. The mobile platform could be moved as desired.

The control vehicle was parked about 100 metres away from the rocket with the launching team positioned in slit trenches. When fired it could fly up to 3,600 mph at an altitude of 50 to 60 miles, and through controlled instruments the range could be altered accordingly, the maximum distance being 225 miles.

Von Braun arrested

THE rocket team under Werner von Braun's leadership was immensely proud that it had designed and built a missile capable of exploring the universe and, perhaps one day, carrying men into space. Captain Walter Dornberger is reputed to have said to von Braun after the first successful firing of the A4 took place — "This, October 3, 1942, is the first day of a new age of traffic technology; today space travel was born".

The German High Command, more interested in the military capabilities of the rocket, was keen for the SS to take control of the project with Dr Klammer in charge. A power struggle developed and in February 1944 von Braun was called to Gestapo headquarters where Heinrich Himmler tried, in vain, to persuade him to leave the Wehrmacht and work exclusively for the SS. The scientist refused and three weeks later was arrested on the grounds that his object all along had been space exploration and not weapon development. Also arrested were some of his colleagues, including his brother Magnus.

As the programme could not proceed without them Dornberger managed to secure their release. But the SS took control of the rocket project and Klammer became one of the fastest rising Nazi stars in the Third Reich.

With further technical problems delaying the A4 and Peenemunde being bombed twice again in July and August 1944, the scientists soon forgot about their part in the power struggle and concentrated on getting the project completed. On July 25 Blizna was evacuated and a new firing range was set up farther west at Tuchel where the vibration problems were resolved.

Polish commandos

AS soon as the experiments with V-weapons moved from Peenemunde, eastwards into Poland, the agents of the Polish Home Army Units reacted and reports of the first trials of the new weapon were frequently, and bravely, fed down the underground line to London via Rzeszow and Warsaw.

At Blizna, where the Germans built their new firing range, the Polish inhabitants were expelled but, in the woods inside the firing range, commandos of the Polish Home Army Unit operated silently by night, picking up splinters of the missiles which had sometimes exploded prematurely in the air. For many months they worked in this Nazi military zone, knowing that such unauthorised entry carried the death penalty should they be discovered.

In January, 1944 the range of the rockets on trial increased and the Polish commandos were able to detect the routes of the missiles, find the points where they fell, beat the Germans to the sites and send vital parts to Warsaw.

The commander of one partisan unit was Henryk Pawelec who lived in the mountain village of Goryswigtokrayskie, 100 miles south-east of Warsaw and close to the rocket range. He carried a false identity card and operated with stealth and extreme caution in an area densely populated by a vigilant and merciless enemy.

Henryk and his commandos discovered valuable material such as the remnants of fuselage and a turbo compression unit. They made sketches and plans and explored the secrets of the A4, ignoring the peril which faced them every day. On one occasion Henryk and his unit, *Wybranreccy*, found an unexploded missile, hid it from the Germans, carefully dismantled it and, through the Polish underground Intelligence Service, transported the parts to London via several secret landing grounds. The dramatic operation concluded with the delivery to London of rocket parts in various parcels, examined at once by Dr Jones.

Several hundred members of the Polish Resistance Movement died fighting anonymously in what became known as the "underground rocket chase". Many suffered terrible torture at the hands of the Gestapo and Henryk Pawelec lost his entire unit in this way. He was lucky. When his work was completed he escaped to Italy and then finally to England.

Three senior members of the rocket team stand in front of the first A4 to be successfully test-fired. Left to right: Werner Gengelbach, an electrical specialist, Walter Thiel, rocket engine specialist and Hans Hüter, senior engineer at the Test Stand V11, Peenemunde. In the background is the A4, also known as the V4 with its "moon maiden" motif. Hüter wears an official issue leather coat as protection against the cold Baltic weather on the test site. Walter Thiel was killed in the bombing of Peenemunde in 1943.

First rocket lands in Paris

BY the beginning of September, 1944 the Nazis were ready at last for the rocket offensive. The A4 became known as the V2, or Vergeltungswaffe-zwei (vengeance weapon two) and two batteries were moved into position for firing — one directed at Paris and the second at London. By this time all northern France and most of Belgium had been liberated by the Allies and what remained of the prepared rocket-launching sites in Pas de Calais was now the tramping ground of Allied troops. Hitler's orders were to attack Paris first and Batterie 444 positioned itself at Euskirchen, 15 miles south west of Bonn while the 2nd Batterie of Artillery Detachment 485 of Gruppe Nord moved into The Hague to prepare for a double launch against London.

On Wednesday September 6 two V2s were aligned with Paris and eight tons of volatile fuel were pumped into each. The first was ignited shortly after 9 am but the motor cut out just as it was about to lift off. The rocket fell back onto the firing table where it tottered but remained upright. The same happened with the second rocket some 40 minutes later. So far the V2 rocket assault was more like a damp squib!

The technicians discovered the fault and by dawn on Thursday morning were ready to fire again. The first rocket lifted off haphazardly and disappeared into the distance never to be seen again; the second was a perfect launch. It rose into the stratosphere and five minutes later came down to earth in the Paris suburb of Maisons Alfort, killing six people.

Three more shots were fired at Paris, a distance of 200 miles, but the Americans were advancing so fast that the detachment had to withdraw from Euskirchen and join the batteries at The Hague for the attack on Britain. Paris was spared.

Death from the stratosphere

THERE was a great air of optimism in London and south-east England on Friday September 8, despite the false news of the German surrender three days earlier. The Allied armies were rolling inexorably eastwards through Belgium and towards the borders of Adolf Hitler's Fatherland. Everywhere there was serious talk of the end of the war before Christmas. After five years of hardship, ending with those terrible doodlebugs, the end of hostilities was now a reality.

As the people of London dispersed from their offices, shops and factories on this fine autumn evening with the weekend ahead, they were blissfully ignorant of the fact that fifty miles above the earth a long dark rocket, weighing 13 tons, armed with a ton of high explosive, travelling at more than 3,000 mph was hurtling towards London from the Dutch coast. No-one heard it, no-one saw it.

At 6.43 pm the rocket ended its brief but deadly flight, plummeting from the

This was Staveley Road, Chiswick after the first V2 had exploded. Three people were killed, Mrs Ada Harrison and a little girl from next door, Rosemary Clarke, aged three. The third victim was army private Frank Browning who was crossing the road when the rocket fell. Germany made no formal announcement of the incident and the British Government, meeting without Churchill who was on his way to Canada, imposed a total news black-out.

....four times the speed of sound

stratosphere at four times the speed of sound into the ground in the western suburb of Chiswick. The explosion in Staveley Road created a 30-foot wide crater. Three people died, 17 were seriously injured, six houses were totally destroyed and many others severely damaged. As the missile impacted into the concrete, a thunderous explosion echoed right across London; there was immediate confusion for no-one had heard the sound of a German bomber or the drone of a flying bomb, or an air-raid alert. Those living in West London heard a double thunderclap, after the impact — the noise of the rocket breaking the sound barrier.

This was the turning point in the history of warfare. The V2 rocket offensive had begun and from this moment in time military strategy was revolutionised. Chiswick in West London was the first place in England to be introduced to the long-range ballistic missile.

There followed a conspiracy of silence. The question on everyone's lips remained unanswered for several weeks. The official euphemism for this and the following explosions was that gas mains had blown up. Those who felt the pavement shake under their feet, looked up to see a white vapour trail hanging vertically in the air and then heard the double boom, were more sceptical. Could this, they wondered, be Hitler's much-vaunted long-range rocket which Duncan Sandys had refused to discuss at his conference a few days earlier? He said he knew about the V2 and in a few days time the press would be walking over the abandoned launching sites in France.

THIS map of Northern Europe and England shows the locations of the principal towns in the V2 campaign. By the time the first missile was launched, France and most of Belgium had been liberated and two of the rocket assembly plants, at **Watten** and **Wizernes** in Pas de Calais, overrun by the advancing troops. Watten, in fact, was the world's largest bunker and 130,000 tons of concrete went into its construction. The heavy Allied bombing could only knock a few lumps out of its vast walls.

It was from **Euskirchen**, south of Bonn, that the first rocket was fired at Paris. The Germans then withdrew to **The Hague** and **Walcheren Island** where they joined the other batteries for the attack on England. From here, the first two rockets fell at **Chiswick** and **Epping**. On September 25 an attack was opened on a number of Continental targets, notably **Antwerp, Brussels, Liege** and **Lille.** It was on that day that rockets were fired from **Staveren** in Friesland towards targets in **East Anglia**.

Other locations on this map include **Kummersdorf West**, south of Berlin, where the German Army Weapons Department was first established, **Peenemunde**, where the missile was developed, **Blizna** and then **Tuchel**, the firing ranges in Poland and **Nordhausen**, where the V2 was assembled in vast factories under the Harz mountains.

The little town of **Oberammergau** has yet to figure in the V2 story, but it was to this peaceful spot in the Bavarian Alps that the rocket men eventually moved.

The "flying gas mains"

Dr Jones and his colleague in Scientific Intelligence, Charles Frank were in their office at the Air Ministry when they heard a double bang. The two men looked at each other and said almost simultaneously — "that's the first one". A few moments later came another boom made by a missile on its supersonic descent. This one had landed at Parndon Wood, near Epping.

The two incidents made a complete mockery of the day's headlines which had actually proclaimed the end of the flying bomb battle. They also coincided with the news that the Allied armies were held up in their advance across Belgium by the rivers Scheldt and Rhine, and so there was an area around the Hook of Holland still in German hands — an area destined to remain so throughout the winter.

The third V2, on September 10, came down at Fambridge, near Southend, the fourth blew up in a field at Crockenhill, near Swanley and the fifth at Magdalen Laver. There was little damage and no casualties. On Tuesday September 12 there were four more — at Paglesham, near Rochford, Keston, near Biggin Hill, Dagenham and Kew Gardens. The casualty list so far was eight killed and 28 seriously injured.

There were no official announcements apart from Ministry references to "gas main explosions", which led the public to christen them the "flying gas mains".

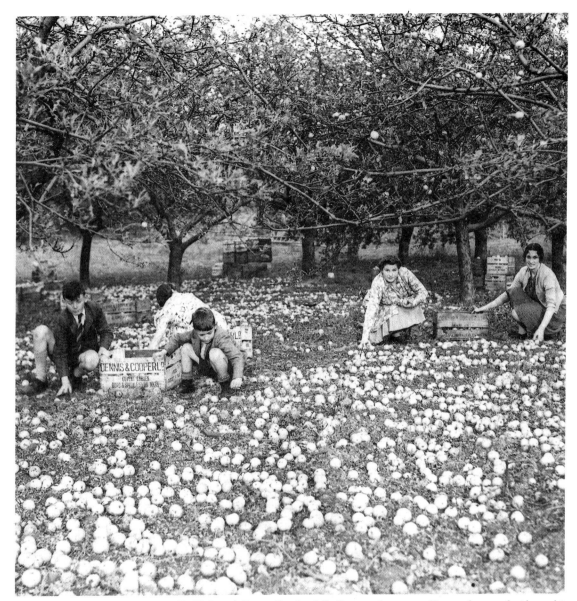

The first V2 to fall in Kent was at Field Crouch Farm, Crockenhill. It caused no casualties or damage but brought down thousands of apples from a nearby orchard and gave the farmer his quickest apple picking season ever.

Big bangs attract the 'big noises'

EDWARD Carter, Chief Warden for the Urban District of Waltham Holy Cross from 1939 to 1945 kept a diary in which he recorded all the main incidents and took many photographs. Some years after the war the diary was published by Waltham Abbey Historical Society. Here are some extracts beginning on Saturday September 9, 1944 when Ted, like most people, was rather confused by the "mysterious explosions".

Saturday September 9: So now what? Last evening at about 1845 two large explosions heard, but apparently some distance off, though they shook doors and windows. I thought the first one must be thunder, so loud did it seem and so long did it rumble and echo.

At the scene of the incident we found Harris from Group 7, Smith, the bomb recce man and several others. Crater about 8 ft deep and 20 ft across and trees and shrubs all round, just wiped out. Clearly not a PAC, nor Compo, not ordinary bomb. Must be something out of the ordinary to attract all the "big noises". An odd feature is that no-one seems to have heard it coming.

Tuesday September 12: More of the "mysterious missiles" have fallen. They appear to be stratosphere-rocket-shells,

Wednesday September 20: Out of the east came the deep throbbing of a late doodlebug. I was just in time to see the fiery tail swing rapidly sideways and plunge headlong down against a pale white background of searchlights. Control said "Green Man" area of Waltham Cross. I went poste haste to the incident. Confusion reigned for a time, when it seemed that everyone was milling around in all directions. Converted my car into a control point after turning into Eastbrook Road. The bomb had fallen smack into Cobbins Brook. Houses in Honey Lane facing the Larsen Rec were in a sorry state and the damage extended in varying degrees up many roads. All around was the tinkling of glass and the "smack" of tiles falling, and householders were busy sweeping glass and plaster into the roads. 400 houses were affected. Photograph shows the incident post at The Green Man, Bill Beanse looking over the shoulder of Kath Stewart.

possibly launched from Jutland or inside Germany itself. The terrific height and speed at which they travel makes them invisible and inaudible and apparently they travel to earth considerably faster than their own sound.

Wednesday September 13: Went with Ellis to Dagenham this pm to see the effects of a "mysterious missile". Not so bad as I had expected, and not so bad as doodlebug damage.

Thursday September 14: A loud explosion (another gas main!) Fell at Walthamstow right alongside Group 7 HQ. Crater 25 ft deep filling with water from a broken main. Transformer station in the ground of the new Town Hall with walls sucked out and reinforced concrete roof curved down to the ground, all cracked and broken. A long shapeless heap of rubble and dust was all that was left of a row of houses - about 11 in all. Here and there, an odd piece of wall stood dejectedly, and at one end a bedroom opened to the four winds retained its bed and bedding.

Soft 'pop' in Woolwich

I worked for the Ministry of Supply at Woolwich for the whole of the war and experienced more than 60 ordinary bombing raids. Often I had to walk home from Woolwich to Welling because of damage to the tram lines.

It was in September, 1944 that we began to hear loud bangs at intervals and were told that gas mains were exploding in different areas. On the morning of September 14, I was sitting in the kitchen eating my breakfast when there was a soft 'pop' and all the windows shot open. I went into the hall and was aghast to see that the front door was hanging off and the frame was falling outwards. Then the silence ended; the air became dark with debris raining down and I could hear screams.

I had to get to work but my sister and other neighbours helped anyone they could, because a row of houses in Dairsee Road had received a direct hit, killing seven people and injuring dozens of others. A girl I knew had just come back from leave but was met at the station to be told that her mother and sister had been killed. Her father was discovered amid the debris unscathed.

Joan Smith, Tenterden, Kent

A blinding flash from the direction of Central London — the sight often witnessed by Len Northrop.

A blinding flash

The V2's four-minute journey to London was as fast and silent as the fastest shooting star, but without its beauty. Many times in that weary winter of 1944-5, with peace already in the wings, I would walk home at night after going to a cinema at Rochester. When the night was clear and starlit I enjoyed the three-mile stroll and it had the added bonus of keeping me fit for my football games.

On occasions, as I walked the tree-lined route to my village and looked across the darkened hills to London, there would come a blinding flash, silence for perhaps 15 seconds, then a heavy thud that shook the night. Death and destruction from the sky was 30 miles away and here was I on a lonely road thinking of my football game the next day.

Such was the drama of those weeks. The emotions played all kinds of tricks but, to a youth of the time, life was dangerous, dramatic and highly exciting.

Len Northrop, Herstmonceux, Near Hailsham

Doodlebug Alley moves to Essex

THE statement by Mr Duncan Sandys that the flying bomb launching sites in France and Belgium had been captured and the menace was finally over, was premature. As refugees came streaming back, many to roofless houses, Colonel Wachtel's men had regrouped in north-west Germany and were now ready to launch from specially-adapted Heinkel aircraft. Doodlebug Alley was about to move to a new county; Essex was under the direct firing line.

At dawn on Saturday September 16, nine bombs were released. Five were shot down, two crashed in open country and one got through to Woolwich. The ninth fell in St Awdry's Road, Barking, killing 13 people and injuring more than 100.

The following evening the roar of a flying bomb brought hundreds of people into the streets of Colchester. They saw the thrilling sight of a V1 being chased by a fighter. Machine gun fire was heard as it crossed the town followed, a few minutes later, by an explosion as the robot fell harmlessly in a village field.

The *Essex County Standard* reported how another bomb, which fell at Little Baddow, cost the life of Mrs Gregory Nicholson, secretary of the Essex Drama League, whose house was demolished. "The bombs", said the newspaper, "were now flying at a much lower altitude and on September 20 one flew into a hill at Maldon. There were 12 casualties. Among those who escaped were a couple rescued unhurt from a Morrison shelter in a wrecked house.

"During the following week, bombs roared over Colchester every night and in the early hours of September 27 one crashed in Ardleigh, destroying four thatched cottages. Four people were killed — Mrs Ada Cheeseman, her two children and Mr Wilfred Jaggard. The doodlebug was heard approaching the village. Its engine stopped and the inhabitants heard it gliding on. One man described the sound as 'like the whistling of a bomb'. Then there was a terrific bang which seemed to last for more than a minute."

Just before this incident, the villagers of Marks Tey, Copford and Easthorpe had appealed to the Regional Commissioner of the Eastern Civil Defence, requesting that an air raid siren be installed in the vicinity. The appeal, representing 900 residents, was turned down owing to the "limitations of the supply of equipment and the lack of minimum conditions of population density."

In Colchester, flying bomb alerts were now a nightly occurrence. There were explosions at Inworth, Sudbury and Ware and "on the black moonless night of October 5, a robot damaged by anti-aircraft fire, missed houses near the Abbey Field, struck a tree and

Four thatched cottages stood on this site at Ardleigh, near Colchester. They were destroyed on the morning of September 27, 1944. One person was killed.

exploded at Reeds Hall'. The tree in direct line with an army hut crowded with soldiers, probably saved scores of lives.

The village of Marks Tey, its people angry that the petition for a siren had been rejected, was now being peppered with flying bombs. There were no fatalities but many houses, stables, barns and glasshouses were completely wrecked. The railway line was damaged and, on one occasion, customers of the Trowel and Hammer public house were showered with glass.

Air-launched V1s continued to fall in Essex throughout October, November and up to Christmas, 1944, when the Allied occupation of key bases near the German frontier gave Essex a brief respite. In this time, however, the doodlebugs caused considerable damage at Thorrington, Little Bentley, Eight Ash Green (destroying the parish church), Great Bentley, West Mersea and Fingringhoe.

One bomb hit allotments near Berechurch Road, Colchester, demolished a number of houses and blew all the windows out of the Queen's Hotel. The landlord, Mr Joe Girling, twice previously bombed out, opened as usual, selling what he described as "real draught beer".

A bridge too far

One of the V1 launching sites overrun by Canadian forces sweeping through Holland. This ramp was used to launch flying bombs against Antwerp. Just before pulling out the Germans blew up as many sites and bombs as they could.

FIVE members of one family, the Shins, were killed when a rocket struck their terraced house in Adelaide Avenue, Lewisham on September 17. It was the 25th to reach England — and the worst to date. The blast destroyed 11 homes in the road, 14 people died and 29 were seriously injured.

By this time the Home Office had received serious warnings from British agents on the Continent about the likely severity of the attacks and new stringent precautions were taken to protect Londoners, who would have been shocked if they knew of the plans being made for their safety.

It was decided to select suitable assembly points outside a radius of about five miles from the centre of London. Those refugees escaping on foot would be picked up by buses and transported to these points, which were mostly schools, cinemas, dance halls and football stadiums.

The people of Sidcup, and those who arrived there by bus, would have been required to make their way to the Central School at Alma Road, or to the Odeon Cinema from where they would be driven to Maidstone. The evacuees from Beckenham, so it was planned, would go to the Regal Cinema and then on to Sevenoaks. Bromley and Orpington would also be evacuated to Sevenoaks. Altogether there were 87 top-secret routes in the fringe areas and the picking up points were chosen at random. If the emergency plan had been put into operation the police and the WVS would have played a vital part.

On the same day as the Adelaide Avenue disaster at Lewisham, British airborne forces began landing on their dropping zones at Arnhem in the Allied operation to capture the Rhine Bridges. This heroic operation, code-named "Market Garden" severely threatened Hans Klammer's rocket units who, fearful his men would be cut off, hastily withdrew and the firings ceased for about a week. There was one parting shot. A rocket landed in Chatsworth Way, West Norwood scoring a direct hit on the church. Two died and 51 were injured.

After holding the bridgehead at Arnhem for nine days against overwhelming odds, the British and Polish troops surrendered and the operation was abandoned. On September 25 the rocket attacks re-commenced but the aiming point now was East Anglia, and Norwich appeared to be the centre of the target.

The Wermacht had set up shop in south-west Friesland.

Rockets on East Anglia

FEWER than 30 missiles had been launched from the German rocket sites in the suburbs of The Hague and on Walcheren Island before the ill-fated Market Garden operation forced Versuchsbatterie 444 to withdraw. Dr Klammer instructed his unit to move forward to the Gaasterland district of south-west Friesland, where they found an ideal site in a thickly wooded area close to the hamlet of Rijs and well concealed from the prying cameras of Allied reconnaissance aircraft. The V2 had a 200-mile maximum range and the cities of Ipswich and Norwich were the only centres of sizeable population now within firing range.

On the afternoon of Tuesday September 26, the village of Ranworth in Norfolk was shaken by the ear-splitting double explosion which shattered windows for a radius of a half mile from the centre of the blast. The rocket had impacted in a field of stubble, creating a crater 25 feet deep and 40 feet in diameter. A column of black smoke could be seen from Norwich, eight miles away, a clear indication that the V2 offensive had moved into East Anglia.

During the next 16 days more than 30 rockets were destined to land in the two eastern counties and more than a dozen in Essex. For the Rijs rocket team the operation was a complete flop for the missiles repeatedly fell harmlessly in rural areas; there were no fatal casualties and only 51 people were injured — mainly by flying glass.

The worst incident, and one which could have been far more tragic, occurred on October 4 at 1.40 pm when a rocket landed just 100 yards from the village school of Rockland St Mary about five miles from Norwich. The children were changing classes at the time when their world was turned upside down by a blinding flash and loud explosion. Seven children were injured and taken to hospital and 21 others and a teacher were slightly hurt. A man who had been leading horses across a nearby field was badly injured by a piece of the shattered rocket which had struck him on the neck.

One of the most eventful days was Tuesday October 3 when six missiles were fired at Norfolk. At regular intervals the earth shook, windows were shattered and huge columns of black smoke mushroomed into the sky. Not one of those six found a populated area. The first arrived at Beeston St Lawrence Park, the second plunged into the sea, the third made a crater near Valley Farm, Hopton in Suffolk — from where six people were taken to hospital —the fourth hit meadowland at Witchingham, not far from Attlebridge airfield, the fifth fell onto Hellesdon Golf Course, damaging 400

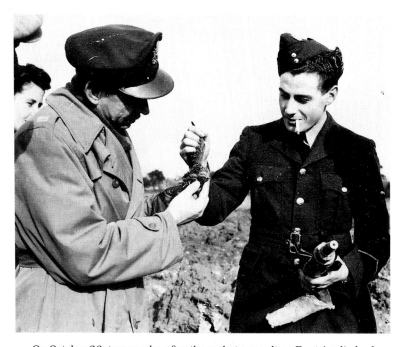

On October 26, two weeks after the rocket assault on East Anglia had ended, a stray missile fell at Welborne, near Mattishall, Norfolk. The V2 caused a crater 15 feet deep by 41 feet wide and damage was caused to 15 farm buildings, a school and 15 houses. Two men were slightly hurt and a wing was broken off a passing skylark. Photograph shows the bird being examined by LAC Dunthorne (right) and a USAAF officer from Attlebridge airfield and comes to us by courtesy of P.A. Dunthorne (via Bob Collis). Bob is an aviation historian from Lowestoft.

houses — and the sixth exploded in a field at Darrow Farm, Denton, 11 miles away.

The last rocket to leave Rijs Wood for East Anglia was at 7.40 am on October 12. It fell harmlessly in open country at Manor Farm, Ingworth, causing minor damage to 24 houses. Characterising the failure of this episode of the campaign, it was to be the last V2, not intended for London, to fall on British soil.

The attacks on Ipswich and Norwich were over but the Germans did not abandon Rijs Wood. Information had reached the unit that the Belgian port of Antwerp was now in Allied hands and massive quantities of equipment for the troops were being unloaded.

Hans Klammer instructed his men to change the direction of the rockets and tilt them towards Antwerp.

The Belgian town of Antwerp was now in Allied hands and, critical to the success of the continuing advance, it was imperative to bring the port into operation as soon as possible in order to provide a shorter supply route to the front. Hitler, of course, was aware of this. On October 13, the German High Command instructed Hans Klammer to switch his emphasis from Norfolk to Antwerp and destroy it completely. Between October 13 and 20, 23 rockets were launched from Rijs towards the harbour installations. On October 21, at 4.50 pm. Batterie 444 left Rijs Wood. Some 20 minutes later seven Tempests of No 274 Squadron arrived overhead and, flying in a line astern, strafed the now-abandoned rocket base. The army, however, were well clear, having themselves blown up what was left behind. This damaged rocket, found later in the campaign by advancing commandos, shows that the retreating Nazis were leaving behind no souvenirs.

Between October 4 and 11, 62 flying bombs were launched from Heinkel 111s, of which nine fell on London. During this period 16 people were killed at Hornsey, six at Chertsey, four at Harrow and two at Surbiton. All the air launches took place during the hours of darkness and night fighters could not approach closer to the coast than six miles to seaward and five miles landward. Many Heinkels and their bombs were destroyed by fighters but it was the gunners in the new belt, northwards from Clacton to Great Yarmouth, who were again achieving the greater rate of success. The balloon barrage, too, had its moments. On October 8, a doodlebug caught in the cable crashed onto the village of Fawkham, near Gravesend, demolishing several houses. There were many casualties.

Heaven in Hellfire Corner

WITH all fears of a German invasion of Britain finally over, the Home Office made the decision to stand down the Home Guard. On Sunday October 15, more than 3,000 men and officers drawn from 50 battalions throughout Kent were among the first in the country to attend a stand-down service. The men, accompanied by bands of the 1st (Ashford) and the 18th (Dartford) fell in at the Chaucer Barracks, Canterbury and marched through the city to the Cathedral.

Lord Cornwallis, the new Lord Lieutenant of the County, took the salute outside the city walls after the service where he said: "When we in deep anguish received into our little Kentish ports our hard-pressed armies retreating from Dunkirk and when we saw endless train loads being taken back to the west through our county for rest and refitting, we might have thought there was little hope. But always remember with pride that when those tired armies were going back west, a citizens' army was rising in the south-east, ready to fight on the beaches, in the fields and in the streets to secure the breathing space the nation so urgently required. That citizen army was you — the Home Guard of Kent — and today I give to you all the humble and completely sincere thanks of the people of your country."

Three days later the now-peaceful front-line towns of Folkestone and Dover received a visit from King George VI and Queen Elizabeth who paid their personal tribute to members of the town's Civil Defence services. After all the bombing raids, the doodlebugs, anti-aircraft guns and intensive cross-Channel shelling, there was a strange silence in Dover and Folkestone. There were no explosions and people were actually sleeping in their own beds.

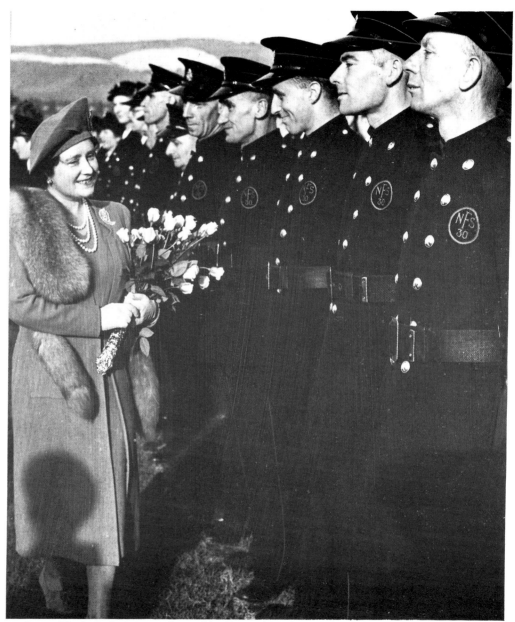

Queen Elizabeth chats to members of the National Fire Service during her visit to Folkestone on October 18, 1944.

The Southend rocket is removed for examination.

Southend under fire

THE Market Garden debacle allowed Hans Klammer to send two rocket batteries back to The Hague to resume the attack on London, confident that the Allied advance from the south had been successfully halted. East London and Essex were now in the firing line and in the next few days V2s plunged to earth in Leytonstone, killing eight people, Tilbury, Wanstead and Walthamstow.

Southend was also subjected to assault by the V2; missiles fell at Pitsea and Rawreth and, on October 11 at 6.50 am, one exploded in the soft mud of the foreshore about 70 yards west of Southend Pier and left the inhabitants reflecting on what might have been, for had the V2 fallen a few yards inland the casualties would have been severe.

As it was, windows were blasted and roofs torn away from houses, shops and hotels in The Royal Terrace, Marine Parade and the High Street. Parts of the missile crashed through the Pier Pavilion and a large section embedded itself in the sea wall which surrounded the boating pool.

The incident happened at a time when there was still a total news ban on the V2, partly for morale at home but also to keep the Germans guessing. It also had the people of Southend guessing, especially those who touched the metal soon after the missile landed and found their fingers blistered and seared. The burns were due to the intense heat of the metal caused by its supersonic race through space. One white hot piece crashed through the roof of a house in Pleasant Road and fell on a bed in which 71-year-old Mrs Alice Gaylor was sleeping. The bed caught fire but Mrs Gaylor escaped with slight burns.

In the weeks that followed the people of south-east Essex became accustomed to hearing the explosions of the rockets as they bombarded the district, fortunately without any serious casualties. Damage was done at Rawreth, Wickford, Little Wakering, Fambridge, Rayleigh, Fobbing, Laindon, Canvey and many places in the Dengie Hundred and Billericay urban district.

BIG BEN INCIDENTS: SEPT/OCT 1944

This list shows the date, time and location of almost every Big Ben (V2) incident in the UK during September and October. Other months follow until the end of the rocket campaign in March

September 1944

8th (18.43) **Chiswick**
(18.43) Parndon Wood, nr **Epping**
10th (21.30) **Fambridge**, nr Southend
11th (09.07) **Lullingstone**, nr Crockenhill
(09.30) **Magdalen Laver**
12th (06.15) **Kew Gardens**
(08.19) **Dagenham**
(08.52) **Keston, nr** Biggin Hill
(17.55) **Paglesham**, nr Rochford
14th (04.53) **Walthamstow** (date corr.)
13th (11.05) Sea off **Colne Point**
14th (07.25) **Woolwich**
(13.16) **Rotherfield**
15th (04.09) **Sunbury**
(14.20) River N of **All Hallows**
16th (07.33) **Southgate**
(08.28) **Wembley**
(10.28) **Yiewsley**
(15.20) **Willingdon**, nr Eastbourne
(22.38) Noak Hill, nr **Romford**
17th (05.11) **Knockholt**
(06.04) **East Ham**
(12.05) **Hockley**, nr Southend
(13.11) **Coulsdon**
(18.56) **Brockley**, Lewisham
18th (19.02) **Lambeth**
25th (19.10) **Hoxne**
26th (16.30) **Ranworth**
27th (10.47) **Horsford**, N of Norwich
(16.25) **Kirby Bedon**, SE of Norwich
(17.50) **Beighton**, ESE Norwich
28th (14.20) 8 miles NE **Happisburgh**
29th (13.12) **Hemsby**, nr Yarmouth
(19.45) **Horstead**
(20.42) **Witlingham**, nr Norwich
30th (12.14) **Tunstall**, E of Norwich

October

1st (17.55) **Bedingham**, NW Bungay
3rd (09.32) **Beeston St Lawrence**
(14.41) **Hopton**, NW Lowestoft
(16.55) Mill Farm, **Gt Witchingham**
(19.45) **Hellesdon**
(20.10) Darrow Farm, **Denton**
(23.05) **Wanstead (**Leytonstone in original Fighter Comm. list)
4th (08.15) **Eastchurch**, Isle of Sheppey
(12.22) Sea 8 miles off **Yarmouth**
(13.40) **Rockland St Mary**, Norwich
(16.47) **Crostwick**, nr Norwich
(17.36) **Spixworth**
5th (04.22) **Goose Green**, Hoddesdon
(07.36) Sea off **Great Yarmouth**
(09.04) Taverham Hall Fm, **Norwich**
(11.38) **Peasenhall**
(13.28) **Surlingham**
(16.09) **Acle**
(17.44) **Little Plumstead**
6th (09.25) **Shotesham** All Saints
7th (08.53) **Pitsea**, nr Southend

8th (08.03) **Tilbury**
9th (05.52) **Wanstead Flats**
(09.50) **Havengore Island**
(10.45) **Langley**, SE Norwich
(10.50) **Brooke**, SE Norwich
(13.50) Hyde Marsh, nr **Fambridge**
(18.30) Sea off **Orfordness**
10th (07.19) Sea off **Clacton**
(10.25) **Navestock**, NW Brentwood
(16.00) **Harwick Harbour** (air burst)
(17.35) **Bramerton**, SE Norwich
11th (00.45) **Rawreth**, NW Southend
(05.20) North of **Ockendon**
(06.50) **Southend**
(08.10) **Haddiscoe**, nr Beccles
(10.51) **Rockland St Mary**, Norwich
(14.21) **Playford**, NE Ipswich
12th (00.12) **Walthamstow**
(02.53) Sea off **Southend**
(07.40) **Ingworth**, N of Aylsham
(10.58) **Rawreth**, NW Southend
13th (06.48) **Great Burstead**, Brentwood
(07.24) **Little Wakering**, Southend

14th (02.22) 1 mile E of Northaw
(23.50) Nr **Fairlop** airfield
15th (05.05) **Rettenden**, SE Chelmsford
17th (15.50) **Little Baddow**, Chelmsford
18th (06.32) **Chislet**, NE Canterbury
19th (07.17) **Borough Green**
20th (20.15) **South Norwood**
21st (01.15) **Hayes**
23rd (03.44) Sea 1 mile SW **Clacton**
(14.10) Felmore Farm, **Billericay**
(16.53) St Mary's at **Hoo**, Chatham
(19.18) **Navestock Heath**
24th (00.28) **Langdon Hill**, Tilbury
(02.07) Sea nr **Queenborough**
(05.02) **Rushmere St Andrew**
(20.44) **Wickford**, Essex
(20.47) **Fobbing**, Essex
(22.27) Nr **Southminster**
25th (12.40) **Rawreth**, Essex
26th (08.10) **Walthamstow**
(08.40) **Bermondsey**
(09.00) **Barley**, 3m SE of Royston

(10.14) **Welborne**, 10m W of Norwich
(11.35) **Sheering**
(13.41) Sea off **Clacton**
(18.45) **Palmers Green**
(22.50) **Ilford**
27th (06.55) nr **Slough**
(10.15) In field nr **Swanley**
(11.21) **Wanstead**
(12.05) **Chingford**, forest land
(18.54) **Wanstead**
(23.25) **West Ham**
(23.47) **Lewisham**
28th (04.59) **Ashford**, nr Staines
(11.07) **Deptford** (mid-air burst)
(18.15) **Shalford**, nr Braintree
(18.20) **Camberwell**
29th (23.57) **Shenfield**, Essex
30th (05.15) **Beckton**, nr Barking
(12.30) **West Ham**, Victoria Dock
(12.31) **West Ham**, Forest Lane
(16.23) **Woolwich**
(18.47) **Wapping**, Hermitage Wharf
(20.38) **Elstree**, Ridge Hill
31st (02.56) **Hanwell** Golf Course
(07.40) **Surrey Commercial Docks**
(18.11) **Bexleyheath**
(18.36) NE **Woolwich**
(21.03) **Hendon**, Kingsbury area
(23.40) **Orpington**

Throughout the duration of the war, the people of Dover suffered more consistent bombardment and more heartbreak than any other town in the south-east, outside of London. More than 10,000 properties were damaged, 199 people were killed and 307 seriously injured. Here are some of the survivors holding gifts sent by the people of Salford to help in "some small way to compensate their suffering". The scheme was run by the WVS.

As Canadian and British commandos, joined by Dutch and French units, advanced towards Walcheren Island where a rocket base had been established, the Germans were forced to retreat even further eastwards. Field Marshal Montgomery had an early opportunity to examine the remains of a V2 which crashed in open country near Antwerp on October 30, close to the headquarters of Major General Hobart, GOC 79th Armoured Division who is seen in the photograph.

Churchill admits: we are under attack again

ON Wednesday November 10, the Prime Minister finally admitted that Britain was under attack by the secret long-range German weapon, the V2. He told the House of Commons that almost 100 had landed since the first hit Chiswick but the information had been suppressed for very good reasons. Winston Churchill's statement followed an announcement on German radio that London "was devastated" by the weapon. The Prime Minister denied this.

"For the last few weeks the enemy has been using his new weapon, the long-range rocket, and a number have landed at widely scattered points in this country. In all, the casualties and damage have so far not been heavy, though I am sure the House will wish me to express my sympathy with the victims of this as with other attacks,

No official statement about this attack has hitherto been issued. The reason for this silence was that any announcement might have given information useful to the enemy, and we were confirmed in this course by the fact that, until two days ago, the enemy had made no mention of this weapon in his communiques. Last Wednesday an official announcement followed by a number of highly coloured accounts of attacks on this country was issued by German High Command. I do not wish to comment upon it, except to say that the statements in this announcement are a good reflection of what the German Government would wish their people to believe, and of their desperate need to afford them some encouragement.

I may however, mention a few facts. The rocket contains approximately the same quantity of explosive as the flying bomb. However, it is designed to penetrate rather deeper before exploding. The result is somewhat heavier damage in the immediate vicinity of the crater, but rather less extensive blast effect. The rocket flies through the stratosphere, going up to 60 or 70 miles, and outstrips sound. Because of its high speed. no reliable or sufficient public warning can, in present circumstances, be given. There is, however, no need to exaggerate the danger. The scale and effect of the attack have not hitherto been significant.

Some rockets have been fired at us from the island of Walcheren.

DAILY HERALD

No. 8962 — SATURDAY NOVEMBER 11 1944 — ONE PENNY

The V2 Rocket Comes To Southern England

THESE pictures, taken in Southern England, show damage caused by German long-range rockets. The use of this weapon is another attempt by the enemy to attack the morale of our civil population, said Mr. Churchill yesterday.

1,000 Tanks In Third Army's Loraine Drive

ONE THOUSAND tanks were locked in battle on the American Third Army front last night, according to German reports.

The clash occurred some miles east of Delme, a village 17 miles north-east of Nancy.

Earlier in the day Americans had captured the 1,200ft. high Delme ridge, the enemy's most important observation point in the sector.

General Patton's tanks pushed on more than five miles to the north-east and captured the village of Fremery.

Then German resistance stiffened.

Two more five-mile advances farther north led to the capture of Buchy, a village midway between Delme and Metz, and Tragny.

To the south, Chateau Salins was taken, and tanks struck on another three miles to the village of Hampont.

Nearer Border

The position on this sector, after three days of attack, is that the great quadrilateral formed by the main roads linking Pont-à-Mousson, Buchy, Chateau Salins and Nancy has been almost entirely cleared of German troops.

General Patton's left flank was last night only two and a half miles from the German frontier.

This northward stab was achieved by a rapid widening of the Third Army's new bridgehead over the Moselle north-east of Thionville.

It is now nearly seven miles long and three miles deep at points.

It is now known that Patton is using at least eight divisions—two armoured and six infantry—in wide sweeping moves which threaten to outflank Metz completely.

Another two-to-tire advance of 400 yards was made by General Hodges' troops in the Forest of Hontracht which west of Aachen.

A similar advance was made south-west of Hoengen village, but the gain was lost to a German counter-attack.

Surrender Call

In this battle front line loudspeakers suddenly boomed out:

BUILDING NEW WEST DEFENCES

From WALLACE KING

STOCKHOLM, Friday

THE German General Staff is building a huge new defence belt from Emden to the Swiss frontier.

Plans have been made to evacuate the entire population west of this line.

Military circles in Berlin speak of this scheme as a development of defensive tactics which have proved successful in the West at Aachen and in East Prussia.

Realising that Atlantic Wall type defences were outdated the German General Staff summoned a conference of specialists.

Bigger Obstacles

At this General Guderian, leading Nazi tank expert, who was routed to East Prussia to stem the Red Army's drive, convinced everybody that a "rolling" defence system based on armoured vehicles, self-propelled guns and transportable concrete bunkers was the only method of preventing the Fatherland's frontiers.

In this new defence zone mines, released in wood, clay, and glass that are claimed to defy detection by existing detectors, are being used.

"Pyramid" tank obstacles, like those in front of the Siegfried

'COMETS' THAT DIVE FROM 70 MILES

Antwerp Under Fire— Berlin

PARIS and Antwerp, as well as London, are being attacked by rockets, the Germans claimed last night.

A few hours after Mr. Churchill announced that V2s had been fall...

Ten-ft. Parts Recovered

From W. A. E. JONES, Southern England, Friday

BRITAIN'S front line at home is under fire again—from a stratosphere rocket that is dropping on us from 60 to 70 miles up in the air, a rocket that travels faster than sound and flashes across the sky like a "comet trailing fire."

I am writing this story in this front line. There is no siren warning now. No time to take shelter.

For this is the most indiscriminate weapon of this or any other war. It is a sinister, eerie form of war.

I have just come away from a district hit recently by "V2." It dropped at teatime. It hurtled through a house, exploded and dug a deep crater.

Several people were killed. Children at a birthday party in a tiny, old house died as they sat at their table with the cake and its candles fascinating them.

People poke around the debris. Cranes are at work.

LINE TO BUDAPEST IS CUT

"HERALD" REPORTER

This is now in our hands, and other areas from which rockets have been or can at present be fired against this country will doubtless be overrun by our forces in due course. We cannot, however, be certain that the enemy will not be able to increase the range, either by reducing the weight of the warhead or by other methods. Nor, on the other hand, can we be certain that any new launching areas which he may establish further back will not also in turn be overrun by the advancing Allied armies.

The use of this weapon is another attempt by the enemy to attack the morale of our civil population in the vain hope that he may somehow by this means stave off the defeat which faces him in the field. Doubtless the enemy has hoped by his announcement to induce us to give him information which he had failed to get otherwise. I am sure that this House, the Press and the public will refuse to oblige him in this respect."

157

Churchill spoke about the vain attempt by the enemy to attack the morale of the British people. With his process of indiscriminate slaughter and destruction, lasting for five long years, Hitler managed to kindle, in British hearts, a great fire of defiance which is brilliantly illustrated in this photograph of an old couple salvaging household goods from their bombed home — perhaps for the umpteenth time.

Carnage in Antwerp

ALTHOUGH the great Belgian port of Antwerp had been on the receiving end of V1 and V2 attacks since early October, Hitler was so desperate to deny the Allies the use of the port that he ordered the attacks to be increased. This, he thought, would give him time to mount his master plan — a breakthrough in the Ardennes, cutting the Allies in two, as he had done in 1940.

For the rest of October more than 150 flying bombs and 100 rockets pounded the city, destroying many buildings and killing hundreds of people. The assault continued throughout November and, on the 27th of that month, a V2 landed on Terniers Square in the heart of the city. A military convoy was crossing a road junction at the time and 29 servicemen were among the 157 killed.

The most horrifying incident of the vengeance campaign occurred on December 16, the day the Ardennes offensives began, when a rocket landed on top of the Rex Cinema in Antwerp. The cinema was packed to capacity at the time and the carnage was terrible — 567 killed of which 296 were Allied servicemen and women.

By the end of the campaign, in March 1945, Antwerp had received 2,248 V1s and 1,712 V2s.

Heavy censorship on press reports and photographs continued to apply. "Do not publish the report of the sounding of an air-raid warning in London", editors were told. "Do not publish obituary notices for people killed by enemy action." Do not publish the shooting down or the crashing of an aircraft, whether pilotless or piloted." Photographs were submitted to the censor's office before they could be used and easily-identified buildings were blacked out.
The caption of this Associated Press picture reads: Furniture and other household belongings from wrecked homes are piled in the street after a robot weapon had crashed in Southern England. Where is it ? Readers may be able to identify.

Thameside suffers

AFTER a relatively quiet October and a growing feeling of optimism that Kent would now be spared from any more damage, the month of November proved to be busy for the emergency services — especially in the Thameside towns. A flying bomb fell in the Grafton Avenue/Jackson Avenue area of Rochester on November 8 at 8.45 pm. More than 500 homes were damaged and the casualty detector unit was needed to help find some of the victims. Eight people were killed.

Five days later, Gravesend suffered Kent's first serious V2 incident when a missile exploded in Portland Avenue damaging the town's Co-op stores. Five were killed and 16 seriously injured. A mortar bomb hit Chatham on November 13 and towards the end of the month, Gravesend suffered a second rocket attack. This one came down in the town centre near Milton Place.

Among the eight people killed was a young serviceman who was spending his last evening on leave with his fiancée. The couple were trapped in the explosion and rescuers, including many sailors, worked for hours in the glare of floodlights to reach them. They found the man dead with his arms around his girlfriend, who was alive and conscious. He had died protecting her.

The highest V1 casualty toll in the new phase of the assault occurred at Purley in Surrey when a bomb, released from a Heinkel, dived onto the St Marie Hotel, Purley, killed 19 people and injured 30. Many guests were buried alive under the wreckage and rescue teams, with Alsatian dogs, worked all night to reach them.

This was Wilson Avenue, Rochester on the morning of November 9, after the rocket attack of the previous evening. Help was at hand for the hundreds of people whose homes had suffered. Blast damage was supposed to be less for rocket attacks.

Gigantic wall of blast

FOR London, and particularly south-east London, November was also a disastrous month. It started on the first day with three V2s falling within a few miles, all causing multiple fatalities. The first hit Eglinton Road, Woolwich, killing seven people including four members of one family, the second was at Dulwich in which 24 people died and the third was at Brockley.

In his book *Bolts from the Blue*, Lewis Blake writes: *"Among the stars made pale by the moonlight a more fiery glow suddenly appeared, a man-made intruder in the firmament. It grew larger and brighter by the second, shooting earthwards at a speed almost too great for the human eye to follow. Brockley's crowded Victorian Terrace lay directly in its path, but there was no sound to warn the inhabitants of their immediate peril. A brilliant flash of light, a gigantic wall of blast, a mighty roar — in an instant the damage was done. The tram-track passing the corner of Shardeloes Road and St. Donatt's Road was blown skyhigh in a huge fountain of debris. A dozen three-up one-down dwellings sagged and tumbled to the ground like so much builder's rubble. The very earth seemed to jerk upwards and fall back."*

By dawn only 11 bodies at Brockley had been recovered; the death toll eventually reached 35 with another 155 injured. In these harrowing conditions the rescue services worked feverishly through the night and several awards for courage and devotion to duty were won.

A few days later the same rescuers were at another battlefield. On the gloomy evening of November 11 an enormous explosion filled the air from the direction of Shooters Hill; a V2 had impacted in the roadway and created a scene of utter horror. A bus with its top deck missing and the rest of the vehicle in flames was caught in the explosion and its 16 passengers never stood a chance. The Brook public house had collapsed, burying many customers, none of whom survived. The ambulance station alongside the Brook Hospital was in ruins and, in the hospital itself, there were more trapped victims. Some were located by an Alsatian search dog. Twenty six people died.

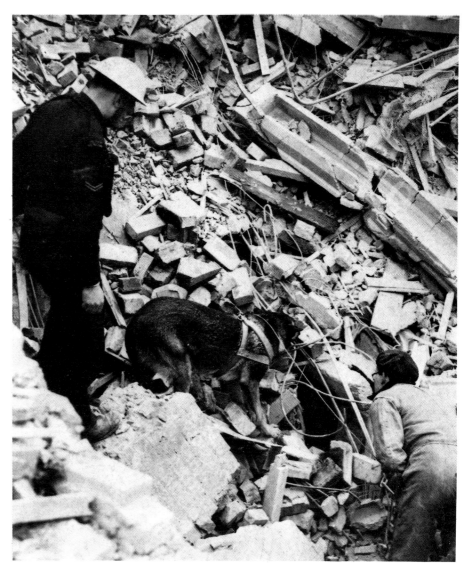

Rescue workers led by Thorn, the tail-wagging Alsatian with a habit of locating the exact whereabouts of V-bomb victims, searched among the debris for those who might still be trapped beneath the crushed wards of Brook Hospital, Woolwich.

This is the crater caused by the V2 rocket which exploded at Southborough, near Tunbridge Wells on Monday November 13 at 10.47 pm. Villagers recall hearing a massive explosion followed by the rush and hiss of the missile's descent. Fortunately no-one died as a result of this incident although six people were taken to hospital, including the occupants of the house in the background.

Saved — by the bus

ON Sunday November 19, 1944 my husband and I met some friends at Bromley Common where we enjoyed tea together. When we left their house about 8.30 pm it was pouring with rain so we waited outside the Crooked Billet in Southborough Lane for a 94 bus to take us to Grove Park. We decided to go into the pub for a drink but at that moment the bus appeared, so we boarded it. As we turned into Crown Lane, Bromley there was an enormous explosion and the bus shook and stopped. After a while we continued our journey home and it was only later that we discovered the Crooked Billet had received a direct hit from a V2. Our friends from Bromley Common were among those killed. We were very, very lucky.

Helen Wythe (Mrs), Edenbridge

This was Bromley's worst V2 incident. The missile hit the forecourt of the Crooked Billet and demolished the entire four-storey building which was crowded with evening customers More than 100 firemen and four heavy rescue teams toiled through the night and all of the next day to recover victims from the rubble. Because no-one knew for certain how many people were in the building at the time of the explosion, the rescue work was doubly difficult. The death toll finally reached 24. The 65 seriously injured were taken to Bromley and Farnborough hospitals.

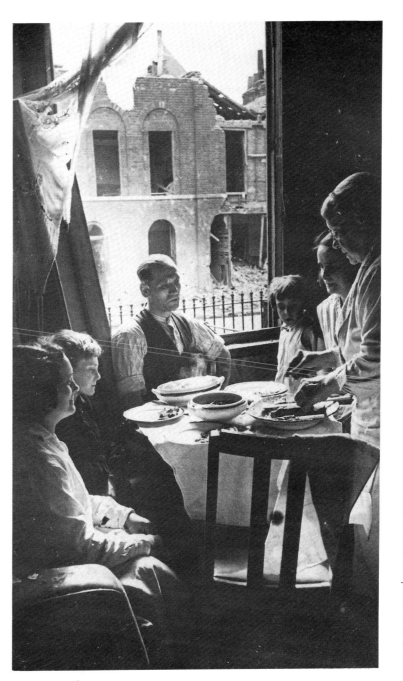

Even today East-enders talk of that "wartime spirit" — the respect and affection shown by neighbours in a real crisis. This was certainly the case in those critical autumn days of 1944. In this photograph a family is shown hospitality by neighbours. Through the window, across the road, are the ruins of their house, damaged by a doodlebug.

Unlike a flying bomb there was fire when a rocket exploded. One such was at Middlesex Street (Petticoat Lane) on November 10. It exploded on the Brunswick Buildings at 2.51 pm just after Churchill had revealed to Parliament that V2s were falling on Britain. The blaze seared through the Norwegian naval stores and the fire fighters were soon on the scene. Eight people died, with 79 seriously injured.

The battlefield at New Cross

ALMOST every day throughout November there were reports of rocket incidents in the London boroughs. The Light and Heavy Rescue teams, the Express Casualty Service, ambulancemen and firemen, ARP workers, the WVS and those operating the mortuary vehicles and mobile canteens were regularly finding a huge crater in the midst of yet another devastated community. As stretcher bearers carried out the dead and Alsatian dogs helped to look for buried victims, policemen took charge of personal possessions that lay amongst the debris. Eleven died at Forest Hill, nine at Peckham, four at Welling, 31 at Deptford, 19 at Aldgate, 25 at Bethnal Green, 18 at Poplar, 24 at Greenwich, 33 at Wandsworth and 16 at Greenwich again. On top of this the Germans produced more aircraft from which to launch V1 attacks, which increased both in scale and duration. They came across the East Anglian coast and the Thames Estuary. London was under incessant fire — and the war was almost won !

By Saturday November 25 — the day on which Hans Klammer was preparing to launch his 250th rocket against England — most Londoners had grown accustomed to the sound of explosions which rolled across the sky. They frequently wondered if they would be next.

The 250th was an innocuous affair for it burst in the air over open country above Cookham Road between Sidcup and St Paul's Cray. The next one, however, was to cause Britain's worst disaster in the whole of the V-weapon campaign. The missile fell at 12.26 pm to the rear of Woolworth's in New Cross Road. The store, which was full of women and children, bulged slightly outwards and then collapsed inwards in a great cloud of dust and smoke which mushroomed high into the air. Those inside the shop stood no chance.

Next door to Woolworth's, the Co-op also disintegrated killing more people. Passers-by were lifted into the air and thrown great distances, a bus in the New Cross Road spun round like a top and then completely buckled, lorries overturned, people in offices were killed at their desks, parked cars and delivery vans burst into flames.

Lewis Blake in *Bolts from the Blue* describes the scene: *"Wrecked shops and houses stretched from New Cross Gate station to Deptford Town Hall on both sides of the road and for much of Goodwood Road. Tumbled masonry completely blocked the A2 and everywhere lay ankle deep in broken glass. A traffic hold-up in Deptford had brought a temporary lull in the usual busy stream of tramcars, otherwise the carnage would have been greater still. As it was, scores of dazed and blood-covered victims moaned on the pavements, or ran hysterically they knew not where. Others were silent and motionless."*

"Such were some of the scenes that confronted the C.D. services which rushed to New Cross from all over SE boroughs. No need to visit Europe to view a battlefield; here in an ordinary London shopping street was one as bloody as the front line could offer. The small borough of Deptford had experienced more of its share of a "people's war" since 1940, but this calamity exceeded all in its scale of suffering.

It took many days and nights to extricate the bodies of the dead and badly injured from underneath the mountain of rubble that once had been two of the most popular stores in the road. All the usual rescue services were there including many sailors from the Royal Naval College at Greenwich. Floodlights were set up and mobile cranes were brought in to lift clear the huge pieces of masonry which spilled across the road. The bodies were taken to the municipal mortuary but that was soon full and a nearby firm offered to accommodate the dead.

Officially the death toll was 160 but it was obviously higher for 11 people were missing, including two women who had gone to Woolworth's for tea with their babies in prams. They were never seen again. More than 120 people were seriously injured and an unknown number slightly injured.

The Civil Defence Controller said after the incident: "We bled the Group white for services at New Cross Road. We could not have dealt with another incident at the same time".

THE LOUDEST OF ALL

ONE of the greatest explosions in Britain during November 1944 was not caused by a V1 or V2 but a beach land mine. At 5.00 am on November 22, a barge carrying 180 tons of high explosive broke its tow during a storm in the Channel and drifted ashore to the west of Newhaven where it struck the mine. Hundreds of houses were damaged by the blast which was felt up to seven miles away. A naval rating, crushed by a falling wall, was the only person to die but many others suffered from shock and injury.

This is the scene at New Cross after Britain's worst V-bomb disaster. So great was the explosion that a delivery boy some 400 yards away felt the wave of blast warm to his face and others at a similar distance were physically pushed backwards. This photograph shows the junction between New Cross Road and Goodwood Road.

Mr Ron Paskell of Fareham, Hampshire sent us this photograph of Christ Church, Battersea which was destroyed by a V2 rocket at 11.14 pm on November 21, 1944. He writes: "As an 11-year-old Battersea boy I knew the church well because every weekday I would stand at the bus stop facing the side of the building to catch a No 31 or No 12 tram to school. The photograph was taken by a local resident just after the bomb had fallen and is just about at the position of the tram stop. For me memories of the V1 and V2 were recalled when watching the Cruise missiles during the bombing of Baghdad during the Gulf war."

Rocket watch

IT was possible, in theory, to give London a four-minute warning of a V2 rocket launch. They came from five selected radar stations at Bawdsey and High Street in Suffolk, Great Bromley in Essex and Dunkirk and Swingate (Dover) in Kent. Here young women, who had learned to detect the "echoes" of V2s by watching cathode tubes, were on a continuous round-the-clock Big Ben rocket watch.

When the women had identified the "echoes" as coming in England's direction they would report each one to the RAF Filter Room at No 11 Group HQ who would then put the usual alert procedures into effect. It was, in the early days, a hit and miss affair because the warning was given when the rocket was still climbing and it was likely to fall anywhere, including into the sea.

Later in the campaign the problem was largely solved by a special setting of gun-laying (GL) radars located at Southwold, Aldeburgh and Walmer. When a rocket crossed these radar beams between certain limits it would indicate if it was likely to fall in the London area. The warning time was less than two minutes.

BIG BEN INCIDENTS: NOVEMBER 1944

1st (02.15) **Woolwich**
(05.13) **Dulwich**
(18.32) **Wanstead Flats**
(18.32) **Deptford**
(22.45) **Dartford**
2nd (03.30) **Ditton**
(10.05) **Lewisham**
(17.00) **Banstead**
(20.58) **Long Reach**
3rd (00.58) **Hornchurch**
(04.38) **Lewisham**
(10.45) **Barking**, Creekmouth
4th (10.56) **Ilford**
(17.25) **Sutton-at-Hone**
(18.05) Wakering Stairs, **Southend**
(21.17) N of **Romford**
5th (00.36) **Romford**
(01.30) **Penshurst**
(07.45) **Wandsworth**
(10.55) **Bermondsey**
(12.45) **Rainham**, nr Barking
(16.41) **Dagenham**
(17.12) **Islington**
6th (09.45) **Luton**
(10.51) **Yalding**, SW of Maidstone
(14.58) **Bexleyheath**
(17.50) **Little Warley**, nr Brentwood
7th (1.08) **Weeley**, nr Clacton
(09.04) **Canvey Island** area
10th (06.45) Sea off **Shoeburyness**
(08.15) **Hornsey**
(11.50) **Belvedere**
(14.51) **Middlesex Street,**
(15.10) **Fulbourne**, nr Cambridge
11th (15.40) **Cliffe-at-Hooe** (in woods)
(18.37) Shooters Hill, **Greenwich**
(19.09) S of **Birchington**, Kent
(23.44) Brook Place, **Ide Hill**, Sevenoaks
12th (00.08) Rochester Gardens, **Ilford**
(02.29) Noak Hill, NE **Romford**
(11.35) **Nazeing**, Essex
(17.30) **Stone**, nr Dartford

(20.53) **Westminster**
(21.56) **West Ham**
(23.43) **Swanscombe**
13th (04.32) **Ockendon**
(05.08) **West Ham**
(08.12) Sea, NE of **Clacton**
(12.49) **Erith**
(16.38) **Gravesend**
(22.17) Langdon Hills, **Brentwood**
(22.47) **Southborough**
14th (06.21) **Orpington**
(09.38) **Eltham**
(09.40) **Greenwich**
(21.37) **Tifford** area
(22.16) **Rayleigh**
(22.25) **Bermondsey**
15th (00.08) **Stratford**, Leytonstone
Road
(02.06) **Southgate**
(05.12) **Romford**
(05.50) Between **Hertford & Harlow**
(09.19) Sea off **Southend**
(12.50) **Lewisham**
(16.43) **High Ongar**
(17.18) **Finchley**
(02.45) **Islington**
(07.40) **Collier Row**
17th (02.40) **Barking**
(03.27) North of **Dartford**
(04.50) **West Ham**
(09.15) **Poplar** (mid-air burst)
(10.56) Sea off **Clacton**
(21.45) **Rainham**
18th (11.13) **Stanford Rivers**
(11.16) **Chadwell Heath**
(11.28) **Woolwich**
(16.07) **Theydon Mount**, SE Epping
(16.08) **Erith**
(19.48) **East Ham**
(22.32) **Dagenham**
19th (02.10) **Walthamstow**
(07.05) **Peckham**
(08.31) **Wandsworth**

(10.58) **Hackney**
(16.25) Warren Hill, **Chigwell**
(19.22) **Welling**
(21.18) **Bromley**
20th (01.02) **Pinner**
(10.00) **East Ham**
(13.15) **Abridge**, nr Epping
(18.52) **Plumstead** Marshes
(20.54) **Woodford Bridge** (airburst)
21st (02.52) **Tilbury** area
(05.37) **Erith** Marshes
(12.00) **Walthamstow**
(12.03) **Little Waltham**
(13.20) **Erith**
(15.17) **Laindon**
(18.02) **Orpington**
(23.14) **Battersea**
22nd (13.27) **Bradwell** Marshes
(15.04) **All Hallows**
(16.02) **Great Wakering**
(19.40) **Bethnal Green**
(20.34) **Welling**
(21.07) **Ilford**
(23.15) **Dagenham** Marshes
23rd (01.55) **Silvertown**
(19.32) **Westwick**
(20.13) **Finsbury**
(20.15) **Bowers Gifford**
24th (03.37) **West Ham**
(08.00) **Waltham Cross**
(10.45) **Braughing**, Herts
(10.52) **Ilford**
(12.02) **West Ham**
(12.07) **Tillingham**
(20.32) **Poplar**
25th (09.25) **Wanstead**
(10.35) **Chislehurst** (mid-air burst)
(11.16) **High Holborn**
(11.30) **Great Warley**
(12.26) **Deptford**
26th (02.25) 9m SE of **Clacton**
(05.40) **Ilford**
(08.10) In sea off **Orfordness**

(11.01) **Rainham**
(11.34) **Chigwell**
(12.51) **Walthamstow**
(13.45) **Poplar**
(13.55) **Billericay**
(17.43) **Cranham**, 4m SE of Romford
(20.06) **Horndon**, 5m NE of Tilbury
(21.07) **Hertford**
(23.25) **Canvey Island**
27th (16.16) **Sidcup**
(22.05) **Woolwich**
(23.13) **Chingford**
28th (16.20) Sea 8m S of **Foulness Point**

(20.15) **Stepney** (mid-air burst)
(22.03) **East Newlands**
(23.35) **Burwash**
29th (03.13) **Barling**
(10.55) **Sandon**
(15.14) **Bradwell**
(19.50) **Polsingford**
(20.20) **Woolwich**
(21.11) **Bexley**
(23.38) **Gravesend**
(23.55) **Edmonton**
30th (00.09) **Leytonstone**
(01.10) **Greenwich**
(22.05) 2m N of **Foulness Point**

Erith in the firing line

STAFF at Erith Oil Works were leaving their canteen just after lunchtime on Tuesday November 21 when a missile exploded. Nine people caught the full force of the blast and were blown to pieces and others were stripped of their clothing. There was a thorough search for the victims over a wide area, including the roofs of the buildings.

More than 70 people were in the canteen at the time and the majority were seriously injured. A shuttle of ambulances took them away to the emergency underground hospital.

Erith received several rockets. Two fell in the Thames and, on one of these occasions, two police sergeants in their station a mile away felt earth tremors before the explosion was heard. Two also fell on the Callender Cable Works but there were no casualties. One of the worst in the borough was at Belmont Road in February 1945 when five people were killed and 62 injured.

Towards the end of November, the boroughs of Woolwich and Greenwich were under bombardment from both V1s and V2s. Six people were killed and 54 injured when a rocket fell on Green Lane, New Eltham on the 29th and 19 died when one impacted in the centre of the road at Sunfields Place, Greenwich on the 30th.

Eee, they'd a doodlebug in Oswaldtwistle !

EVERYONE said the war would be over by Christmas 1944 but, as the festive season approached, it seemed more than ever like an endless, bitter slog. The German counter offensive in the Ardennes, designed to recapture the strategically-placed port of Antwerp, was pushing back the Allies. Rockets were still pounding Greater London several times a day. The occasional air-launched doodlebug was hitting south-east England and particularly Essex. To cap a miserable year the weather was bad, with fog, drizzle and finally snow.

Only those who lived north of the Pennines felt relatively secure from the V-bomb attacks. The newspaper reports of "another tragedy in south-east England", seemed remote to the people in Lancashire, Yorkshire and Durham.

The Luftwaffe had other ideas about the North of England. In the early hours of Christmas Eve, Sunday December 24, 50 Heinkels of KG 53, each one carrying a flying bomb, crossed the coast between Skegness and Mablethorpe and released the missiles in the direction of Manchester. It was an attempt by the Nazis to outflank the east coast defences and create panic in a part of the country which had never seen a doodlebug.

Many of the missiles crashed immediately and some vanished, never to be seen again. One went down with its parent Heinkel in the North Sea and another was caught by a night fighter. The rest, 31 of them, droned on in the darkness towards the large industrial target.

Of those that went astray, one fell into the River Humber, another crashed harmlessly at Redbourne in Lincolnshire and one near Worksop. Many heard the unfamiliar sound in the sky like the rattle of a badly-tuned motorbike and evacuated London children had to explain what was happening. A teacher from Dartford in Kent was astonished when she heard a V1 during her second night in Darwen and another, which crashed near a small Lancashire village, prompted the amazed comment — "Eee, they'd a doodlebug in Oswaldtwistle".

The first to get near its target crashed, in the early morning darkness, at Hewngate Farm, Brindle, near Chorley. The Oswaldtwistle missile also crashed into farmland, close to the Haslingden to Blackburn road. A third exploded harmlessly on a golf course at Didsbury, not far from the densely populated Manchester suburb of Wythenshawe. There were casualties,

however, at Davenport, near Hyde and in Worsley, where a small boy was killed.

The worst incident was at Oldham. The bomb exploded on terraced houses at the junction of Abbey Hills Road and Warren Lane where 32 people were killed and 49 badly injured. Those who died included four members of a wedding party — the bride and groom escaped — and several infants. In one house, four people were killed and five injured. Next door were three small children, evacuated from Streatham where they had already been bombed out from three homes. Their parents, Mr and Mrs Hyman, fearful of the flying bombs in London, took their little ones to "the safety" of Oldham and were actually in the house spending Christmas with them when the missile came down. Mrs Hyman was injured but the rest of the family escaped.

The only other bad incident of this raid was at Chapel Street, Tottington where seven people were killed. The missile hit a row of terraced houses, completely destroyed two of them and a shop, damaged a church and 350 other houses. Two evacuee families from London lived in one of the destroyed houses but they too escaped, having left the previous afternoon to spend Christmas in London.

The Manchester raid was notable on two counts — it provided the last serious flying bomb incident and the strangest delivery of Christmas letters ever known. Some of the missiles carried leaflets headed Vl POW post in which there were printed letters from wounded prisoners-of-war in Germany, whose homes were in the Manchester area. They were scattered about Oldham and picked up by local people who were ordered to hand them over to the police.

The letters implied the good treatment the prisoner was having and suggested that the Germans were really nice people. The intention was also to induce the addressee to write to the prisoner and disclose where the bomb had actually fallen. It was an ingenious piece of propaganda.

After the Manchester raid 60 heavy guns were moved from the east coast to the fringe Diver area between Skegness and Filey, followed by four troops of light AA guns and some searchlight detachments. The caution was understandable but KG 53 was now short of fuel and very few more V1s were fired from the air. The last one, in fact, landed at Hornsey in north-east London on January 14, 1945.

CHRISTMAS EVE IN THE NORTH OF ENGLAND

Many people in the North of England knew nothing about the flying bomb attacks on London, then suddenly they were in the thick of the action as more than 30 were scattered widely and indiscriminately across the country. The map below shows the approximate location of 28 V1s, the figure corresponding to the name of the town or village in each county.

CHESHIRE (6 flying bombs)

1 **Kelsail** 6.22 am
2 **Ollerton** 6.05 am
3 **Henbury** 6.45 am
4 **Macclesfield Forest** 6.10 am
5 **Stockport** 5.30 am
6 **Hyde** 6.25 am

SHROPSHIRE (1 flying bomb)

7 **Newport** 5.40 am

LANCASHIRE (8 flying bombs)
8 **Oldham** 5.50 am
9 **Didsbury** 5.30 am
10 **Worsley** 5.30 am
11 **Radcliffe** 5.56 am
12 **Tottington** 5.50 am
13 **Turton** 5.44 am
14 **Oswaldtwistle** 6.00 am
15 **Brindle** 5.28 am

DERBYSHIRE (3 flying bombs)
16 **Buxton** 5.50 am
17 **Chapel-en-le Frith** 5.45 am
18 **Beighton** 5.40 am

NOTTINGHAMSHIRE (1 flyingbomb)
19 **Sturton le Steeple** 5.45 am

LINCOLNSHIRE (2 flying bombs)
20 **Redbourne** 5.40 am
21 **Epworth** 5.48 am

YORKSHIRE (7 flying bombs)
22 **Rossington** 6.00 am
23 **Grange Moor** 5.35 am
24 **Midhope Moor** 5.45
25 **Sowerby Bridge** 6.0 am
26 **Willerby** 5.45 am
27 **South Cliffe** 5.45 am
28 **Pocklington** 5.50 am

Three fell in areas not included in this map — at Tudhoe, Spennymoor in County Durham, Woodford, Northamptonshire and on Reads Island in the Humber Estuary.

BIG BEN INCIDENTS: DECEMBER 1944

1st(08.03)**Enfield**

(08.03)**Eltham**

(09.00)**Barking Marshes**

(09.31)**Lapwater Hall, nr Brentwood**

(10.24)**Barking**

(10.24)**Leyton**

(13.01)**Hornchurch**

(13.08)**Great Burstead**

(18.25)**Muswell Hill**

(21.12)**Paglesham, Southend**

(21 47)**Walthamstow**

2nd(07.35)**Ramsholt**

(08.20)**Sea off Clacton**

(08.31)**Benfleet**

(11.08)**Dagenham**

(20.29)**Lambeth**

(21.34)**Grays Thurrock**

3rd((06.13)**Rainham**

(07.41)**Wennington, SE of Rainham**

(09.29)**Burnham-on-Crouch**

(09.46)**Greenwich** (mid-air burst)

(10.30)**Herongate, SE Brentwood**

(12.31)**Wickford**

(14.51)In River Thames, **Erith**

(17.08)**Grays Thurrock**

(21.00)**Bexley**

4th(02.31)**Tilbury**

(09.36)**Canewdon, E of Rochford**

5th(21.38)**Dagenham**

(22.30)**Woodham Ferrers**

6th(02.31)**Great Burstead**

(02.33)**Camberwell**

(04.46)nr **Woodham Ferrers**

(05.47)25m **E of Foulness**

(07.15)**Crayford**

(10.04)15m E of **Naze**

(23.07)**Marylebone, Duke Street**

7th(01.23)**Hackney**

(02.03)**Braintree**

(20.08)**Hayes**

(03.24)**Woodford**

8th(12.45)**Canewdon**

(22.11) mile S of **Brentwood**

(23.51)E of **Tiptree**

9th(04.49)**Hornchurch**

(05.24)**Canvey Island**

(07.45)**Enfield**

(22.36)**Bowers Gifford**

10th(00.38)**Erith**

(04.50)**Lewisham**

(20.50)20m N of **North Foreland**

12th(01.21)10m SW of **Clacton**

(04.24)**Southwark**

(05.15)**Greenwich**

(06.23)**Burnham-on-Crouch**

(17.58)**Sidcup**

(20.34)**Creeksea**

(22.42)**Notting Hill**

13th(00.18)Sea SW of **Clacton**

(03.23)**Little Warley**

(07.21)**Woolwich**

(22.05)2m N of **Foulness Point**

(22.33)**Pitsea Marshes**

14th(01.09)Mouth of **River Roach**

(02.16)**Bowes Park**

(05.01)**Nuthampstead, Herts**

(17.17)**Southwark**

(20.42)4m E of **Foulness Point**

(21.06)**Great Stanbridge**

(23.39)**Highwood, nr Chelmsford**

15th(00.14)In **River Crouch, Rayleigh**

(02.03)**High Ongar**

(02.50)9m E of **Shoeburyness**

(04.05)**Mottingham, Sidcup**

(21.48)3m E of **Clacton**

(10.43)Sea 9m SW of **Clacton**

(20.13)7m SE of **Foulness Point**

17th(16.02)**Leyton**

(18.54)**Camberwell**

18th(00.57)**Tillingham Marshes**

(16.29)**Clacton** foreshore

19th(00.47)**Hazeleigh Lodge, Maldon**

(01.25)1m N of **Chelmsford**

(06.05)**Ilford**

(11.31)**Bradwell Marshes**

(23.25)**Lewisham**

20th(02.59)**Crayford**

(12.08)**Brentwood**

(14.15)**Little Berkhamstead Hill**

(17.00)**Cuffley**

(19.20)Sea, **Foulness Point**

(20.01)**Nevendon**

21st(01.44)**Noak Hill** area

(04.34)**Brentwood**

(04.40)**Rayleigh**

(09.42)**Bradwell-on-Sea**

(10.43)**Firstead**

(16.17) **Barking**

23rd(18.49)**Bexley**

(19.40)**Hackney** (mid-air burst)

(20.28)20m E of **Shoeburyness**

(23.46)**Mildenhall** area

24th(07.37)**Wanstead**

(09.37)**Eastwood**

(23.23)4m SW of **Epping**

26th(21.05)**Nazeing**

(21.26)**Islington**

(21.45)**Pitsea**

(21.56)**Dartford Marshes**

27th(01.19)**Navestock**

(02.48)**Downham** area

(04.56)**Waltham Holy Cross**

29th(06.14)1m S of **Southminster**

(09.06)1m NE of **Mundon**

(09.16)1m NE **Burnham-on-Crouch**

(19.31)**Tillingham**

(19.54)3m E of **Brentwood**

(20.06)**Barking**

(22.38)**Croydon**

(23.20)**Shotgate, 2m E of Wickford**

30th(08.59)**West Ham**, Prince Regent Lane

(20.58)**Ilford**

(21.34)**Northfleet**

(22.34)**Sutton-at-Hone**

(22.47)**Stansgate Abbey, nr Maldon**

(22.49)**Orsett, Essex**

31st(00.35)**Ramsden Heath**

(02.09)**Enfield**

(02.55)**Rush Green, Romford**

(03.40)**Noak Hill, nr Brentwood**

(19.12)**Stow Maries, nr Maldon**

(19.46)In Sea E of **Shoeburyness**

(20.41)**Canvey Island**

(23.40)**Islington**

Boxing Day slaughter

IT was Boxing Day, 1944 and the Prince of Wales public house in Mackenzie Road, Islington had more customers than usual because the pub along the road had run out of beer and many had "transferred" before closing time. With an hour to go to closing time at 10.30 the atmosphere was noisy and convivial.

The party was abruptly and cruelly broken up by an enormous explosion. The floor of the bar collapsed and customers crashed into the cellar followed by tons of masonry. Outside a column of grey and brown smoke rose into the wintry sky. Victims, covered in blood and horribly injured but alive, tried to claw their way to safety. Someone was yelling hysterically. Others were silent and motionless.

This was the scene which greeted the rescue services in Islington on that Boxing Day evening. The rocket had exploded a few yards from the Prince of Wales in Mackenzie Road. Hundreds of houses in that heavily populated community were destroyed and the injured lay in their ruins.

One of the first on the scene was Divisional Fire Officer Cyril Demarne. "The glow of a number of fires could be seen through swirling fog as a trailer pump operator set his suction hose into an emergency water dam. He attempted to draw water without success. A horrible thought entered his mind; surely it was not empty? He shone his torch through the door and saw that the water was frozen with the suction strainer lying on the ice. He smashed the ice with a large axe and soon the water was flowing and the men were bringing the fires under control."

Throughout the night and into the next day Civil Defence rescue squads and firemen tunnelled carefully into the debris to reach those trapped in the pub cellar. One by one they lifted out the dead and injured. It was a grim and arduous task that was fraught with danger for both rescuers and victims. When the last of the bodies was recovered the next morning, the death toll had reached 68.

Unhappy New Year

THE New Year began with still no sign that the relentless pounding of London and its environs would soon end. There were hopes and there were rumours but, like a mirage, they faded. New Year V2 attacks were now averaging 10 a day and there was an increase in the number of doodlebugs. During the night of January 3/4, more than 50 V1s were launched in an attack lasting almost three hours — the longest assault since the sites were captured four months earlier. One reached London, the rest were scattered far and wide over East Anglia.

Fewer were launched on January 5 but one exploded behind the High Street in Beckenham, killing 13 people and destroying 20 houses. The next day a V2 plummeted to earth at Adolphus Road, Deptford and 20 people died. By now there were sub zero temperatures in south-east England, most of which was blanketed by heavy falls of snow. When the Deptford missile fell, burning coals from the open fires were scattered amongst the debris, setting alight many houses.

There were more tragic incidents in the suburbs — 20 killed at West Ham, 15 at Hackney, 41 at Lambeth, 29 at Islington, 14 at Rainham, Essex, 21 at Potters Bar, 12 at East Barnet, 23 at Tottenham, 30 at Southwark, 15 at Battersea and 30 again at West Ham.

The old railway tunnel at Swanscombe in Kent which led to the local lime pits, was fitted out by the local authority as an air raid shelter and was in regular use in those scary early days of 1945 when the south-east was under attack from both vengeance weapons. During the Christmas holiday, children often used to troop obediently down to the shelter and remain there for hours at a time. In January, when the new term began, the children took their chance with everyone else, for the Government was determined that schools should not close. Many argued that this was courting risk of a great tragedy; a single incident would have caused enormous public outrage. Fortunately, there were no such disasters — the closest being on December 12 when a V2 hit Morden Terrace School at 5.15 am, four hours before the children were due to assemble.

BIG BENS: JANUARY 1945

1st (01.55) **Laindon**
(04.58) **Leyton**
(05.25) **Halstead**
(06.22) **Sandon**
(08.52) **Off Foulness Point**
(20.40) **30m E of Bradwell**
2nd (03.35) **Barnes**
(09.20) **Waltham Cross**
(12.15) **Beckenham**
(15.35) **Greenwich**
(15.46) **Doddinghurst**
(18.19) **Stapleford**
(18.51) **Ramsden Heath**
(21.42) **Greenwich**
3rd (03.32) **Billericay** area
(08.39) **Edmonton**
(08.50) **Chelsea**
(13.05) **Southminster**
(18.51) **Harlow/Sheering**
(20.03) **Tonbridge**
(23.50) **Hornsey**
4th (04.19) **Hoddesdon**
(12.30) **West Ham**
(12.36) **Titsey Hill**
(12.56) **Rayleigh**
(15.43) **Runwell**
(16.13) **Hackney**
(16.13) **Little Thurrock**
(18.35) **Clothall**
(19.32) **Ilford**
(20.29) **Lambeth**
(21.06) **Stepney**
(21.21) Sea off **Southwold**
(22.54) **Dulwich**
5th (00.12) **Beckenham**
(00.43) **Navestock Side**
(03.36) **Wanstead**
(09.27) **Raydon** area
(14.12) **E of Billericay**
(15.25) **Tolleshunt D'Arcy**
(22.45) **Addington**
6th (02.15) **Dartford** area
(07.49) **SE Hatfield**
(08.32) **Ongar Park Wood**
(13.43) **Deptford**
(16.28) **Northaw**

(16.46) **West Ham**
(17.06) **Dulwich**
(19.46) **Erith**
(22.01) **Beazley End**
(22.46) **Camberwell**
7th (01.45) **Dagenham**
(02.16) **Teddington**
(04.56) **Tottenham**
(05.25) **Guildford** (Hog's Back)
(06.12) **Great Baddow**
(12.14) **Leytonstone**
(15.40) **Cheshunt**
(16.48) **Ilford**
(17.15) **Islington**
(17.36) **Hutton**
(18.13) **Brightlingsea**
8th (10.43) **High Beech**
(11.23) **Islington**
(12.13) **Sydenham**
(12.37) **Hornsey**
(13.14) **Wilmington**
(14.13) **Barking Marshes**
(15.18) **Barking**
(16.02) **Datchworth**
(16.33) **West Hampstead**
(18.22) **Clapham Common**
(19.44) **Sidcup**
(22.29) **Stoke Newington**
9th (10.50) **Beckenham**
(14.05) **South Ockendon**
(17.16) **E of Sawbridgeworth**
(18.02) **Basildon**
(19.28) **Deptford**
(22.15) **Great Warley Street**
10th (00.27) **Edmonton**
(11.00) **Great Totham**
(11.14) **Stoke Newington**
(14.20) **Henlow/Arlsley**
(14.31) **Broomfield**
11th (10.25) **Battlesbridge**
12th (11.04) **South Green**
(17.38) **Marden Ash**
(17.39) **Trimley**
(17.55) **Writtle**
(19.35) **Boreham**
(20.45) **Ilford**

(22.16) **Biddlestead**
13th (00.59) **Toot Hill**
(02.31) **Wood Green**
(06.00) **Islington**
(07.08) **Poplar**
(07.49) **Watton at Stone**
(08.57) **Broadoak End**
(11.30) **Chigwell**
(11.53) **Enfield**
(12.58) **West Ham**
(14.11) **South Hornchurch**
(16.35) **West Tilbury**
(17.58) **Hockley**
14th (10.56) **Foulness Island**
(11.35) **Abbess Roding**
(12.12) **Barking**
(13.47) **Beaumont**
(15.29) **Cheshunt**
(15.50) **Ilford**
(16.13) **Lewisham**
(17.38) **Shoreditch**
(20.59) **Barking**
15th (05.18) Off **Shoeburyness**
(09.07) **Chingford**
(11.13) Nr **Whitstable**
(17.17) **Off Polling**
(18.54) **Hackney**
(23.12) **Rainham**
16th (03.00) **Noak Hill**
(09.09) **Nr Herne Bay**
(10.59) **Chigwell**
(15.00) **Goldhanger**
(19.10) **Sidcup**
(20.32) **Cock Clarks**
(21.01) **Harlow**
(21.54) **Nr Banstead**
17th (08.18) **Mayland**
(11.42) **Bengeo**
(12.17) **Essendon**
(14.17) **Corringham Marshes**
(16.42) **East Horndon**
(16.59) **Hatfield Broad Oak**
(18.34) **Much Hadham**
(19.37) **Chingford**
19th (23.09) **Barking**

Continued on page 174

The cave dwellers

THE thousands of South Londoners who had made their home in the ancient network of caves at Chislehurst during the Blitz returned in 1944 as the rocket attacks on London increased. They were there by courtesy of the Chislehurst and Sidcup UDC's caves committee who charged 6d a week for a family "pitch". They did not have to sleep in the caves every night but lost their pitch if it were not used for three successive weeks.

At one time more than 15,000 people lived in Chislehurst caves; a small town below ground that ran with clockwork efficiency. There was water and electricity, the WVS ran canteens and supplied clothing to those who had been bombed out. There was a cinema, church, telephone kiosk, national savings bank, first aid post and shops. The committee elected marshals whose job it was to police the caves; there was a dance hall, a barber's shop and a brownie pack.

Among the distinguished visitors was Charles de Gaulle who lived for a while at 41 Birchwood Road, Petts Wood. The caves continued to be occupied up to the end of the war.

The rules of the caves (see picture) demanded that the "cave captain" control his section,, that lights must be out by 10.30 pm , that music must cease by 9 pm and that all dwellers must arrive early and "stay put". This notice survived for many years.

Children queue up at the first aid post in Chislehurst caves for their weekly dose of cough medicine from Nurse Throndsen. They were not ill - the cough mixture was a substitute for sweets. The normal temperature of the caves was 48 F but this increased to 80F plus when there were 15,000 shelterers.

BIG BENS: JANUARY 1945

(continued from page 172)

(23.10) **Wanstead/Woodford**	**25th** (07.12) **Enfield**
(23.41) **Great Parndon**	(08.19) **Willesden**
20th(01.16) **Upminster**	(08.33) **Langdon Hills**
(02.57) **Canewdon**	(12.01) **Hatfield Heath**
(05.00) **Walthamstow**	(19.18) **Off Clacton**
(06.39) **East Ham**	(21.45) **Greenwich**
(08.55) **Takeley**	**26th** (06.11) **Shenley**
(10.06) **Bishop's Stortford**	(06.24) **Wanstead/Woodford**
(10.52) **Potter's Bar**	(06.32) **Woolwich**
(11.21) **Barking**	(09.05) **Leyton**
(13.15) **East Barnet**	(09.40) **Ardleigh Green, Hornchurch**
(16.09) **East Horndon**	(09.54) **Aveley**
(16.10) **Navestock**	(10.40) **Clapham**
(16.37) **Riverhead**	(12.10) **Dagenham**
(18.08) **Broxbourne**	(14.43) **Ilford**
(19.23) **Greenwich**	(18.17) **Croydon**
(19.52) **Tottenham**	(23.01) **Woolwich**
(22.49) **Wanstead/Woodford**	**27th** (00.04) **East Ham**
21st (02.05) **Plaxtol**	(02.14) **Wickford**
(12.11) **Hendon**	(03.40) **Latchingdon** area
(14.43) **Laindon**	(03.45) **East Ham**
(15.46) **Noak Hill**	(03.55) **Stanmore**
(16.50) **Greenwich**	(03.56) **Wanstead/Woodford**
(18.52) **Rainham**	(09.45) **Mountnessing**
(18.57) **Woolwich**	(12.26) **Tillingham**
(19.12) **South Ockendon**	(16.01) **Battersea**
22nd (10.12) **West Thurrock**	(16.25) **Datchworth Green**
(12.15) **Friern Barnet**	**28th** (00.19) **Forest Row**
(14.37) **Kingston-on-Thames**	(00.43) **West Ham**
(17.14) **Southwark**	(02.29) **Willesden**
23rd (08.37) **Hither Green**	(03.30) **Benenden**
(09.26) **Waltham Holy Cross**	(05.07) **Bromley**
(air burst)	(06.51) **Sidcup**
(10.50) **Mayland**	(07.30) **Kirby-le-Soken**
(11.45) **Edmonton**	(10.30) **East Ham**
(15.51) **Nr Stapleford Abbots**	**29th** (05.55) **Bradwell**
(19.14) **Dagenham**	(06.33) **Waltham Holy Cross**
(21.52) **Horton Kirby**	(07.36) **Great Amwell**
24th (09.07) **Waltham Holy Cross**	(08.52) **Darenth**
(10.50) **Enfield**	(09.22) **Shotgate**
(11.43) **Enfield**	(09.53) **Bridgemarsh Island**
(16.19) **Greenwich**	(10.02) **Stoke Newington**
(20.05) **Navestock**	(15.35) **Bradwell Bay airfield**

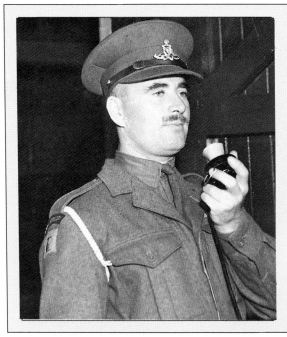

One of the gunners employed on the south-coast before the move to the east coast Diver Belt was Battery, later Regimental Sergeant Major Douglas Henry of 138 AA Regiment. Doug saw plenty of doodlebugs and is proud of the fact that the gunners became the first line of defence and achieved so much success. One lingering doubt still troubles him, however, and that concerns the last flight by the Band Leader Glenn Miller who took off from England on December 16, 1944 to play in Paris and went missing. It would have been a busy day for the gunners with the increased activity of air-launched V1s over East Anglia and the Thames Estuary. "Is it possible", wonders Doug, "that Glenn Miller's plane was shot down by an anti-aircraft battery?"

Brook Hospital hit again

BY the end of January, 1945 the American First Army had regained for the Allies most of the ground lost in the Ardennes, the Red Army were within 165 miles of Berlin, having established a Government of their own in Poland, Churchill and Roosevelt had met Stalin at Yalta and the flying bomb attacks on Britain had ended — for the time being. But the rockets kept coming, with many serious incidents in East London and Essex.

Communities that had already experienced the traumas of a V2 explosion were suffering again. Twenty eight were killed at West Ham, 25 at Leyton, 18 at Walthamstow, 24 at Deptford and 31 at St Pancras. It appeared those close to where a first rocket had fallen were more likely to receive another.

It was perhaps for this reason that all the patients of Brook Hospital, Woolwich, which had been badly hit by the missile of November 11, 1944, were taken to a basement shelter, leaving behind the maintenance staff on fireguard duty. It was a wise decision by the hospital authorities. In the early hours of February 20 the hospital received a direct hit and two wards were completely demolished as well as the kitchen, stores, mess room the nurses', maids' and sisters' homes, dispensary and reception rooms. Three of the fireguards were killed.

BIG BEN INCIDENTS: FEBRUARY 1945

1st (01.33) E of North Weald
(02.08) Althorne
(03.03) West Ham
(04.03) Harrow
(05.19) Chiddingstone
(06.11) Walthamstow
(07.31) Walkern
(07.46) Chingford
(10.10) Chingford
(14.00) Hackney
(14.06) Chingford
2nd (06.13) Woodham Mortimer
(08.08) Southminster
(08.22) Deptford
(10.13) Dagenham
(10.41) East Ham
(12.43) East Ham
(12.55) Walthamstow
3rd (11.25) Epping Forest
(13.16) Barking
(15.15) Ilford
4th (14.48) Nr Danbury
(15.05) Ilford
(15.06) Dagenham
(17.26) West Ham
(17.31) Ilford
(17.37) Theydon Garnon
(18.13) Doddinghurst
(18.15) Hackney
(22.21) Wanstead/Woodford
(23.51) Nr Hornchurch
(23.57) Rettendon
5th (01.59) Chingford
(02.39) Hackney
(05.35) Epping Upland
(08.14) Willingale
(09.41) Watton-at-Stone
(21.09) Waltham Holy Cross
6th (04.58) Paglesham
(06.38) Essendon
(07.34) Tottenham
(09.48) St Mary Cray
(09.51) Ramsden Heath
(12.56) Bradwell Bay
(18.05) Crockenhill

(19.16) Wanstead Flats
(21.46) Woolwich
7th (11.52) Ilford
(12.10) Barking
(15.59) Waltham Holy Cross
8th (00.32) Bacton
(01.08) Walthamstow
(02.18) In sea, Sheringham
(03.03) Chislehurst
(09.18) Fobbing
(10.57) Bethnal Green
(12.06) Erith
(12.35) Ilford
(15.43) Rettendon
(17.43) Chislehurst/Sidcup
(17.50) Greenwich
(20.12) Cock Clarks
(22.38) Dagenham
9th (05.42) Navestock
(07.26) Stow Maries
(14.08) Poplar
(16.08) St Pancras
(17.25) Hayes, nr Bromley
(19.03) In sea south of Clacton
(21.34) Chislehurst
10th (00.33) Basildon
(04.59) Welling, Bexley
(06.34) Radley Green
(08.28) Leyton
(09.24) In sea at Bradwell
(10.58) Woolwich
(11.27) Rawreth
(12.47) Purleigh
(15.03) In sea at Clacton
(15.29) Margaretting
(16.01) Purfleet
(19.14) Oxted
(20.01) Widford
11th (01.03) Romford
(01.50) Chertsey Mead
(04.40) Stoke Common
(12.31) Stratford
(13.31) Bromley
(14.51) Walthamstow
(16.07) Romford

(18.16) East Ham
(22.00) Lewisham
12th (05.15) Leatherhead
(07.16) Sea off Clacton
(07.22) Beauchamp Roding
(10.30) Bayford
(13.46) Mountnessing
(16.04) Great Warley
(18.45) Great Totham
(18.46) Dengie
(20.28) Walthamstow
(23.05) Hackney
13th (02.24) Sea off Orfordness
(03.42) W of Halstead
(06.17) Cheshunt
(15.49) High Laver
(15.53) Thameshaven
(16.15) Braxted Park
(16.33) Erith
(16.39) Depden
(16.44) Wood Green
(18.45) Harold Wood
(18.52) West Ham
(19.15) Bexley
(22.58) Ilford
(23.47) Hordon-on-the-Hill
14th (00.32) Platt
(02.21) Farningham
(03.02) Cranham
(05.03) Rawreth
(05.36) Canvey Island
(09.55) Camberwell
(14.41) Chislehurst/Sidcup
(14.55) Havering
(17.00) Havering
(17.11) Finsbury
(17.12) Mountnessing
(20.23) South Green
(21.58) Hammersmith
(22.31) Hackney
(23.57) Latchingdon/Shoreham
15th (00.55) Erith
(07.04) Crayford
(09.30) Iver Heath
(11.22) Shoreham

(11.36) Corringham Marshes
(14.47) Sea SE of Foulness
16th (16.10) N of Shenfield
(21.24) Nr West Hanningfield
(21.34) West Hanningfield
(21.54) Woolwich
(23.44) Leyton
17th (00.41) Nr Steeple
(00.49) Upper Kirby
(00.54) Dunton
(03.32) Aylesford
(03.41) Althorne
(04.28) Garston Park
(05.42) Ilford
(05.33) Poplar
(06.22) Rawreth
(08.10) Lynstead
(08.49) Brentwood
(11.32) Willingale
(14.22) St Mary's at Hoo
18th (00.55) Chingford
(01.16) Canvey Island area
(04.25) Ilford
(07.32) Woodham Ferrers
(08.10) Wickford Ramsden
(08.17) Nr Pitsea
(09.40) Aveley
(10.15) Dartford Heath
(12.01) Rochester
(12.18) Bexley
(14.41) Poplar
(15.21) Canewdon
(18.06) Sea off Clacton
(19.44) Erith
(19.52) Woolwich
19th (00.44) Ilford
(04.46) Off East Anglian coast
(04.56) Abbess Roding
(07.19) Epping Forest
(07.27) Wanstead/Woodford
(07.42) Crayford
(11.06) Woolwich
(11.44) Greenwich
(13.57) Off Clacton
(14.19) Walthamstow

(22.21) Stoke
(22.55) Laindon
20th (01.16) Greenwich
(04.32) Poplar
(08.44) Mundon
(09.57) Earl Stonham
(11.21) Upminster
(11.37) Ilford
(13.23) Rainham
(13.37) Waltham Holy Cross
(15.38) Highwood
(17.56) Woolwich
(20.35) Romford
(20.47) Chingford
(22.55) Foulness Island
(23.29) Barking
21st (09.17) Sidcup
(11.21) Beckenham
(12.58) Ilford
(16.17) South Ockendon
(22.18) Ilford
22nd (09.21) Epping
(14.46) Eynsford
(17.53) Heston
(20.11) Sea off Clacton
(21.02) West Romford
(21.48) Althorne
(22.48) Warley
(22.51) Greenwich
23rd (00.04) East Ham
(01.03) Waltham Holy Cross
(04.37) Chigwell
(07.46) Dagenham
(09.08) Chigwell
(09.45) Sevenoaks
(11.24) Cheshunt
(12.42) Sea off Folkestone
(13.39) 1m NW of Epping
(14.25) Blackmore
(16.43) Cold Norton
(16.59) Chelmsford
24th (07.40) Dagenham
26th (09.10) Woolwich
(09.11) Bobbingworth
(09.35) Ilford
(11.27) Belvedere, Erith
(18.26) Leyton
(20.25) West Ham
(23.05) Pitsea Marshes

Crisis for Germany but the rockets keep coming

MARCH, 1945 was the crisis month for the Germans, but who in south and east of England would have believed it. Unremitting fire came from the rocket batteries in The Hague. Flying bombs reappeared after a gap of several weeks. Attacks by manned aircraft were carried out on the heaviest scale since D Day. Machine gunning, cannon fire, heavy explosives and incendiaries were all reported and in the first week of March alone civilian fatalities from all causes totalled 169.

Bomber Command was retaliating with a series of heavy raids on German cities, designed to force the Nazis to capitulate. The Russians were advancing in the east, but most of Holland was still in German hands and Col Wachtel, despite his dwindling command, was now equipped with the longer range flying bomb. New ground-launch ramps were built in The Hague and more than 100 set course for London. General Pile's men on the east coast defences, helped by the new radar techniques, were now red-hot shots and the guns accounted for 86 of the 125 which approached Britain.

There was nothing the gunners could do about the rockets. Even the more enlightened thought that was an impossible problem for AA Command. Pile and his men had other ideas. They produced a scheme, entailing the use of special radar stations to detect rockets at a height of more than 30,000 feet, predict the point of fall and burst shells in their path. The guns would have to be fired when the rockets were still 30 miles from London.

General Pile wrote: "It was variously estimated that we could blow up in the air between three and 10 per cent of all the V2s we fired at. However, Monty beat us to it and before we could wring permission out of the War Cabinet to try our plan, the rocket area of Holland was cut off by the liberation armies."

Before that happened the rockets hit London so frequently that at least one incident was reported every day of the month, up to March 27. Inevitably one hit West Ham where 31 people died. There were 52 killed at Deptford, 25 at Poplar, 23 at Leyton and 33 at Heston.

At Stepney a rocket hit Hughes Mansions and demolished two five-storey blocks of flats. The rescue teams spent hours extracting the bodies from underneath a mountain of rubble and, when they completed their gruesome task, the death toll was approaching 100. It rose eventually to 131 killed and 40 seriously injured.

This was the second biggest disaster of the entire V-weapon campaign.

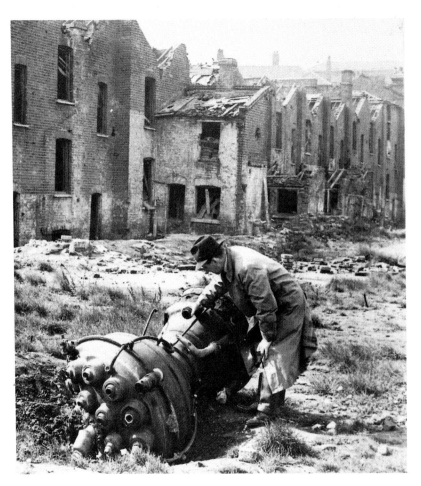

Some people claim to have seen, on a clear day in a cloudless sky, a V2 rocket in its descent. It was an unusual sighting for it was visible for only four seconds during its rapid dive from about 20,000 feet, and it was far more usual for the vapour trail to be seen. This remained in the sky for up to 30 seconds. The first thing the majority of people knew about the V2 was the explosion itself, followed by another boom and then the descending whistle indicating that the rocket had broken the sound barrier. The picture above shows the damage caused by a V2 which crashed at Limehouse in March. In the foreground a missile expert examines the propulsion unit.

Two rockets fell in the Earlham Grove area of Forest Gate in the beleagured Borough of West Ham, one on October 30, 1944 and the second on Tuesday March 6, 1945. The impact point of the second rocket can be clearly seen.

BIG BENS

FEB 1945

(continued P175)

27th (01.23) **West Thurrock Marshes**
(01.25) **Dagenham**
(02.24) **Kelvedon Hatch**
(02.29) **Ilford**
(04.43) **Chevening**
(05.33) **Theydon Garnon**
(07.45) **North Stifford**
(09.21) **Swanscombe**
(10.51) **Ingatestone**
28th (00.22) **New Hall Green**
(01.21) **Enfield**
(03.14) **East Ham**
(05.07) **Erith**

Part of the activity in Highbridge Street, Waltham Abbey where a V2, had impacted. Ted Carter and his colleagues worked non-stop for 30 hours, searching for bodies, pulling down dangerous buildings and bulldozing away the rubble. In the background is Waltham Abbey, burial place of King Harold, slain by an earlier foe. With the main road through the town closed, Ted had to drive 10 miles to get his car back to the depot. "Perhaps", he said, "someone will wake up now to the sore necessity of a by-pass."

Crater in town centre

FROM the diary of Ted Carter, Chief Warden of Waltham Holy Cross, come these extracts about the rocket which caused a huge crater right across the town's one and only main road and sucked in part of the Drill Hall, several houses and a wardens' post.

Wednesday March 7: So terrific had been the flow of water from the broken mains that the crater, itself 75 ft in diameter and probably at least half that in depth, was flooded to a level above that of the adjoining road. Across the crater the whole front of the Home Guard Drill Hall had collapsed in a heap of bricks and girders. The two larger houses were only open shells, with doors, ceilings, windows and frames, stairways smashed into rubble.

Our new control room was out of action and all telephone lines westward were gone completely, and shadow control in the Abbey crypt had to function as best as it could. The NFS ran out emergency field telephones to link up Control Centre.

The bodies of two children had been found, and I watched the searcher dog looking for a third. With its trainer it sat crouched and tense on a heap of rubble, and giving it an encouraging pat the trainer led it off, and work started again.

As we searched I half dreaded finding anything, but when we did, it wasn't as bad as I had expected. First there was a leg. with the foot complete and uninjured but the larger bones toward the knee showing horribly between the mangled flesh. A moment or two later, another foot was found, with the shoe completely missing. The third child's body was recovered, making the total of deaths four, and injured 53.

With the dawn of the next morning, the incident came to life again; repair gangs came in from every direction, naval working parties arrived in charabancs, until Highbridge Street was busier than it had ever been before in all its long history, and cars and lorries jostled and bumped each other as they came and went.

The last rocket to cause great loss of life in Central London, dived directly onto the centre of Smithfield Market on Thursday morning March 8, at a time when the market was packed with traders and customers. It penetrated the floor and exploded in the underground railway network beneath. The buildings collapsed into the crater and the shops which had a frontage onto Farringdon Road were completely levelled. Many people dropped into the crater as the floor of Smithfield gave way and others, on the pavement outside the building, were buried by the rubble which rained down on them several seconds later. The death toll was even greater than the Boxing Day blast at Mackenzie Road — 110 people killed and many more severely injured.

Six rockets landed within a quarter-mile radius of this spot in the Wanstead Park area of Ilford. The sixth struck on Thursday March 8 between Endsleigh Gardens and Kensington Gardens, damaging most of the homes in this aerial photograph. Nine people were killed and 15 seriously injured.

BIG BEN INCIDENTS: MARCH 1945

1st (01.08) **Billericay**
(02.34) **Little Leighs**
(05.07) **Barnet**
(05.09) **Stapleford Tawney**
(05.46) **Woolwich**
(08.06) **Shoreditch**
(08.23) **Orpington**
(15.27) **Walthamstow**
(16.10) **Wickford**
(17.28) **Horndon-on-the-Hill**
(23.13) **West Ham**
2nd (01.02) **Ashington**
(02.19) **Havering**
(04.49) **Greenwich**
(04.52) **Orpington**
(05.41) **Chigwell**
(05.48) **Chigwell**
(05.51) **1m N of N Fambridge**
(07.39) **Herongate**
(07.50) **Egypt Bay**
(08.18) **Sea off Southend**
(09.22) **Brentwood**
(11.06) **Greenwich**
(12.21) **Orpington**
(23.03) **Chigwell**
(23.11) **Bermondsey**
(23.15) **Woking**
3rd (01.14) **Foulness Island**
(02.32) **Edmonton**
(03.35) **Theydon Bois**
(03.47) **Woolwich** (air burst)
(04.39) **Woolwich** (air burst)
(04.49) **Sevenoaks**
(06.01) **Ilford**
(06.14) **Sea off Clacton**
(12.17) **Deptford**
4th (01.35) **Havering-atte-Bower**
(04.52) **Penshurst**
(05.38) **Bermondsey** (air burst)
(08.20) **Chingford**
(09.08) Mouth of the Thames
5th (20.07) **Woolwich**
(22.32) **Rainham**
6th (00.57) **Bexley**
(03.07) **Rainham**

(03.09) **West Ham**
(04.35) **Sidcup**
(06.18) **Barking**
(08.35) **Woolwich**
(12.33) **Bowers Marshes**
(12.57) **Wandsworth**
(16.58) **Walthamstow**
(19.38) **Wandsworth**
(19.38) **West Ham**
(21.44) **Woolwich**
(23.24) **Ilford**
(23.26) **Chigwell**
7th (01.59) **Nr Navestock**
(03.13) **Stanford Rivers**
(03.20) **Deptford**
(06.03) **Edmonton**
(08.37) **Greenwich**
(10.33) **Sidcup area**
(12.57) **Poplar**
(14.55) **Brundish (Norfolk)**
(17.00) **Waltham Holy Cross**
(21.59) **Ilford**
(23.32) **Dagenham**
8th (00.49) **Chigwell**
(01.37) **Woolwich**
(03.24) **Writtle**
(04.21) **12m ESE of Clacton**
(04.36) **St Mary Cray**
(05.04) **Ilford**
(09.12) **West Ham**
(11.02) **Finsbury**
(11.10) **Farringdon Road**
(12.06) **Blackheath**
(14.55) **Sidcup**
(19.53) **Horton Kirby**
(20.17) **Dunton**
(21.46) **Bennington**
(21.51) **Harold Park**
(23.03) Sea off **Canvey Island**
9th (00.40) **Kenton**
(02.18) **Marden**
(04.06) **Pitsea**
(04.27) **Greenwich**
(08.29) **Greenwich**
(08.38) **Sea 3m SSW of Southend**

(11.06) **In Thames**
(13.51) **Waltham Holy Cross**
(22.59) **South Ockendon**
10th (00.01) **Beckenham**
(00.16) **Biggin Hill**
(01.26) **Pilgrims Hatch**
(01.50) **Enfield**
(04.22) **1m SSW of Rawreth**
(09.57) **West Mill**
(10.01) **Bexley**
11th (07.09) **Nr mouth of River Crouch**
(07.40) **West Ham**
(10.02) **Westerham**
(20.04) **Deptford**
(20.40) **Canvey Island**
(21.51) **Bulphan**
12th (00.11) **Ilford**
(00.26) **Upminster**
(01.29) **Greenstead**
(02.05) Sea 6-7m SE of **Clacton**
(02.33) **Sidcup**
(02.40) **Sidcup**
(04.45) **Little Warley**
(04.47) **Hainault Forest**
(05.05) NW of **Hornchurch**
(07.01) **Woolwich**
(07.18) **Althorne**
(09.03) **Thames Estuary**
(11.17) **Lower Kirby**
(21.19) **Epping**
(23.46) **Nazeing**
13th (03.27) **Tillingham Marshes**
(06.29) **1.75m NE of Brentwood**
(08.30) **Erith**
14th (00.30) **Havering**
(21.22) **Rainham**
(23.27) **Sutton-at-Hone**
15th (00.16) In Thames at **Dagenham**
(03.33) In Thames at **Woolwich**
(06.24) **Rayleigh**
(09.11) **Richmond**
(13.27) **Tottenham**
(22.26) **Hornchurch**
(22.57) **Neasden**

(23.45) **Nr Maldon**
16th (02.34) **Willesden**
(02.54) Sea off **North Foreland**
(06.34) **Leyton**
(06.51) **Stock**
(08.53) **East Ham**
(09.37) **Dengie**
(23.06) **Basildon**
17th (00.09) 3m S of **Upminster**
(00.55) **Nr Hornchurch**
(03.34) **Wennington Marshes**
(05.16) **Hampstead**
(07.36) **Dartford**
(08.11) **Woolwich**
(12.45) **Greenwich**
(13.20) **Stepney**
(22.26) **Barking**
18th (00.38) **West Ham**
(01.33) **Cranham**
(01.41) **Battlesbridge**
(02.03) **Epping**
(03.40) **Ightham**
(06.30) **Aylesford**
(06.40) **Hutton**
(06.46) **Barking**
(09.34) **Marble Arch**
19th (00.04) **Theydon Garnon**
(00.06) 2m S of **Harlow**
(01.33) **South Hornchurch**
(01.37) **Nutfield**
(10.08) **Wargrave**
(10.31) **Erith**
(15.55) **Woolwich**
(22.20) **Theydon Bois**
(22.45) **Hatfield Broad Oak**
20th (01.28) **Little Warley**
(04.10) **West Hanningfield**
(05.37) **Hornchurch**
(07.03) **Parslow Common**
(08.20) **Sidcup**
(09.53) **Mayland**
21st (00.40) **Wanstead/Woodford**
(09.36) **Heston and Isleworth**
(11.39) **Hampstead**
(13.43) **Ruislip**

(18.44) **NE Romford**
(21.33) **6m NW Braintree**
(22.40) **Woodham Ferrers**
(23.55) 4m E **Bishops Stortford**
22nd (02.06) **Off Blackwater River**
(02.36) **Nr Canewdon**
(02.43) **Epping, Fairfield**
(03.35) **Harrow**
(03.57) **Hoo, Nr Strood**
(05.22) **Stock**
(05.47) **Boreham**, NNE Chelmsford
(06.02) **Leyton**
(07.02) **Brightlingsea**
(07.44) Sea 5m off **Bradwell**
(08.13) **Dagenham**
(09.52) **South Woodham**
(10.30) **Dagenham**
(21.45) 20m SE **Yarmouth**
(23.21) **Dartford**
(23.42) **Southminster**
23rd (01.40) **Greenwich**
(03.15) Sea off **Clacton**
(04.30) **Stepney**
(06.26) **North Weald**
(06.49) **Little Gaddesden**
(09.41) W of **Althorne**
(12.32) **Stapleford**
(23.16) **Waltham Holy Cross**
24th (01.31) **Poplar**
25th (22.33) **St Pancras**
(23.00) **Enfield**
(23.44) **Stepney**
26th (00.05) **Lambourne**
(04.04) **Cheshunt**
(04.20) **Bermondsey**
(04.42) **Hornchurch**
(09.03) **Navestock**
(14.43) **Ilford**
(15.22) **Bromley**
(19.08) **Romford**
(22.30) **Noak Hill**
27th (00.22) **Edmonton**
(03.02) **Cheshunt**
(03.30) **Ilford**
(04.04) **Hutton Park**
(07.21) **Stepney**
(16.54) **Orpington**

Wickenden Road, Sevenoaks - where four homes were levelled to the ground.

Sevenoaks — a safe haven?

THE market town of Sevenoaks, 25 miles from the centre of London, was considered to be sufficiently safe from V2 rocket attacks to enable the authorities to compulsorily evacuate south-east Londoners there, had there been a saturation attack on the capital.

They would not have found a haven of safety. From September 17 when one crashed in the nearby village of Knockholt, rockets peppered the Sevenoaks area. There were explosions at Borough Green, Penshurst (twice), Ide Hill, Chevening, Riverhead, Plaxtol, Platt, Farningham, Shoreham, Eynsford, Westerham and Ightham — all within a few miles of the town centre.

Although most of them fell harmlessly in open country, there were some injuries and much damage to property. The worst attack of all came on Saturday March 3 when a V2 fell on Wickenden Road, a residential area

just north of Sevenoaks town centre, which had already received a land mine earlier in the war. The rocket impacted on a semi-detached house which was blown to pieces in the explosion. Three other houses collapsed and blast damage was extensive.

Nine people were killed including a young couple, Leonard and Gladys Webb and their two children, David, aged two and Deidre, aged five months. In a nearby house the four members of one family were trapped in their bedrooms. Rescue work went on throughout the night with the help of searchlights and they, along with other injured victims still wearing their nightclothes, were finally freed.

This was the second rocket to hit Sevenoaks. The first was on February 23 when one dived into the middle of Ash Platt Road, less than half a mile from Wickenden Road. One person died in this incident.

Wickenden Road, Sevenoaks showing the exact spot where the rocket landed. In the foreground is Mr James Tomlin, a fireman in 1944, who lost his wife and six-year-old daughter, Rosemary in the disaster. This photograph was taken in 1985.

The man who died in the Westerham rocket explosion was George Blake who had earlier complained that there was an unexploded bomb, under the earth, somewhere in his garden. Bomb disposal experts could find no trace of it, but George continued to complain. It may have been an uncanny premonition of what was to come, for the rocket landed at the bottom of his garden in Madan Road, near to the Westerham railway station car park. George was the only person to die, but seven people were seriously injured and there was considerable damage to more than 300 houses. The famous train, The Westerham Flyer which ran the branch line to Dunton Green was not damaged in the incident.

Rocket in Westerham

THE Germans on the V2 launchers in Holland would not have known how close they came to hitting Winston Churchill's country home at Chartwell with the rocket they fired soon after 10.00 am on Sunday March 11. Although the Prime Minister often visited Chartwell at the weekend it was more likely that he would have been at Downing Street during those hectic days before Germany capitulated. The rocket landed in Madan Road, near the centre of Westerham, killing Mr George Blake who was alone in his house at the time.

Three days later, on Wednesday March 14, a rocket landed in front of a bootmaker's shop in Sutton-at-Hone, near Dartford, killing 10 people. A butcher's shop next door to the bootmaker was wrecked and a couple killed. Their three-year-old son had one of the most remarkable escapes of the whole campaign. Asleep in his cot when the rocket fell, he was hurled out of the house by the explosion and found dazed, distressed but alive in his cot at the bottom of the garden.

Another survivor was an RAF pilot home on leave but his parents and a younger brother were killed.

There was one more serious incident in Kent before the war ended and it occurred just a few miles from where the first flying bomb landed in the potato field at Swanscombe in June 1944. This one was also a V1 and it was also in the early hours of the morning. It crashed in Dartford but, on this occasion, four people died.

Final rocket falls in Orpington

IVY MILDRED MILLICHAMP
BELOVED WIFE OF ERIC
27TH MARCH 1945 AGE 34

THE LAST PERSON IN BRITAIN
TO BE KILLED BY ENEMY ACTION
ALWAYS IN OUR HEARTS
REMEMBERED WITH LOVE

TIME was running out for Hitler and for his rocket troops in The Hague. On Wednesday March 24, the Western Allies advanced across the Rhine and SS Gruppenführer Klammler was virtually cornered. He had time for a few parting shots before moving his men out of Holland, placing Britain beyond range of the V2. Before they packed their bags and left, on the afternoon of Monday March 27, they launched two final rockets — one to Antwerp, which killed 27 people — and one to England.

It landed at Orpington, 15 miles from the centre of London, between Court Road, part of the Orpington by-pass, and Kynaston Road gouging a hole 40 feet across and 20 feet deep in the gardens which separated the two roads. People for miles around heard the explosion. Buildings shook, windows shattered, pavements shuddered and many dived instinctively for cover.

In Kynaston Road, two small boys who had gone into the Anderson shelter at No 96 were saved from certain death. A married couple in their garden at No 84 were injured. Two old age pensioners at No 86 were more seriously hurt, as were the elderly occupants of No 82, whose roof was lifted off in the blast.

In Court Road, the owner of No 63 was shopping at the time in Petts Wood and heard the explosion. She returned to find her home gone. A police inspector at No 69 was listening to a radio programme about the war being over when the house fell on top of him. He survived.

On that spring afternoon 23 people from Kynaston Road and Court Road were seriously injured and one woman was killed. Mrs Ivy Millichamp, aged 34 of No 88 Kynaston Road, was in her kitchen when the rocket fell. She was pulled clear of the wreckage by her husband Eric but she had caught the full force of the blast and was already dead.

Ivy Millichamp was the last civilian in Britain to be killed by enemy action. She was the daughter of Mr and Mrs Benjamin Croughton who raised their large family of seven daughters and five sons in Tottenham before moving to Rayleigh in Essex. Ivy, the eighth born, married Eric Millichamp in 1938 when she was 27 and went to live in a small bungalow at Kynaston Road which was convenient for Eric's employment as an engineer.

In January, 1945 a flying bomb landed in Court Road, killing eight people but Ivy and Eric escaped unharmed. Then, just over two months later came the rocket, and Ivy suffered the cruel fate of being the last civilian to die in Britain after a long, bitter battle. She was laid to rest in All Saints Churchyard on April 3. The grave was never marked and the death certificate gave her address as No 86 Court Road but, thanks to the editor and authors of the book *"The Blitz — Then and Now — Volume Three"* the certificate was corrected. They also arranged for a suitable headstone to be erected and, on Remembrance Sunday, 1989 a memorial service was held.

The gardens behind No 88 Kynaston Road, Orpington where the final V2 rocket fell killing Mrs Ivy Millichamp.

United States soldiers who captured a flying bombs site in Northern France before the Nazis had time to complete it. The launching ramp is camouflaged

Wachtel's parting shots

THE days of the V2 rocket were over but not so the flying bomb. The third and last phase of the V1 offensive began on March 3, 1945 when Flakregiment 155 (W) launched a few doodlebugs from ground ramps at Ypenburg, Vlaardingen, and a site near Delft. The first two were attacked by fighter bombers and put out of action but the RAF never discovered the Delft site and from here came the closing shots of the campaign.

On March 28, the day after the Orpington explosion, two flying bombs came down at Waltham Abbey and one at Chislehurst. In the evening, and the early hours of March 29, 21 were launched but only one managed to evade the guns and the fighters and dived to

earth in a sewage farm at Datchworth, near Hatfield. One hour later the anti-aircraft gunners triumphantly claimed what was to be the last V1 to land on British soil. It exploded in open country at Iwade, near Sittingbourne, close to the A2 road — and therefore on the same route as the Swanscombe bomb, 262 days earlier.

Back in June 1944, Colonel Wachtel had told his men that their hard work was soon to be rewarded; the V1 was a weapon with which they could win the war for the Fatherland. The fact that they failed was due to all those who parried the blow — the bomber crews who doggedly attacked the factories, the depots and the launching sites, the fighter pilots who found three methods of destroying the bomb thus barring its way to the capital and the skill, courage and endurance of the men and women of AA Command.

WHEN the 1st US Army reached the vast underground factory at Nordhausen in April, 1945, they found 10 miles of interlaced tunnels driven deep under the Hartz Mountains where 60,000 prisoners had helped the Nazis to produce Hitler's "miracle weapons". The lines of V1 and V2 assemblies had been left undisturbed and the American soldiers realised that they had found one of history's greatest technical prizes. All the rocket equipment was transported by road and rail to Antwerp and then on to the States. Enough parts were captured to fill 300 large railway wagons — sufficient to construct 75 V2s. The last trainload left Nordhausen on May 31, 1945, the day before the Russians were expected to arrive. Before they left the Americans blew up the tunnel entrance to seal the complex.

While the Americans were transporting rockets from the underground caves at Nordhausen to Antwerp, the Germans were attempting to salvage a few V2s from other sites. At Oyle, on April 16, 1945, a trainload was shot up by the RAF while being carried on the railway. Most of the train was badly smashed and rockets destroyed but this one, almost complete, was undamaged.

The Eagle has landed

EVEN as the Third Reich faced extinction, von Braun and Dornberger were still actively engaged in their work at Peenemunde; in fact they were working on a new project, the A4b, a standard V2 modified to permit the attachment of supersonic wings. But the game was nearly up, and the rocket men realised it. They met secretly with their senior staff to decide whether to remain at Peenemunde and surrender to the Russians or move to an area likely to be occupied by the US Army.

They decided that the American option was the lesser of two evils and, ignoring orders from their Nazi bosses, von Braun, Dornberger and 4,000 employees and their families packed up large quantities of drawings and documents and headed south. Avoiding the Gestapo and the SS they finally reached the town of Bleicherode in the Harz Mountains and set about continuing with their research work.

In early April, the two men and 500 other scientists and technicians moved into Bavaria and waited in villages around the town of Oberammergau for the arrival of the Americans. They surrendered to a unit of the 44th Infantry Division on May 2, 1945 and asked if they could go to America and continue their work in rocket development there.

The Americans realised that this was an extraordinary coup. Von Braun was the outstanding spirit in the entire rocket project and his scientists had invaluable experience in rocketry and its development. About 500 of the former Peenemunde team were offered contracts to go to America. The majority accepted and there they worked happily with their old adversaries.

The great dream eventually came true. On July 20, 1969, Professor Dr Werner von Braun, as director of the Apollo Space Project, heard these historic words from Commander Neil Armstrong — "Houston. Tranquility Base here. The Eagle has landed."

Wachtel also surrenders

Colonel Wachtel of Flakregiment 155 (W) also surrendered. Driven from Holland, he retreated to Luneberg in north-west Germany and reformed his troops into infantry to fight the advancing British on the ground. On May 4, 1945, along with other German forces, he surrendered unconditionally to Field Marshal Montgomery.

Like the rocket men, the men of Flakregiment 155 (W) were not tried as war criminals and Colonel Wachtel, at the end of hostilities, secured a post in a different kind of aviation as the manager of Hamburg airport.

Dr Werner von Braun, with a broken arm, at the moment he surrendered to the troops of the 44th Division of the US Army. With him are (left) Major General Walter Dornberger, commandant of Peenemunde and (hatless) Lt. Col. Herbert Axter, senior scientist.

Hanna Reitsch and the suicide squadron

THE diminutive aviator, Flugkapitan Hanna Reitsch, who risked her life by flying the early prototype of the flying bomb in order to find out why it was going out of control, was one of Germany's most remarkable test pilots. She frequently achieved speeds in excess of 500 mph, survived terrible crashes and enjoyed tea parties with Adolf Hitler. Later in the war when the Allies were gaining air superiority, Hanna initiated the idea of an even more remarkable phase of warfare — a suicide squadron, with pilots trained to fly a V1 bomb directly at selected targets.

This brave woman, who was prepared to die for her country, had received considerable acclaim by flying the Messerschmitt 163A, a delta glider, fitted with a liquid-filled lightweight rocket engine. The Me 163 had already broken the world air-speed record when pilot Heine Dittmaar flew it at 571, then 623 mph. Hanna described her experience as "like riding on a cannonball".

Hanna survived her flights in the 163A and, in 1943, went on to fly the first pre-production prototypes of the Me 163B, a military fighter version with a more powerful engine, better known as the Komet. She made four powered flights but the fifth ended in disaster when the engine stalled and then went out of control. Hanna received appalling injuries, including a skull fractured in four places and severe spinal injuries. Her nose was almost torn from her face.

A few days after the accident Hanna was told she had won the Iron Cross. She spent five months in hospital, musing over her plan to make Germany stronger by forming a suicide squadron and, in August 1943, made her proposals public. Field Marshal Milch turned down the idea as "contrary to the German mentality" but others were more open minded and endorsed them "in principle".

On February 28, 1944 Hanna was summoned to the Führer's mountain chalet, the Berghof at Berchtesgaden. She decided that instead of the post-presentation small talk over cups of tea, she would present to Hitler her bizarre idea of a suicide squadron, known as the Reichenberg project. Hitler was horrified and rejected the idea in a series of lengthy monologues. Later on, however, as the Allies were gaining strength, he did concede that a suicide unit might be conceivable but he, and only he, would decide when it should become operational.

With Hitler's reluctant patronage granted and other members of the Nazi party enthusiastically endorsing the plan on the basis that the R-weapons could snatch victory out of defeat, the formation of the squadron was soon under way. Cockpit instruments and conventional controls were built into the FZG76 under a cloak of utmost secrecy and the now piloted V1 was coded F1 103 R, the R signifying Reichenberg.

Hanna wanted volunteers to come forward to pilot this projectile into the centre of its target, destroying it completely. She said at the time: "It should be possible to deliver, while sparing the enemy civil population, a rapid succession of devastating blows at generating stations, waterworks, key production centres and, in the event of an invasion, at naval and merchant shipping".

Hanna Reitsch with Adolf Hitler shortly after receiving the Iron Cross.

Although several hundred piloted V1s were manufactured and about 100 pilots trained, this most desperate project was never put into effect, due to lack of enthusiasm in the highest Nazi circles. The scheme was abandoned.

When the Allied armies finally penetrated into Nazi held Europe, many examples of the R-weapon were found almost intact — including almost 200 Reichenberg 4s, which British Intelligence named the V4.

Instead of killing herself in an English city, or at a European bridgehead where the advancing troops were concentrated, Hanna Reitsch lived for another 34 years.

She died in 1979.

Several types of the Reichenberg flying bomb were produced, the final operational version being the R4. This looked little different from the ordinary flying bomb but the nose was reshaped and space was made for the pilot by removing one of the two large globes which contained compressed air. This made it no longer necessary to operate controls automatically. There are a few Fieseler Fi 103 R4s in Great Britain including one at the Lashendon Air Warfare Museum at Headcorn in Kent, which has been well restored by Trevor Matthews and his colleagues.

This would be similar to Hanna Reitsch's personal R4 which she test-flew at Peenemunde, where it was discovered. She had about 10 uneventful flights and two narrow escapes. On one of these occasions when water was being used as ballast, the draining hole designed to empty the tank before landing, froze up. Hanna said at the time: "I gripped and clawed at the lever till my fingers were bleeding. With a few hundred feet to go the lever suddenly moved and there was time to drain out most of the water."

Hanna landed the piloted V1 by skidding across the earth. The undercarriage of the Headcorn model is badly dented indicating a rather heavy landing and Trevor Matthews is convinced that he has the most famous "suicide doodlebug" of them all.

Throughout the V weapon campaign, the county of Kent was in the front line and became known as Hellfire Corner. 1,444 flying bombs and 67 rockets fell in Kent, and now it was all over. God bless our boys, says the banner in this street in Canterbury, where the lady on the accordion led the procession on VE Day.

Back from the jaws of death

THE Battle of the Flying Bombs was over. The German retreat became a rout. President Roosevelt died on April 12 and the next day the concentration camps at Belsen and Buchenwald were taken by the British. The Russian noose tightened around Berlin. Mussolini was executed on April 28. The survivors of Dachau death camp were liberated. On Sunday April 30, Adolf Hitler and Eva Braun, his bride of 36 hours, committed suicide in their Berlin bunker. The war was almost over.

The cost of the V weapon campaign could now be counted — 8,958 dead and 24,504 injured, a total that could well have been higher if the V3 had ever been put to use. This was a gigantic long range gun capable of firing rocket shells against London. A battery of these guns were discovered by the advancing forces in a great concrete structure at Mimoyecques, Pas de Calais. By then it had been heavily bombed and could probably have never come into action but it contained 50 smooth bore barrels approximately six inches in diameter and 416 feet long which would have fired finned projectiles, each weighing 300 pounds at a combined rate of up to 10 a minute at London.

The War Office felt that British Intelligence should have known about it, but thanks to Bomber Command the third "miracle weapon" was never more than a Nazi dream.

On Tuesday May 8 at 3pm Winston Churchill told the nation on the BBC that representatives of the German High Command had signed the act of unconditional surrender. Hostilities were to end officially at one minute after midnight.

There were wild celebrations but, coming so soon after the end of the V for Vengeance campaign, the news in many homes was greeted in a more sober fashion. These included the many families either bereaved by the bombs, or whose members bore the scars of terrible injury. They included members of the Civil Defence who had seen at first hand the hideous nature of warfare. They included the fighter and the bomber pilots who lost more than 2,900 colleagues in the V weapon battle. And they included those who mourned the loss of loved homes and prized possessions.

On Tuesday May 8, 1945, Churchill said: "The lights went out and the bombs came down. But every man, woman and child in the country had no thought of quitting the struggle. London can take it. So we came back after long months from the jaws of death, out of the mouth of hell, while all the world wondered. When shall the reputation and faith of this generation of English men and women fail ? I say that in the long years to come not only will the people of this island, but of the world, wherever the bird of freedom chirps in human hearts, look back to what we've done and they will say 'do not despair, do not yield to violence and tyranny, march straight forward and die if need be — unconquered'. Now we have emerged from one deadly struggle — a terrible foe has been cast on the ground and awaits our judgement and our mercy".

Frank Wootton's painting shows a Mustang of 170 Squadron 35 Wing PRU on aerial reconnaissance duty over a "ski" site in northern France. Photographs taken by Mustang and Mosquito pilots in November 1943 revealed construction sites with numerous small buildings of identical design on each site, including concrete platforms with a central axis bearing on London. Each site contained sheds shaped like skies on their sides. By the end of that year, 83 "ski" sites had been detected and bombers had released 3.210 tons of bombs over them.

The whole weight of Bomber Command was brought to bear against Peenemunde on the moonlit night of August 17, 1943. 596 bombers of 54 Squadrons set off across the North Sea in a bid to destroy the workshops and laboratories where the V2 was being designed and manufactured. Hundreds of airmen went on the raid. Many didn't return and many more died in subsequent bombing missions. Some 49 years later, at RAF Hendon, members of the Bomber Command Association, met for their regular summer get-together. Peenemunde was on the menu, as it always is, and here are some of the survivors representing, for the purpose of this book, the hundreds of brave men who took part in Operation Hydra, one of greatest bombing raids in history. Left to right: Warrant Officer Jack Slaughter DFM, navigator with Pathfinder Force 83 Squadron; Squadron Leader 'Pil' Pilgrim DFC FCA. pilot with 44 Squadron; Flight Lieutenant James Chapman DFC, Rear Gunner with 61 Squadron; Flight Lieutenant John Wilkin DFM, Navigator with Pathfinder Force 156 Squadron (John was one of the deputy master bombers to Squadron Leader John Searby); Flight Lieutenant Dave Francis DFC, Navigator with 460 Squadron. In the background is the bomb bay of Avro Lancaster R5868 which served with Squadrons 83 and 467. During the war this Lancaster flew on more than 120 confirmed bombing sorties. The Lancaster bomber is, of course, immortalised as the aircraft used in the attacks on the Mohner and Eder dams.

Where the doodlebugs landed in London

81 **Croydon** 141
68 **Wandsworth** 122
84 **Lewisham** 114
71 **Camberwell** 80
76 **Woolwich** 77
75 **Greenwich** 73
70 **Lambeth** 71
83 **Beckenham** 70
95 **Orpington** 63
58 **West Ham** 58
94 **Coulsdon** 54
86 **Chislehurst** 45
80 **Mitcham** 43
56 **Poplar** 39
60 **Barking** 37
85 **Bromley** 37
93 **Beddington** 36
59 **East Ham** 36
49 **Hackney** 36
62 **Esher** 35
79 **Merton** 35
90 **Banstead** 35
69 **Battersea** 34
91 **Sutton** 34
30 **Ilford** 34
67 **Wimbledon** 33
73 **Bermondsey** 30
74 **Deptford** 30
54 **Stepney** 30
89 **Epsom** 29
42 **Westminster** 29
61 **Dagenham** 28
92 **Carlshalton** 27
35 **Twickenham** 27
87 **Bexley** 25
57 **Leyton** 24
29 **Wanstead** 23
64 **Malden** 21
78 **Surbiton** 20
39 **Kensington** 20
16 **Chigwell** 20
5 **Enfield** 20
46 **St Pancras** 19
28 **Walthamstow** 17
82 **Penge** 17

This plan of the London Civil Defence Region, as it was in 1944, shows the number of flying bombs which landed in each borough or urban district within the region during the main attack from June 13 to September 1, 1944. The first figure indicates the number of the borough to correspond with the map. The last figure is the number which fell.

Major incidents

The Guards Chapel, Westminster:
121 killed
Sloane Court, Chelsea:
74 killed
Lewisham High Street:
58 killed
Aldwych, WC2:
48 killed
Beckenham, Bromley:
44 killed
Clapham Junction:
24 killed
St Pancras Station:
24 killed

The number of incidents in London makes it impossible to list them individually here

53 **City of London** 17
40 **Fulham** 15
25 **Hornsey** 15
34 **Heston** 15
47 **Islington** 15
22 **Willesden** 15
21 **Wembley** 14
38 **Hammersmith** 14
72 **Southwark** 14
11 **Hendon** 13
44 **St Marylebone** 12

77 **Erith** 12
88 **Crayford** 11
10 **Harrow** 11
20 **Ealing** 11
7 **Waltham Holy Cross** 11
55 **Bethnal Green** 9
66 **Barnes** 9
45 **Hampstead** 8
65 **Richmond** 8
63 **Kingston** 8
37 **Acton** 7

31 **Staines** 7
50 **Shoreditch** 7
19 **Southall** 7
48 **Stoke Newington** 7
14 **Edmonton** 7
6 **Cheshunt** 6
4 **East Barnet** 6
18 **Hayes** 6
23 **Finchley** 6
13 **Southgate** 6

26 **Wood Green** 5
51 **Finsbury** 5
8 **Uxbridge** 5
43 **Paddington** 5
33 **Feltham** 5
12 **Barnet UDC** 4
9 **Ruislip** 4
32 **Sunbury** 4
52 **Holborn** 4
27 **Tottenham** 4

17 **Yiewsley** 3
41 **Chelsea** 3
2 **Elstree** 2
1 **Bushey** 1
24 **Frn Barnet** 1
3 **Potters Bar** 1

TOTAL 2,419

... and the counties of England

This map does not include Durham which received a solitary V1.

YORKSHIRE
7

LANCA-
SHIRE
8

CHESHIRE
6

DERBY
3

NOTTS
1

LINCOLN-
SHIRE
2

STAFFORD

SHROPSHIRE
1

LEICESTER-
SHIRE
1

RUT-
LAND
1

NORFOLK
13

WORCS

NORTHANTS
4

HUNTS
2

CAMBS
8

SUFFOLK
93

HEREFORD

BEDS
10

BUCKS
27

OXFORD-
SHIRE
4

HERTS
82

ESSEX
412

GLOUCESTER

BERKS
12

WILTS

SURREY
295

KENT
1444

SOMERSET

HAMPSHIRE
80

SUSSEX
880

DORSET

Isle of Wight

This shows the number of flying bombs falling in each county in England, as the boundaries were at the time, from June 13, 1944 to March 29, 1945. The map excludes the London Civil Defence Region.

Kent, with 1,444, and Sussex,East and West, 880 — the counties in "Doodlebug Alley" — easily came top after London. Essex, third with 412, received most of the air-launched bombs after the main attack. Surrey were the recipients of 295.

The bombs were scattered far and wide over the other counties, including 80 in Hampshire which was the result of the attempt to bombard Portsmouth and Southampton in the middle of July, 1944. Suffolk, suffered with Norfolk in the autumn and winter, and the rest were either "wides" or "overthrows."

The Air Ministry in a report published in November, 1944 acknowledged that the results of the V1 offensive were "greatly in the enemy's favour." It cost the Allies nearly £48 million in aircraft and airmen lost, bombs dropped, shells fired and balloons lost, and that did not include the millions of pounds spent repairing and rebuilding homes that were damaged.

The production cost of each V1 was approximately £150 and the Germans spent in excess of £12 million for constructing launching sites and training the crews.

There is no doubt that the flying bomb and the rocket attacks on England raised German morale and had they come two, or even one year earlier, it is possible that the war may have taken a different course. As it was, the V1 and V2 offensives followed the Normandy landings and the Allies' progress was not affected.

Miss Constance Babington Smith, photographed in 1992 at her home in Cambridge. Miss Babington Smith was the young WAAF officer who first identified a flying bomb at Peenemunde from a mass of photographs which she had been interpreting. She went on to enjoy a distinguished career as editorial researcher with Life Magazine and then as an author of several books including Evidence in Camera, the story of the photographic interpretation unit at Medmenham in Buckinghamshire. Her fascination for aviation has never diminished. She has written a History of British Test Flying and a full biography of Amy Johnson. Miss Babington Smith has edited the letters of Rose McAulay and, more recently, completed her latest book, Champion of Homeopathy. She has lived in Cambridge for more than 20 years.

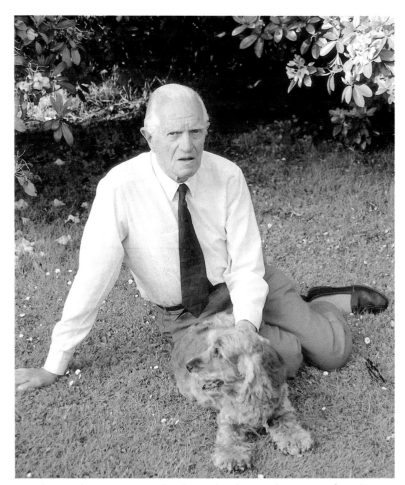

As Military Adviser to Duncan Sandys, Colonel Kenneth Post was, from the start concerned with the battle of the flying bombs and rockets and, in 1992 when this photograph was taken at his home in Tunbridge Wells, he recalled, with great clarity, the Crossbow Committee, meetings of the War Cabinet and the often heated discussions on the prospects of the country being bombarded by Hitler's secret weapons. Colonel Post was closely involved with the decisions to bomb Peenemunde, the "ski sites" and the huge concrete works at Watten and, when the V1s began to arrive he, and others, advised Mr Sandys and the Prime Minister to move the guns to the coast out of the way of the fighters and away from the elevated North Downs. Colonel Post said: "Duncan Sandys was, in effect, heading up the whole of these operations — Bomber Command, Fighter Command, Balloon Command and the Intelligence Service. I was privileged to work alongside him and this was, by far, the most important thing I did in my life."

Mr Edwin Woods, who lived at Rhodes Minnis, near Lyminge in Kent when this photograph was taken, in 1992 was a member of the Royal Observer Corps in 1944. He was on duty at Post Mike Three when he saw a "fighter on fire" heading towards the Kent coast from Boulogne. He gave a reading to Maidstone ROC, and handed over to his colleagues at Dymchurch, unaware that he had made the first sighting of a flying bomb. He then heard the code word "diver, diver" being called for the first time. (See page 28).

Henryk Pawelec with the badge of his Polish underground unit. As commander of a resistance unit, Henryk played a vital role in unveiling the secrets of the V2 rocket and supplying priceless information to the Allies, regardless of torture and death. When this photograph was taken in 1992, Henryk and his wife ran a guest house in the Kentish town of Deal. (See page 141.)

TOP V1 SCORERS IN THE FIGHTER SQUADRONS

Number	Squadron	Aircraft	Base	Score
1:	3	Tempest 5	Newchurch/ Matlask	357
2:	486	Tempest 5	Newchurch	223
3:	91	Spitfire 14	Deanland	185
4:	96	Mosquito 13	Ford	174
5:	322	Spitfire 14	West Malling/ Deanland	108
6:	418	Mosquito 6	Holmesby/Hurn/ Middle Wallop	90
7:	129	Mustang 3	Brenzett	66

V WEAPON CASUALTIES IN EUROPE

The V Weapon casualties in Europe were as follows.

	Antwerp	Brussels	Liege	Others
Military killed	743	7	92	114
Military wounded	1,078	38	336	457
Total	1,812	45	428	571
Civilians killed	2,900	40	221	575
Civilians injured	5,433	153	937	1,643
Total	8,333	193	1,158	2,218
Grand Total	10,145	238	1,586	2,771

Other Continental centres bombed were Remagen, Arras, Cambrai, Diest, Hasselt, Lille, Maastricht, Mons, Paris, Tourcoing and Tournai

Bibliography

In writing this book I have referred to a variety of pamphlets, newspaper articles, documents and official files in the Public Record Office. Much of the information comes from members of the public who so generously responded to my appeal in local newspapers for photographs and anecdotes about the Vengeance weapon campaign. I am grateful to the archivists of various county record offices and to librarians and museum staff who showed me miscellaneous documents, war diaries, ARP reports, letters and diaries. I have also used a number of published and unpublished books.

After The Battle, *The Peenemunde Rocket Centre*, Battle of Britain Prints International
Lewis Blake, *Bromley in the Front Line*
Lewis Blake, *Bolts From the Blue*
The Blitz Then and Now, Volume Three, Battle of Britain Prints International
Bohdan Arct, *Poles against V-Weapons*, Interpress Publications, Warsaw
Constance Babington Smith, *Evidence in Camera*, Chatto and Windus.
Roland Beamont, *My Part of the Sky*, Patrick Stephens Ltd
Croydon Advertiser Ltd, *Croydon Courageous*
Winston S. Churchill, *The Second World War*, Cassell.
Peter G. Cooksley, *Flying Bomb*, Robert Hale Ltd
Joachim Engelmann, *Dawn of the Rocket Age*, Schiffer Military History
Harry Klopper, *History of Fire Fighting in Kent*, Whitefriars Press, Tonbridge
James Farrar, *The Unreturned Spring*, Chatto and Windus
Folkestone and Hythe Herald, *Front Line Folkestone*
Roy Humphreys, *Target Folkestone*, Meresborough Books, Rainham
George Humphrey, *Wartime Eastbourne*, Becket Features Ltd
Charles Graves, *Women in Green*, Heinemann
Hastings and St. Leonards Observer, *Hastings in the Front Line*
David Irving, *The Mares Nest*, Corgi Books
R.V. Jones, *Most Secret War*, Hamish Hamilton
Marcel Julian, *Jean Maridor, Chasseur de V1*, Amiot-Dumont, Paris
Judy Lomax, The Hanna Reitsch Story
Norman Longmate, *The Doodlebugs, The Story of the Flying-Bombs*, Hutchinson
Rudolf Lusar, *German Secret Weapons*, Neville Spearman
E.S.Oak-Rhind, *In Bomb Alley, the Land Girls Wept*, Local Government Service, vol XX111, no 10
General Sir Frederick Pile, *Ack-Ack*, Harrap
H.R.Pratt Boorman, *Kent Unconquered*, Kent Messenger
Andrew Rootes, *Front Line County*, Robert Hale Ltd
Sussex Express and County Herald, *War in East Sussex*
City of Westminster, *War in Westminster*

A special thank you to Mrs Avril Oswald, Miss Constance Babington Smith, Wing Commander Roland Beamont and Colonel Kenneth Post for their help in checking the manuscript.

FLYING BOMB (V.I.)	
Number plotted 9,251	Number to reach London 2,419
Destroyed by fighters 1,979	Destroyed by gunners 1,971
Destroyed by balloons 278	Interception patrols flown 20,000

ROCKETS (V2)	
Number reported 1,115	Number reached London 517
Number other areas 598	Max height attained 328,000feet
Max speed attained 3,500 mph	Weight of explosive 2,000lbs

These two plans were compiled at the end of the war to show the extent of the V1 and V2 offensives on England. They were taken from drawings made by RAF draughtsmen who worked at The Rookery, near Biggin Hill, which was part of "Diver" control.

This excellent example of a flying bomb on its ramp can be found at the Duxford Museum, near Cambridge. After the war, several ramps were brought to Britain for assessment and use in experimental programmes. The ramps were rebuilt and when no longer required, lay abandoned for more than 30 years. A number of sections were brought to Duxford and they were restored and assembled over a period of two years by a team from the Community Programme.

This stained glass window at Staplehurst parish church, Kent was made up of fragments of a previous window which was shattered when a flying bomb landed nearby, on August 8, 1944.

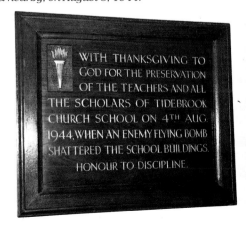

The plaque in Tidebrook church, near Mayfield, East Sussex reads August 4, 1944. In fact it was August 3 when the village schoolchildren had such a miraculous escape. See page 109.

WITH THANKSGIVING TO GOD FOR THE PRESERVATION OF THE TEACHERS AND ALL THE SCHOLARS OF TIDEBROOK CHURCH SCHOOL ON 4TH AUG. 1944, WHEN AN ENEMY FLYING BOMB SHATTERED THE SCHOOL BUILDINGS. HONOUR TO DISCIPLINE.

Launch of a V2 from a field near Wassenaar, The Netherlands during the height of the rocket assault on London. From the first V2, which landed at Chiswick on September 5, 1944 to the one fired on the last day of December, not a single day went by without a launch. The final rocket crashed in Orpington on Monday March 27, 1945.

INDEX

This index contains place names and names of the principal characters in the flying bomb campaign which appear in the general text. It does not include the names of the many contributors who responded to our appeal for reminiscences. They have received individual letters of acknowledgement.

Wing Commander Roland Beamont CBE, DSO, DFC, DL commander, in 1944, of the 150 Tempest Wing was the man who led the battle in the air against the flying bomb. He was one of The Few who fought in the Battle of France, the Battle of Britain and through the war years to the Invasion. On October 12, 1944, Beamont crash-landed his Tempest in Germany and was taken POW. After the war he became a leading Test Pilot, remaining as a highly respected figure in the aviation branch of the Aircraft Industry. He retired from British Aerospace on delivery of the first-production Tornado.

Peter Findley, whose story is told briefly on page 58, has spent more than four years trying to find out more about his mother, Catherine Inwood who was killed when a V1 fell on Weald House, Crockham Hill. His investigations brought him to Edenbridge churchyard where a memorial stone marks the names of those who died in one of the most tragic incidents of all. Peter has met many people who knew his mother vaguely and has received amazing photographs and letters but, by 1992, no relative of his had been found.

There is little evidence today of the destruction wrought by the V-weapons. One exception, however, is the remains of St Mary of the Holy Rood, the church which was destroyed by a flying bomb, shot down by a fighter a few minutes after 8 pm on the evening of Wednesday August 16, 1944. The bomb landed on the tower of the Norman church and six bells came crashing down followed by the walls. Villagers at Little Chart, just south of Charing, campaigned to keep the remains, now covered in ivy, as a symbol of Kent's ordeal in the summer of 1944. A new church, much closer to the village centre, was consecrated in 1958.

Bob Ogley

Bob was a journalist for 30 years until leaving the editorship of *The Sevenoaks Chronicle* in 1989 to become a full-time publisher and author. The overnight success of his first book *In The Wake of The Hurricane*, which became a national bestseller in two editions, launched him into publishing in a most dramatic way.

In 1990, he wrote *Biggin on The Bump*, the *Story of the most Famous Fighter Station in the World*, which received tremendous reviews from national, local and aviation press. The book has raised £12,500 in author's royalties for the RAF Benevolent Fund.

Bob has raised a further £60,000 with the hurricane books for environmental charities and has discovered a supplementary career as speaker to clubs and organisations.

Recently he teamed up with Ian Currie and Mark Davison to research write and publish a series of illustrated county books on the history of the weather. In 1991, *The Kent Weather Book* and *The Sussex Weather Book* were number one county bestsellers.

Froglets Publications Ltd

7961 S